THOSE FASCINATING
PAPER DOLLS

An Illustrated Handbook
for Collectors

Marian B. Howard

With a New Introduction by Barbara Whitton Jendrick

Dover Publications, Inc.
New York

To

the memory of Miss Nellie D. MacLachlan who joined me in adopting this exciting hobby, and Mrs. H. B. Armstrong who, over the years, generously shared with me, results of her own research in the field of paper dolls.

Published in Canada by General Publishing Company, Ltd., 30 Lesmill Road, Don Mills, Toronto, Ontario.
Published in the United Kingdom by Constable and Company, Ltd., 10 Orange Street, London WC2H 7EG.

This Dover edition, first published in 1981, is an unabridged republication of *Those Fascinating Paper Dolls,* originally published by Marian B. Howard in 1965. A new introduction and a new index have been especially prepared for this edition.
Photographs by Gunther Neuman, Miami, Florida, unless otherwise noted.

International Standard Book Number: 0-486-24055-X
Library of Congress Catalog Card Number: 80-70309

Manufactured in the United States of America
Dover Publications, Inc.
180 Varick Street
New York, N.Y. 10014

Introduction to the Dover Edition

When Marian B. Howard began to write *Those Fascinating Paper Dolls,* her plan was to put together a book which would help collectors identify antique paper dolls. The work was written in sections which were published over a period of a year. Miss Howard soon discovered, however, that the entire field of paper dolls could not possibly be covered in one work. She decided, therefore, to concentrate on the paper dolls issued by the largest publisher of paper dolls in America from the 1850's to the turn of the century, the McLoughlin Brothers of New York.

The book, as it was finally produced, deals with many kinds of paper dolls published during the nineteenth and early twentieth century, but by far the largest amount of space is devoted to the paper dolls of the McLoughlin Brothers, who also produced children's books, greeting cards, paper soldiers, games, and paper dollhouses and furniture. It remains the definitive study of McLoughlin paper dolls. Since its original publication, however, several uncut McLoughlin sets have reappeared. On the following pages, we have included photographs of several uncut McLoughlin paper dolls that were either not shown in the original book or were shown in their cut and/or incomplete form.

Often referred to by collectors as "the bible of paper doll collecting," *Those Fascinating Paper Dolls* was originally published in a limited edition. Out of print for more than ten years, it is now considered a collector's item itself. With this reprint, Dover Publications is again making this in-depth study of paper dolls and their manufacturers available to the many collectors who have joined the hobby since the book was first published, and who have been unable to obtain a copy of this much-sought-after research tool.

Barbara Whitton Jendrick

Concord, New Hampshire
October, 1980

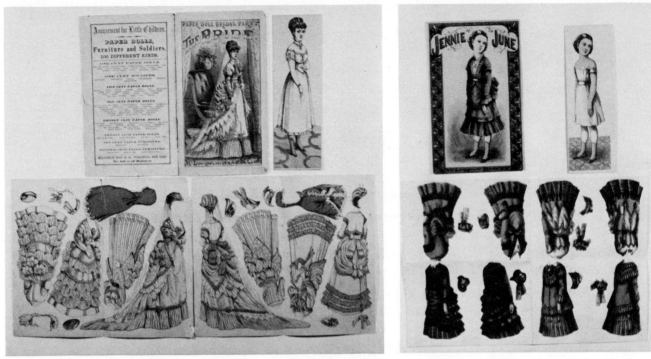

No. A.   THE BRIDE *(see page 102)*. Shown here uncut and complete.

No. B.   JENNIE JUNE *(see page 108)*. Shown here uncut and complete.

No. C.   NELLIE NORTH *(see page 131)*. Shown here uncut and complete.

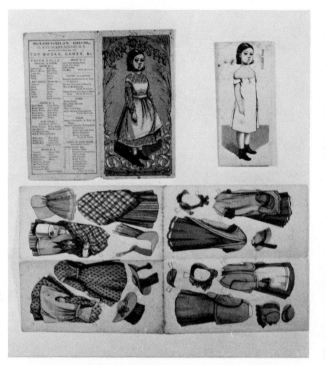

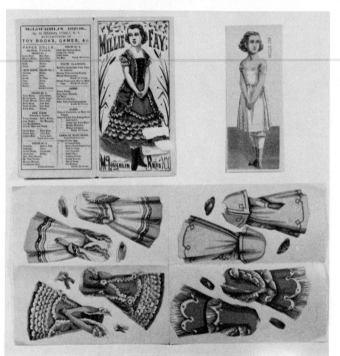

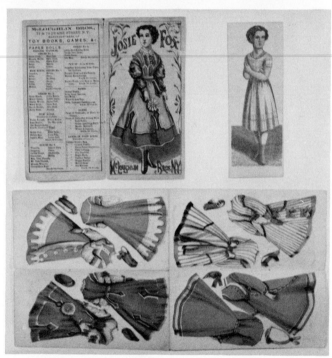

No. D. From "Series No. 2—Twenty-four kinds" *(see page 132)*. Dolls are shown here uncut and complete. Rosa Rustic, page 138; Millie Fay, page 139; Minty Green, page 141 and Josie Fox, page 147.

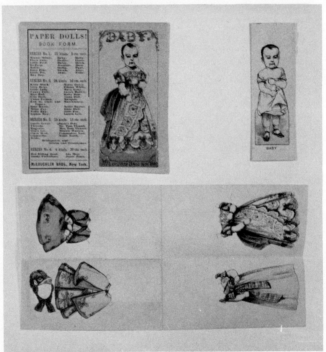

No. E. From "Series No. 1—Twenty-two kinds" *(see page 148)*. Ester Fine, page 151, shown here uncut and complete. Baby, not shown in original book.

THOSE FASCINATING
PAPER DOLLS
An Illustrated Handbook
for Collectors

Author's Preface

With increasing frequency over the past several years, the question has been asked, "What happened to all the old paper dolls?" Today we have the answer; those that survived childish hands are, for the most part, in museums and in the hands of collectors.

Interest in these paper figures has grown rapidly of late, and as it has intensified, the need for factual data has correspondingly increased, and it is in response to requests from various sources that this book has been attempted. It is not complete. No one writer could possibly cover the entire range of the enormous quantity of paper dolls produced during past and present centuries; necessary research is never-ending, unfamiliar specimens continually coming to light. However, I have endeavored to cover the subject as comprehensively as possible. Certain information, to my knowledge not before made available to collectors, is included with the hope that it will prove both useful and interesting.

Of particular importance is the chapter devoted to McLoughlin Brothers. So far as is known, no *illustrated* catalog of this partnership's paper dolls exists. Chapter III of this book, embodying listings from an 1875/76 catalog, together with photographic illustrations of a large part of the listed dolls, virtually supplies such a catalog.

Costume descriptions have generally been omitted since there seems to have been no standard color pattern for a given doll. The early hand-colored ones perhaps were farmed out to different artists, each following his or her own ideas as to appropriate tints, thus resulting in varying sets of the same doll.

Doll measurements, carefully taken, are from the top of each figure's head to the tip of the lower shoe, bases not included unless so stated.

The wonderful cooperation received from museums, publishers and collectors has been heart-warming, and has played a large part in the preparation of this work. If it serves as a guide to properly identifying paper dolls and their correct costumes, as well as proving of value to doll costumers, its purpose will have been accomplished.

Marian B. Howard

July, 1965.

Contents

Acknowledgments

I hereby extend special thanks to Mr. Bart Anderson, Director of the Chester County Historical Society, West Chester, Pennsylvania, for his cooperation, encouragement, and the helpful information furnished for use in this book.

Special appreciation also is expressed to Mrs. William R. Waldron of Wilmington, Delaware, for extensive research and other valuable contributions so generously made to the furtherance of this work.

Grateful appreciation also is expressed to the following for helpful cooperation and assistance, identified by text and illustration captions: The Newark Museum, Newark, New Jersey; the Museum of the City of New York; Brooklyn Children's Museum, Brooklyn, New York; The Historical Society of Pennsylvania, Philadelphia, Pennsylvania; Mr. Herbert H. Hosmer, Founder and Director of the John Greene Chandler Memorial, South Lancaster, Massachusetts; The Valley Forge Historical Society, Valley Forge, Pennsylvania; The London Museum, London, England; The United Press International, New York City; The New York Public Library; Miss Bodil Christensen, Mexico City; Mrs. Sheldon J. Howe, Deerfield, Massachusetts; Mrs. D. J. Ellis, New Smyrna Beach, Florida; Clara Hallard Fawcett, Washington, D.C.; Miss Lillian Faffer, Perth Amboy, New Jersey; Mrs. Charles A. Black (Shirley Temple), Woodside, California; the late Mrs. Earle E. Andrews, Winchester, Massachusetts, as president of The Doll Collectors of America, Inc.; Kimport Dolls, Independence, Missouri; Luella Tilton Hart and Elizabeth Andrews Fisher, writer and publisher respectively of THE JAPANESE DOLL, and to Mr. Paul A. Ruddell, Washington, D.C., who now holds republishing rights; Miss Maude E. Willand, Manchester, New Hampshire; SPINNING WHEEL, Hanover, Pennsylvania; Lightner Publishing Corporation, publishers of HOBBIES, Chicago, Illinois; Marianna, penname for Marian Foster Curtiss, New York, for copy of the 1857 poem, *Nothing to Wear,* and to both Marianna and Lothrop, Lee & Shepard Co., Inc. New York, writer and publisher respectively of the series of *MISS FLORA McFLIMSEY* books; L. C. Page & Company, Inc. a subsidiary of Farrar, Strauss & Cudahy, Inc., New York; Grosset & Dunlap, Inc., Publishers, New York, successors to McLoughlin Brothers; Colonial Williamsburg, Williamsburg, Virginia.

My grateful appreciation also is expressed to the following publishers of paper dolls and pertinent data for full release on their productions: Elizabeth Andrews Fisher, publisher of THE TOY TRADER, Middletown, Connecticut; Milton Bradley Company, Springfield, Massachusetts; Gabriel Industries, Inc., formerly Samuel Gabriel Sons & Co., New York City; Samuel Lowe Company, Kenosha, Wisconsin; Merrill Company, Chicago, Illinois; Whitman Publishing Company, Racine, Wisconsin; The Saalfield Publishing Co., Akron, Ohio; The Curtis Publishing Company, of Philadelphia, publishers of THE LADIES' HOME JOURNAL; McCALL'S, New York; Hearst Corporation, (GOOD HOUSEKEEPING); THE BOSTON GLOBE, Boston, Massachusetts.

Further, I particularly desire to thank the many paper doll collectors who generously entrusted to me, treasures from their collections for photographing and illustrating. The list is long and impressive, and since credit is given on respective captions, (except where omitted by request), an individual listing is not repeated here.

Apologies are offered to those who kindly sent paper dolls not illustrated. Space limitations prevented inclusion of many illustrations of dolls received and actually photographed, and their omission was and is a disappointment. The cooperation nevertheless is as much appreciated as if complete coverage were possible.

Marian B. Howard

Chapter I
Ritual Figures of Paper

Long before paper dolls were produced as fashion models or as playthings for children, figures of various shapes were cut from paper and used in purification and other rites in many different countries.

CHINESE SUPERSTITION FIGURES

In ancient China the offering of living persons as death sacrifices was practiced, once abolished, then reintroduced only to disappear again after the time of Confucius who died in 478 B.C. According to Max Von Boehn in DOLLS AND PUPPETS (English edition) it is believed that even before the era in which living persons were sacrificed, straw or paper images were burned at funerals and the ashes placed in the graves. Thus we learn that paper figures of an unknown form were used as sacrificial offerings long before the time of Christ, and while they do not fall within the category of paper dolls as we know them, they are kindred and well may have inspired such dolls.

What seems to be the first mention of painted figures of the human form was by Marco Polo about the year 1280 when he visited China. He spoke of the male and female figures, as well as figures of animals, clothing, etc., having been burned with the corpse.

Another strange custom in China, believed still to be followed, is the ritual of the Chinese kitchen-god, Tsao Chun. This is a panel of beautiful red paper about six by 11-5/8 inches, printed in the usual fine Oriental art. Some variations in design have been noted, but the one from the writer's collection, pictured in Illus. No. 1, shows Tsao Chun squatting on a floor mat with five attendants grouped about him. For an entire year, in his capacity as watch-dog for the supreme Taoist deity, he gazes down from his post on the wall of the brick stove, observing the carryings-on of the family.

By New Year's Eve, (February 1st in China), he has become grimy from kitchen soot, and is taken down and burned to aid his ascension in smoke to the upper regions, a fresh god replacing him on the stove to do duty for the ensuing year. Since it is the obligation of Tsao Chun to report to the Taoist deity, it behooves the family to follow the prescribed ritual of showing him special attention twice a month, at new and at full moon. Persons who have neglected these attentions during the year attempt to attone for their lapses by smearing honey on the god's mouth on New Year's Eve just before he ascends to the Taoist heaven, so he will say only sweet things of his appeasers.

JAPANESE PURIFICATION FIGURES

What particular substance is there in paper to so endow it with magic in the minds of the less enlightened peoples of the world? In Japan it is the Katashiro.

We are indebted to Luella Tilton Hart and Elizabeth Andrews Fisher for permission to quote from the interesting and informative book, THE JAPANESE DOLL, written by Mrs. Hart and published by Mrs. Fisher, and to Mr. Paul A. Ruddell who holds republishing rights. Little paper figures called Katashiro, (meaning form-token), have been made and used in the Purification or Cleansing ceremony in Japan since the year 900 or even before. Twice a year the Shinto believer goes to his shrine and for a few yen purchases the Katashiro figure which he takes home. On it he writes his name, the year and month of his birth, his sex, then breathes on the figure and rubs it over his body, thus transferring disease and impurities to the Katashiro. This is then returned to the Priest at the Shrine. At the close of the ceremonial period, all of these figures are placed in a boat, taken out to deep water and thrown to the waves.

The Katashiro figure symbolizes the human form, and is made throughout the Kyoto District of Japan. In Illus. 2 the extreme left figure is for a female, the next at right for a male. They measure 2-3/4 by 5½ inches including the "head", are cut double, the head cut from the front and carried upward; side slits seem intended to give the figure some semblance of arms. The two figures are cut from different colors of paper, but Mrs. Hart notes that they also are sometimes cut from white.

The 2½ by 4½ inch figure at extreme right in the illustration, perhaps suggesting a kimono in shape and cut from brown paper, is used for a purification ceremony on the evening of the first day of spring (February 3rd or 4th) at Yoshida Shrine, Kyoto; the figure is common to both male and female.

No. 1. Chinese Kitchen-god 6 by 11 inches. Author's Collection.

8

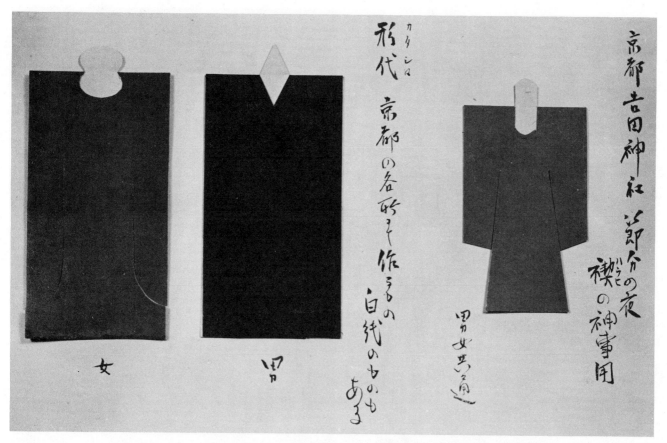

ILLUS. NO. 2. KATASHIRO FIGURES. FROM THE LUELLA T. HART COLLECTION

MEXICAN WITCHCRAFT

In a remote, uncivilized area of Mexico on the border of the states of Puebla and Hidalgo, accessible only by horseback, paper dolls are put to strange uses, as told by Miss Bodil Christensen of Mexico City who has kindly consented to inclusion here of material from her writings as well as information sent to this writer personally.

The inhabitants are Otomi Indians, uncivilized and steeped in superstition. To them everything in nature, the mountain, the well, the earth, the field, the rain, has a Spirit which has to be appeased by making offerings at certain times in ceremonies called costumbres (customs), in order to assure good health, and prosperity in the form of good crops. So-called paper dolls play an important part in these rituals at which only the medicine-man or sorcerer has the power and ability to officiate.

To serve in the ceremony to assure good crops, intricate figures are beautifully cut from tissue paper by the Witch Doctor or Medicine-Man. These are called Seed Dolls, and represent the Spirits of the seeds of various crops. Each figure corresponds in color to the plant it represents, and is easily distinguishable by the fruits that sprout from its sides. The doll for the banana plant, for instance, is green with a cluster of bananas on top of the head and bananas sprouting from the sides.

The 9¾ inch white tissue figure shown in Illus. 3 represents the Lord of the Honey Bee, while the 10½ inch dark figure represents the Spirit of the Green Pepper. Others are cut for corn, beans, and so on.

In the crop control ceremony the sorcerer kills a chicken, dips the applicable paper doll in the blood, then places it under a pile of stones in the center of the field to invoke the auspices of the proper Spirit to bring forth a good crop.

Wierd figures are cut from bark paper made from the bark of certain trees, pounded to paper thinness after a period of cooking and drying. The light colored bark paper dolls are used for good magic—curing, healing and invoking protection; the dark figures for evil magic, as revenge on an enemy in the way of poor crop returns and the like.

Two bark paper figures are shown in Illus. 4. The light colored one is placed in the hand of a dead person for burial to protect him from lurking dangers on his wanderings through the underworld. The black figure is used in a Death ceremony. There is also a fantastic ceremony for the "Spirit of the House" to give thanks for the shelter and protection the house has given to its owner during the first two years of occupancy.

An amusing example of the faith placed by the Otomi in the protective powers of the white paper dolls is that of an Indian who was brought to the nearest village to appear before a judge for some crime he had committed; when a white paper doll with the lips sewn together was found on him, he explained it was to prevent the judge from pronouncing sentence on him!

All this within our own hemisphere though in so remote an area as to seem of another world, but strange and even ludicrous as these costumbres appear to us, to the Otomis they are a natural way of life, faithfully followed in deep sincerity.

9

No. 3. Mexican Green Pepper figure 10½ inches; Lord of the Honey Bee, 9⅜ inches. Author's Collection.

ILLUS. NO. 4. MEXICAN WHITE AND BLACK PAPER-BARK FIGURES, USED IN BURIAL AND DEATH CEREMONIES.
AUTHOR'S COLLECTION.

No. 5-A. Box Cover for Dean & Son's, England, Fanny Grey.

Chapter II
Early American Commercial Paper Dolls

Presumed to be the first paper doll commercially produced in the United States was a toy-book type comprising a series of separate removable costumes enclosed in a small booklet titled "The History and Adventures of Little Henry, exemplified in a series of Figures". This was published by J. Belcher, Boston, Massachusetts in 1812, and while there was no complete paper doll as in our later sets, one head with a neck tab was furnished, which, when inserted in the pocket provided on the back of each costume, converted it into a full figure paper doll. These action costumes were hand-colored and depicted the various happenings in Little Henry's eventful life. Unavailable for definite authentication, details at hand evidence this to be a copy of a booklet of same title and embodying the same characteristics as one published for S. and J. Fuller at the Temple of Fancy, Rathbone Place, London in 1810. (This latter publication is featured in a later chapter devoted to foreign dolls.)

Mr. Herbert H. Hosmer, Jr. in his booklet "A Brief History of Toy Books", 1954, states that copies of many of the Fuller books were published in Boston and Philadelphia in the years 1815/1820. Mostly, however, the American editions come under the classification of toy books rather than paper dolls since, as stated by Mr. Hosmer, illustrations were complete pages bound into the books, not cut-out figures. Therefore, "The History and Adventures of Little Henry", published in Boston in 1812 with removable costumes may be the exception, and the scant available details are given here only to attest the American publication of a type of paper doll early in the century.

A second edition of *Little Henry* is reported to have been published in Philadelphia, Pennsylvania, in 1825, also a copy of the 1810 Fuller book, but with engraved plates bound into the book which automatically places it in the classification of a toy-book. As will be established by similar incidents cited in this work, lacking International copyright regulations prior to December, 1887, copying of published works appears to have been freely indulged in on both sides of the Atlantic.

The next known American commercial paper doll is a boxed set of action costumes also accompanied by a separate head with a neck tab. Published in 1854 by Crosby, Nichols & Co., 111 Washington St., Boston, this boxed set is titled "Fanny Gray, a History of Her Life, Illustrated by Six Colored Figures". The beautiful lithography was by S. W. Chandler & Bro., great-great-uncles of Herbert H. Hosmer, Jr.; the brother in the firm was John Greene Chandler, and

Mr. Hosmer has founded and directs the John Greene Chandler Memorial at South Lancaster, Massachusetts.

Illustration 5 shows the Fanny Gray set and the box in which it was distributed. The cover design of the 6-¾ by 8¼ by one inch deep box is so exquisitely and delicately lithographed in the softest of tones as to constitute a little masterpiece in itself.

In addition to a background scene showing "The Cottage Where Fanny Lived," there are five action costumes representing various episodes as they unfold in her everyday life; Fanny with her kitten, 4-15/16 inches; Fanny selling matches, 5¼ inches; feeding the chickens, 5¼ inches; as a flower girl, 6 inches, and finally as her Uncle's Pet, 6-⅛ inches, the last-named accompanied by a precious little "blue bonnet with pink roses on it." Measurements were taken with the head in place on each costume. Regrettably the little wooden standard furnished with the paper doll is missing from the otherwise complete pictured set.

The small booklet entitled "Fanny Gray, a History of Her Life" tells the story, in verse as was popular at the time, of the child left an orphan by the death of her widowed mother; this necessitated Fanny's roaming the streets selling matches in order to eke out a bare living. Adopted by a prosperous farmer who was touched by her plight, Fanny enjoyed an interlude of affluent living, but when Farmer Weston's crops and his health failed, poor little Fanny was once again forced to the streets. Happily a wealthy uncle who stopped to purchase a nosegay from Fanny's basket of flowers, chanced to recognize her as his only sister's child. Thenceforth Fanny revelled in a life of luxury.

Mr. Hosmer has in his possession the priceless original sketches for this famous paper doll, together with the manuscript for the verses written in ink in a beautiful style. The sketches are brilliantly executed in oil on cardboard, and the one for the cottage where Fanny lived bears the title "Fanny Gray" with the date, "May 1853" which places the original drawings more than a year earlier than the published set. These drawings were preserved in a box the cover of which also bears the name of the published work. A visit to the John Greene Chandler Memorial could be highly rewarding.

While not a duplicate of the toy-book, "The History of Little Fanny—Exemplified in a Series

13

ILLUS. 5. — CHANDLER'S FANNY GRAY. AUTHOR'S COLLECTION.

of Figures", printed for S. and J. Fuller at the Temple of Fancy, London in 1810, the latter well may have furnished the inspiration for the American paper doll.

In the foreword of the little history book accompanying the 1854 Fanny Gray set, the publishers state that they "have spared no expense upon any part of the work, being desirous to present a beautiful specimen of printing in color". The finished work bespeaks fulfillment of their objective.

And here we cite clear example of the obvious copying of a published work, in this instance reversed as to countries. In Illustration 5-A we show the box of an English edition of a *Fanny Grey* paper doll (note changed spelling of the surname) which, in all main details, is a duplicate of the Chandler 1854 set.

Published by Dean & Son, 31 Ludgate Hill, London, this box measures 7 by 8-5/8 by about 7/8 inches deep, only slightly larger over all than the Chandler box. As plainly evidenced by our illustration, the cover design is different and the title changed to FANNY GREY AND HER TRANS-FORMATIONS. The running vine design is lithographed in a dull, darkish green, the box bordered by an embossed floral braid.

Costumes are identical in design and size to the Chandler ones, with the exception that base designs are a little less detailed. Because of this duplication of costumes, we are showing only the box of the Dean & Son production. Unfortunately the original head is missing, but the doll shown in the cover design is identical to the Chandler figure. Whether or not a history book was included in the English set is not known.

Since only the publisher's name and street address appear on the English box, the question immediately arose as to which of the two sets came first. An inquiry addressed to the London publisher brought the response that all of their early records were destroyed during the war, precluding their supplying any information regarding early productions.

Subsequent inquiries finally resulted in the information, kindly provided by the London Museum, that Dean & Son were located at 31 Ludgate Hill from 1855 to 1856. This surely establishes the publication date of *Fanny Grey and her Transformations* as at least a year or two later than the Chandler set, as well as lending credence to the obviousness of Dean & Son's having deliberately copied the Chandler set. If, as is said, mimicry is the sincerest form of flattery, *Fanny Gray* may indulge a justified sense of pride.

Three years later Brown, Taggard & Chase of Boston published a series of charming paper dolls lithographed and copyrighted by J. G. Chandler. These, unlike Fanny Gray, are full-bodied dolls with wardrobes seemingly quaint more than a hundred years later, but high style in 1857. The dolls, with the exception of No. 7, a larger one, were distributed in individual envelopes lithographed in black on white stock, measuring approximately 7-⅜ by 3-⅜ inches. Ornately decorated with fancy scroll work, they proclaimed "HURRAH FOR THE LITTLE FOLKS. Chandler's PAPERDOLLS of the Latest Paris Fashions". Listed below are the known Chandler dolls:

No. 1, Carry.

No. 2, Alice

No. 3, Charley

No. 4, Little Fairy Lightfoot

No. 5, Betty the Milkmaid and all her pets

No. 6, Jack and His Holiday Companions

No. 7, May Queen and Shepherdess

Originals of all of these dolls are reproduced in illustrations Numbers 6 through 12.

Dolls Nos. 1 and 2, *Carry* and *Alice* (Illus. 6 and 7) are similar in design and execution. Costumes appear to have been folded at the shoulder line so when cut out, plain backs are provided exactly following the lines of the fronts, even to the scalloped hemlines.

Doll No. 4, *Little Fairy Lightfoot* (9), uncolored and fragile in appearance, is the daintitst of all. Her costumes, however, are delicately tinted, and imagination imparts life to her little dancing feet.

Betty the Milkmaid (10), *Charley* (8), and *Jack and His Holiday Companions* (11), are re-produced from rarely found uncut original sheets. Confusion has existed in the minds of certain collectors as to which of the last-named dolls is Charley and which Jack. These uncuts serve to dispel all doubt, and we are indeed fortunate to have the privilege of providing this unquestionable proof.

As evidenced by Illustration No. 12, the *May Queen and Shepherdess* is every inch a queen. Eight inches tall, she wears a permanent dress with white flounces and an over-dress of rose pink; there are no separate dresses. For this reason she is posed adorned in her pale green queen's cape with golden crown, the colorful floral wreath upheld by means of ready-cut slots in her closed hands. Divested of this royal raiment she is equally lovely while tending the sheep, at which time she wears her yellow straw hat with its trim of pink roses and ribbons, one of her hand slots serving to accommodate the floral-decorated crook. We consider this doll to be one of Chandler's finest achievements. We are indeed indebted to Mr. Hosmer for generously lending it for inclusion here.

These Chandler paper dolls were lithographed in the fine workmanship for which the brothers were noted. The dolls in underwear have touches of color, flesh tints on the exposed parts of the body, neck-ties on the boys, shoes, gloves and the like on the girls.

In addition to these paper dolls the Chandlers published many juvenile books and toys, one of the latter being a boxed cut-out toy, "The American National Circus" to thrill the heart of any child. A part of this is now in the John Greene Chandler Memorial.

There also is an animated print or card of *St. Nicholas,* dated 1859, but since this work deals mainly with paper dolls other published items are not covered in detail.

NO. 6. CARRY. 3¾ INCHES. HERBERT H. HOSMER COLLECTION.

NO. 7. ALICE. 4-9/16 INCHES. AUTHOR'S COLLECTION.

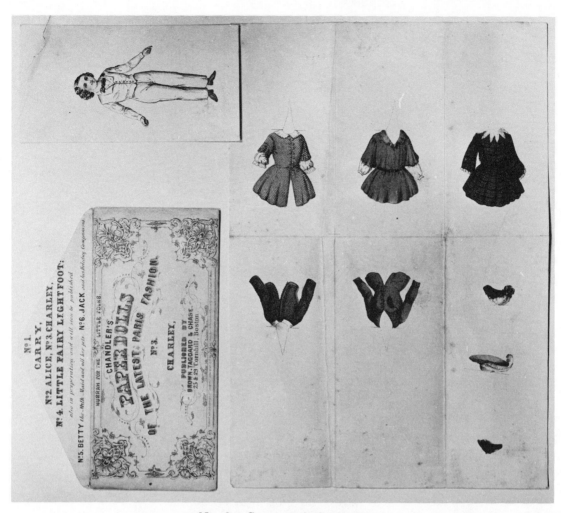

No. 8. CHANDLER'S CHARLEY.

No. 9. LITTLE FAIRY LIGHTFOOT, 3½ INCHES. COURTESY HERBERT H. HOSMER.

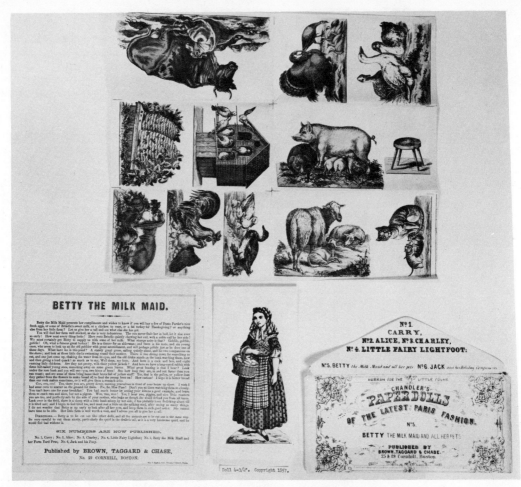

No. 10. BETTY THE MILKMAID, $4^5/_8$ INCHES.

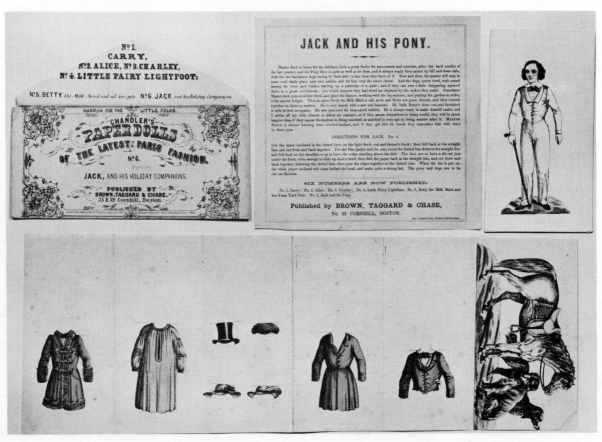

No. 11. JACK AND HIS HOLIDAY COMPANIONS, UNCUT. $4^1/_2$ INCHES.

No. 12. May Queen and Shepherdess, 8 inches. Hosmer Collection.

ARE THEY CHANDLERS?

In Illustration 13 we show two dolls, one in riding position with her mount, the doll 4-⅜ inches, the standing one as pictured minus feet about 4¼. These came together without container or other identification. However, all characteristics point strongly to Chandler workmanship. Note similarity of pose, features and undies to *Carry* and *Alice* of the listed Chandler series. The texture and weight of the light board stock from which all are cut indicate it to be the same. The cape costume came with

both Alice and the two unidentified girls. Presumably it rightly belongs to only one of the dolls, but the fact that a Chandler costume came with the two girls, as did also the pony and dogs rightly belonging to *Jack* of the Chandler series, seems to strengthen our supposition, concurred in by Mr. Hosmer, that the two unidentified dolls probably originated with J. G. Chandler. However, without proof this is, as stated, supposition only. Can anyone supply the answer?

No. 13. Unidentified dolls, possibly Chandler's, 4¼ and 4⅜ inches, respectively. Author's Collection.

In this same year of 1857 and into 1858, Clark, Austin & Smith of New York brought out a series of paper dolls under the heading, THE GIRLS' DELIGHT, front printing only. These were distributed in horizontal-opening envelopes of various sizes to suit the individual dolls. The following list is believed to comprise the total output of this company:

No. 1. Miss Florence.   No. 6. Cinderella

No. 2. Miss Hattie.   No. 7. The Little Pet (dated 1857.)

No. 3. Master Frank (not illus.)   No. 8. Ella. (dated 1858).

No. 4. Nellie   No. 9. Lillie Beers.

No. 5. Clara   No. 10. Emmie and Willie (dated 1858)

Miss Florence, Number 14, is shown by courtesy of Mrs. Margarett Dartt of California, and attention is called that the top right hand duplicate costume "is left plain so that it may be colored according to taste".

In Number 15 we have *Miss Hattie,* doll Number 2 in above schedule, with her four dresses, a cape, one hat, and a bonnet. Like *Miss Florence,* she is an appealing, quaint little girl in precise pose and with tight corkscrew curls.

As will be noted in Number 16, *Nellie* is of different construction from the other Clark, Austin & Smith dolls. She consists of only a head, bust and arms, daintily tinted, cut in one piece with the skirt-shaped uncolored lower body which is without legs or undies. Her right arm is cut out to be brought forward over her dresses. It seems strange that after publishing three full-bodied dolls the company would revert to a less detailed one, but this may have been a whim of the particular artist who designed her. Her wardrobe consists of four elaborate costumes, a fichu and a bonnet.

As disclosed in The Story of Her Life, quoted from the envelope for its amusing content, Nellie was a romantic young lady, to her mother's dismay:

"NELLIE—a young lady of the 'upper ten',—with dresses, etc., sufficient in number and elegance for a princess of 'the blood'.

"Nellie has reached the age when mothers must 'look out' for their daughters, unless they wish some youngster to come along and snatch them away, and take them off out West, or some where else, just as it happened to my friend Nellie.

"A nice young man saw her, was captivated by her many charms—as well he might be—and now she is gone. Her mother has just discovered that she cannot spare her.

"MORAL. Mothers must beware of 'the beaux,' before it is too late."

And so poor Nellie is gone, but she will appear again as *Nellie North* in the following chapter covering McLoughlin Bros.' paper dolls, as she is one of the several like dolls published by both firms. While to our knowledge it never has been definitely established which firm was first in the field, it seems to be the consensus of opinion that Clark, Austin & Smith preceded McLoughlin Bros. Duplication of dolls will be discussed in Chapter III.

Illustration 17 gives us *Clara,** doll No. 5 of the series. This is from the collection of the late Nellie D. MacLachlan, and is one of the hard-to-find paper dolls. She has been reported in no other collection available to us and we are greatly indebted to Miss MacLachlan's nephew, Mr. Alexander MacLachlan, for its inclusion here. Four of the costumes shown are exactly like four of those for McLoughlin Bros.' *Clara West* covered in following chapter; the bodies of the two dolls are alike, the heads different. Only uncut sets would serve to authenticate the costumes of one not included in the other of these cut sets.

Practically the same situation exists with the two Cinderellas, except that the dolls of both companies are exactly alike, the McLoughlin Bros.' set in the author's collection having one additional costume which may or may not have been originally included in the Clark, Austin & Smith set, (Illustration 18). Costumes for the McLoughlin Bros.' *Cinderella* have been verified as correct by an uncut set in the collection of Mrs. Rupert W. Jaques of Marblehead, Massachusetts.

The Little Pet, doll No. 7 of the series (Illustration No. 19), was distributed in an ornately decorated envelope bearing copyright date of 1857, the last of the series to be issued in that year. This is another example of dolls duplicated by McLoughlin Bros., as will be noted in Chapter III, Illustration No. 63.

Ella, Doll No. 8, (Illustration No. 19-A), is 4½ inches tall, and also was duplicated by McLoughlin Bros. The 7-¾ by 3-¾ inch envelope for Clark, Austin & Smith's No. 8 doll is printed in light blue on white stock, and is inscribed, "Entered according to Act of Congress in the year 1858. . . ." *Ella* is the first of the listed dolls produced by this company in 1858, and it follows that Doll No. 9, *Lillie Beers,* must also have been published in the same year though no envelope is available for verification. Likewise, no doll has come in, but in view of the many dolls duplicated by McLoughlin Bros., it well may be presumed that this number falls within that category, as possibly do *Emmie and Willie,* No. 10. Listing for this No. 10 pair was furnished by the late Mrs. H. B. Armstrong of Austin, Texas, who stated, "This container is small with rather elaborate decoration and bearing the date line of 1858". Regrettably we do not have measurements of either the dolls or the container.

It is interesting to note that the envolopes for the first four dolls published by Clark, Austin & Smith were quite plain, the only decoration a not too fancy border-scroll surrounding the printing which describes the doll enclosed; further, that none of these four containers bears a copyright date. Thus it appears that the first four dolls were issued without benefit of patent, since envelopes from the No. 5 doll on did bear copyright dates, also were much decorated. Illustrations of this series of dolls evidence these points.

While, as previously stated, the above is believed to cover the paper dolls produced by Clark, Austin & Smith, they did publish paper furniture. The late Mrs. Armstrong had in her possession an envelope bearing the same heading as that for the paper dolls, THE GIRLS' DELIGHT, and the inscription, "Paper Furniture Number One, for Paper Dolls". This was a much decorated envelope having a rustic border, perhaps to simulate bamboo, and with corner decorations of tiny designs of furniture and accessories. The extent of the company's production of paper furniture is not known.

An attractive little book, titled "PAPER FURNITURE FOR PAPER DOLLS". "For the Amusement of Little Girls", was published by Clark, Austin & Smith. Authored by Amy Ward, New York, this book bears copyright date of 1857, and contains four pages of directions for making paper furniture with eight plates of completed designs.

Data gathered by Miss Lillian Faffer discloses that during the years from 1844 to 1876 there were many changes in the company personnel. Whether or not they published paper dolls after 1858 has not been established, but since so many of their dolls were duplicated by McLoughlin Bros. beginning in 1857-58, and no identified Clark, Austin & Smith doll of a later date than 1858 has come to light, it seems reasonable to suppose that their output was limited to this period.

Whether Mc Loughlin Bros. purchased rights from the former concern, or whether a royalty or other form of agreement was entered into between the two companies, or if possibly piracy existed (which is extremely doubtful), has never been traced to a satisfactory conclusion. However, Miss Faffer's valuable research does prove that Clark, Austin & Smith, under various firm name changes, were listed in New York City directories until 1876, which appears to preclude the question of merger as previously had been considered a possibility.

* * *

*Photograph of *Clara* by Samuel Kravitt, New Haven, Connecticut.

NO. 14. MISS FLORENCE, 4-5/8 INCHES. MARGARETT M. DARTT COLLECTION.

No. 15. Miss Hattie, 3¾ inches. Author's Collection.

No. 16. Nellie, 5-11/16 inches. Author's Collection.

No. 17. Clara, 5½ inches. Collection the late Nellie D. MacLachlan.

No. 18. Cinderella, 4⅝ inches. Author's Collection.

No. 19. The Little Pet, 3-⅛ inches.

An apparently little known publisher of paper dolls was Joseph E. Shaw of Philadelphia. His connection with the paper doll industry was unknown to this writer until some time ago when a beautiful little paper doll, bearing his name as publisher, came in original uncut condition. This is reproduced in Illustration 20.

The Little Favourite, Mary Lee measures 3-7/8 inches, face printing only. Colorings of the entire set are very lovely including the red upholstery and the green fringe of the footstool upon which Mary stands.

The following dolls are listed on the instruction sheet:

PAPER DOLLS.

The little favorite MARY LEE : LITTLE EVA.
AMANDA and her Pet Lamb.
: DOLLIE DUTTON.
LAURA BELL will shortly appear.   : FANNY.
Two kinds of Dolls on card board, with dresses on paper to match.

PAPER SOLDIERS.

Washington's Troops of '76, with Washington on his white charger,—Minute Men of '76.

Also,—MAGIC CARDS.

GAMES—The Snake Game, and the Social Snake, or a Tour through the United States.

While no copyright date appears, the instruction sheet bears address of 733 Spring Garden Street, Philadelphia. Cohen's city directory lists Mr. Shaw as a publisher at this address for the year 1860. For the following year he was listed as a printer, and thereafter was variously listed as a collector, printer and constable. It follows therefore that Mary Lee supposedly was published in 1860, though obviously designed in the late 1850's when heelless shoes were in vogue.

No other Shaw doll is known to us at this time, but the possibility exists that among the many unidentified paper dolls in numerous collections, others might be found were original containers available for authentication.

One such possibilty is the *Little Eva* shown on page 109, Illus. 75, in PAPER DOLLS—A GUIDE TO COSTUME by Clara Hallard Fawcett. Since the doll pictured is not McLoughlin Bros.' *Little Eva,* illustrated in two sizes in the following chapter, might she be the missing Shaw doll of same name?

The lack of importance attached in the past to containers of so many of our early paper dolls is deplorable. Those that show signs of having been played with point to the conclusion that little girls, in their zeal to dress and undress their paper dolls for the parties they arranged, discarded the containers as of no interest in their activities. These same containers would constitute very valuable adjuncts to our collections today.

No. 20. The Little Favourite, Mary Lee, 3-7/8 inches. Author's Collection.

Probably the best known of Anson D. F. Randolph's publications is the quaint little book published in 1856 at 683 Broadway, New York. Titled PAPER DOLLS AND HOW TO MAKE THEM, author unknown, this work enjoyed wide popularity, judging by the many homemade paper dolls that have come to light, patterned after the designs contained between the covers of this small book.

In the following year Mr. Randolph published a companion book, "PAPER DOLL'S FURNITURE: How to Make It", containing 63 pages and 70 pattern drawings and illustrations of completed pieces of furniture. This carries the author's name, C. B. Allair, and was copyrighted under date of 1857.

An interesting side-light developed when, several years after acquiring a copy, a book of similar format titled HOW TO MAKE DOLLS' FURNITURE AND FURNISH A DOLL'S HOUSE came into my possession. This was published by Griffith and Farran, London, and a page-by-page comparison of the two books reveals this English edition to be practically a copy of Mr. Randolph's book. Illustrations are identical with the exception of one added plate in the English edition; text is the same with a minimum of minor changes in phrasing. Names of the two little girls, Annie and Ella, who begged Mrs. Allair to "mark the lines out on paper and then we can cut it out ourselves" are used in both books; however, "Mrs. Allair" of the Randolph book becomes "Mrs. Elliot" in the English edition, while "Bridget" of the New York kitchen becomes "Mary" in London.

This latter book bears no date, but included in a listing of available books at the back is THE GIRL'S OWN TOY MAKER, likewise published by Griffith and Farran and dated 1860. This definitely proves that the London edition of the furniture book could not have been released prior to that date, and establishes the plagiarism in this particular instance.

Ironically, then, comparison of a copy of the 1860 book, THE GIRL'S OWN TOY MAKER, with GODEY'S LADY'S BOOK discloses that at least five of the toys with directions for making included in the former book appeared in GODEY'S during the following year.

Perhaps inspired by the little book on Paper Dolls which he had published in the previous year, Anson D. F. Randolph brought out a seemingly limited number of paper dolls in 1857, but happily, surviving specimens establish that what may have been lacking in quantity was amply offset by quality and the intent to produce toys of an educational nature.

The most pretentious set to come to light is titled *National Costumes: A New and Instructive Amusement for the Young.* This is a fairly large boxed set consisting of a young lady doll with sixteen costumes representing styles native to the countries where they were worn: German Peasant; Finland; Spanish; French Fisher Girl; Turkish; Italian; Circassian; Greek; Russian Peasant; Bohemian; Scotch;

Swiss Canton Berne; French Court of Louis XIV, and Nun Annuncion.

The set shown in Illustration 21, 21a, b and c is from the collection of the late Nellie D. MacLachlan, and is included here by courtesy of The Doll Collectors of America, Inc., publishers of the copyrighted DOLL COLLECTORS MANUAL, 1956-1957 in which duplicate illustrations of this set appeared.

No. 21 shows the box cover design and the copyrighted date of 1857; in 21a we see a likeness of the doll, three of the costumes, and the small booklet containing descriptions of the countries where the various dresses were worn. Illustrations 21b and 21c complete the costume series.

Though slanted to the minds of children, in the light of a changing world these brief glimpses into the century-old history of the featured fourteen foreign countries is interesting:

GERMANY

Germany is divided into a great many duchies and kingdoms. Some parts have mountains and forests; and in others are fine vineyards. There are many famous cities, and old castles, and churches in Germany. The Germans are very much attached to their country, and their homes are happy. They are simple and affectionate, honest, and industrious. The poor women work in the fields. The higher classes are well educated. There are very many learned men in Germany.

The religion of some parts is Roman Catholic, and of others, Protestant.

HUNGARY

Hungary is now subject to the Emperor of Austria, but the Hungarians love their country and hope that it will again be free. There are high mountains at the north and east, which keep off the cold winds, and make the climate mild. There are extensive forests, in which are fierce wolves. The Hungarian nobles are very rich, and oppress the poor who live upon their lands.

The religion is partly Protestant, and partly Roman Catholic.

RUSSIA

Russia is the largest country in the world. The climate of the Northern parts is very cold. There are many forests, containing bears and wolves, which sometimes attack travellers. The Russian noblemen are very rich, and live magnificently; but the peasants, or serfs, who live upon the lands of these noblemen, are poor and ignorant, and have to work very hard; they are bought and sold with the land. Russia is governed by an Emperor, who can do very much as he pleases. The name of the present Emperor is Alexander. The religion is Greek.

FRANCE

France is a very beautiful country, and its climate is delightful and healthy. Its capital is

Paris, a gay and splendid city. The French are very polite and social, and fond of excitement and amusements. They excel in the fine arts. There are many learned men among them. The French language is spoken in most of the courts of Europe. The religion of the country is Roman Catholic, though there are some Protestants. France is now governed by an Emperor, Louis Napoleon.

Louis XIV was King of France at the end of the seventeenth century. His court was very gay and luxurious.

SWEDEN

Sweden and Norway, separated by the Scandinavian mountains, compose one kingdom. Sweden is a cold but very healthy country, with many woods and lakes. A great quantity of iron is found there.

The common people are industrious and fond of reading. The government provides schools in all important places, and the people are intelligent and well educated. The religion is Protestant. The King's palace in Stockholm is considered the most beautiful one in Europe. The name of the present King is Oscar.

ITALY

Italy is famous for its sunny skies, its delightful climate, its paintings and statues, and ruins. Flowers and fruits grow there in the greatest abundance. Rome is its capital. It was once a very grand city, and is full of interesting relics. The church of St. Peter's in Rome, is the largest in the world. The Italians of the lower classes are generally idle, ignorant, and superstitious. Their religion is the Roman Catholic. The Pope lives in Rome.

BOHEMIA

Bohemia now belongs to Austria. It is a flat country, surrounded by mountains. The climate is dry and mild, and many of the people live to a great age. It has large orchards and vineyards, and corn-fields. There are gipsies in some of the forests.

The religion is mostly the Roman Catholic.

FINNLAND

Finnland now belongs to Russia. It is so far north that the climate is very cold. It has many pine forests, and lakes, and mountains of bare rocks, on some of which the snow lies all the year. There are only four months of summer and harvest, when the weather is hot and dry, and vegetation is very rapid. There are great herds of reindeer in the northern parts. The inhabitants are mostly Lutherans. The Governor-general lives in Helsingfors, where is a University, with a library of 40,000 volumes.

CIRCASSIA

Circassia is crossed by branches of the Caucasus, some of whose summits are covered with snow nearly all the year. Those high mountains with their torrents and ravines, and the forests and cultivated fields at their base, make the scenery very wild and grand. The climate is temperate and healthful. The land is not well cultivated, for the people have not good implements, nor much knowledge of agriculture; but corn and wine are raised abundantly. Sheep, goats, and cattle are numerous. Almost every man has his horse, which he treats with the greatest care. The Circassians are celebrated for their fine physical form; and the women for their beauty. The women are subject to the men, and the life of a woman is considered by law, only half as valuable as that of a man. The children must stand in the presence of their father; and when they eat, they go into a corner and turn their backs. The religion of the Circassians is a mixture of Christianity, Mohammedanism, and Paganism.

SWITZERLAND

Switzerland has the grandest scenery in Europe; high mountains with their glaciers, and waterfalls, green valleys, and broad lakes. Roads have been made, at great cost, over the Alps, which are between Switzerland and Italy. Switzerland is divided into cantons, and there is a great variety in the dress, customs, and characters of the people in the different cantons. The religion, too, is different— Protestant in some parts, and Catholic in others. The capital is Berne.

SCOTLAND

Scotland was once a kingdom by itself, but is now a part of Great Britain. It is a beautiful country, celebrated for its lakes and mountains. Its chief city is Edinburgh, which has a famous castle. The climate is cold and the people are hardy. They are simple, honest, industrious, and religious.

SPAIN

Spain is a beautiful country, with a fine, warm climate. It has high mountains and deep valleys, among which are large herds of horses, sheep, and goats. Figs, grapes, olives, oranges, and other fruits grow in great abundance. The Spaniards are excitable, and fond of dress and amusements, especially of bull-fights, which even the women love to witness. Their religion is the Roman Catholic. The name of the present queen is Isabella.

TURKEY

Turkey is an extensive country. Its climate is generally fine and healthy. The soil is fertile, though not well cultivated. Fruits grow abundantly. There are not many roads for carriages in Turkey, but the men are great riders, and have excellent horses. The chief city is Constantinople, which looks finely from the sea, but its streets are narrow and dirty. The Sultan lives in Constantinople. The Turkish women are not respected by their husbands and sons. The men have several wives, who spend their time in dressing, and bathing, and lounging. Their dress is magnificent. The religion is the Mohammedan, and until lately, no other religion has been allowed, but the present Sultan has made laws which permit his subjects to change their religion.

GREECE

Greece was once famous for its beautiful statues, and buildings, and wise men; and is still famous for its fine climate, and scenery, and remains of ancient art. The Greeks are a gay, thoughtless, uncultivated people. The women are handsome, but fond of dress, and uneducated. The religion is that of the Greek Church. The present King is Otho, a German.

* * *

This was indeed an educational toy of the time, and without doubt fulfilled the obvious aim of the publisher to arouse the interest of children in the study of history.

While Randolph published many books for children, the only other set of paper dolls known to us at this time is a set called *The Paper Doll Family*. This was advertised by Mr. Randolph on a flyer page in one edition of his book on Paper Dolls' Furniture, dated 1857, as "consisting of Seven Figures, with Five Dresses for each. Done up in a neat box. Price, 50 cts. In Envelopes containing one Figure, with Wardrobe, 10 Cts. Each." To add lure to his advertisement he incorporated in his copy, reviews apparently lifted from certain publications which provide additional details of this interesting paper doll family:

"The advent of the 'Paper Doll Family' will be hailed with delight by all little girls. The figures are executed on cardboard, the dresses on paper, and by simply cutting them out, are ready for use. The dolls are natural in their form and figure, from the father to the wee baby; the dresses are nicely colored, and constitute a full and handsome wardrobe."—COURIER.

* * *

"Who ever is enriched by the possession of 'Paper Dolls' will wish to add the 'Family' to their treasures. There are seven dolls, suitably colored, father, mother, sister, brother, and Bridget. These are furnished with a full colored wardrobe, ready to be cut out for use."—FARMER.

"Published by ANSON D. F. RANDOLPH,

683 Broadway, Cor. Amity St., N. Y."

"On receipt of seventeen Stamps, a copy of the Set, in a wrapper, will be sent by mail, pre-paid."

* * *

One wonders why only five dolls were listed in the second above quoted review, but from the two we learn the "family" consisted of father to baby,

with a maid or nurse. The flyer also announces three different methods of distribution—complete family, boxed, at 50 cts., individual dolls in envelopes at 10 cts., and the family in a wrapper for seventeen stamps, probably 34 cts. It fires the imagination and it is to be regretted that a full set cannot be illustrated. The only available member is *Miss Adelaide*, No. 3 of the series. Illus. 22 includes the envelope dated 1857, the quaint little lady herself with a bonnet and four costumes, all original except the jacket dress at right of the envelope in the photographic illustration; this is a homemade dress.

We have no knowledge as to when Randolph suspended paper doll production, but a religious paper, THE PRESBYTERIAN, dated Dec. 20, 1884 in the author's possession, and showing an address for Randolph as 900 Broadway, Cor. 20th St., New York, contains two half-column advertisements of books with no mention of paper dolls. This may indicate that none was published as late as 1884, though this is not conclusive since only books of a religious nature were advertised. However, results of a search of New York City directories by Miss Faffer disclosed that Mr. Randolph was listed at the 683 Broadway address as a bookseller for years 1852/53, and as a publisher at the same address for years 1857/58. No listing is given for 1859/60, while in 1861/62 he is again listed as a bookseller. For 1869/70 the listing was changed to A.D.F. Randolph & Co.

In 1897 A.D.F. Randolph Co., New York, published an apparent twelve-sheet set of Indian villages. Eight of these uncut sheets are now in the Chester County Historical Society, Pennsylvania. They portray families, wigwams, tepees, canoes, and other appurtenances natural to the Indians' way of life. All figures are equipped with fold-back standards, each numbered as a guide to proper placement in an assembled village. The Indians themselves are depicted in active pursuits, the later numbered sheets showing them on the war-path with white soldiers on the scene. Sheet X gives us mounted and marching soldiers in blue with an unfurled flag atop a tall flagpole, indicating victory for the white men. Sheet XII shows a fine log mission house, and these 14 x 11-⅛ inch sheets are marked "Kindergarten in Missions, copyright, 1897, by the A.D.F. Randolph Co., New York." The name John Booth appears in the lower right hand corner, presumably the artist for this interesting paper toy.

While this set does not come under the heading of paper dolls, we have briefly covered it here since the date is the latest recorded one known to us for this company. It also strengthens our opinion that almost from the start books and paper toys constituted the main output of Mr. Randolph and his later associates and perhaps survivors.

A recent inquiry directed to the Randolph Publishing Institute of New York elicited the response that they are in no way connected with Anson D. F. Randolph or his former associates, and that their own inquiries in various directions have failed to produce anyone who knows of Mr. Randolph or what has happened to the company.

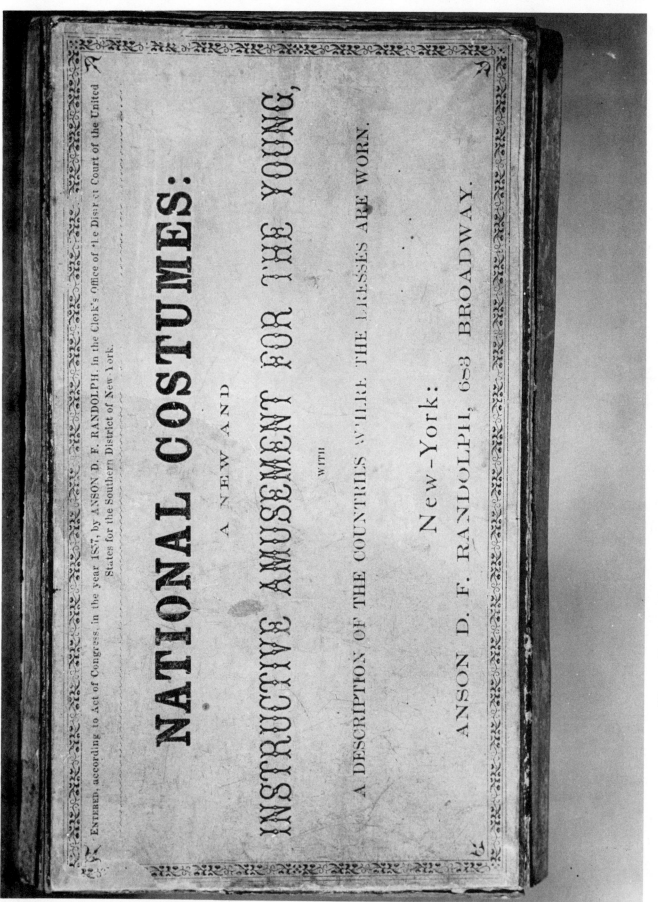

NATIONAL COSTUMES:

A NEW AND

INSTRUCTIVE AMUSEMENT FOR THE YOUNG,

WITH

A DESCRIPTION OF THE COUNTRIES WHERE THE DRESSES ARE WORN.

New-York:

ANSON D. F. RANDOLPH, 683 BROADWAY.

ENTERED, according to Act of Congress, in the year 1857, by ANSON D. F. RANDOLPH, in the Clerk's Office of the District Court of the United States for the Southern District of New-York.

No. 21. BOX FOR NATIONAL COSTUMES. COLLECTION THE LATE NELLIE MACLACHLAN.

GERMAN PEASANT.

FINNLAND

SPANISH.

NATIONAL COSTUMES:

AN

ELEGANT AND INSTRUCTIVE

AMUSEMENT.

WITH A DESCRIPTION OF THE COUNTRIES WHERE THESE
DRESSES ARE WORN.

NEW-YORK:
ANSON D. F. RANDOLPH, 683 BROADWAY.
1857.

No. 21a. DOLL, BOOKLET AND 3 COSTUMES FOR NATIONAL COSTUMES.

FRENCH FISHER GIRL   TURKISH   SWEDISH   HUNGARIAN

ITALIAN   CIRCASSIAN.   GREEK.   RUSSIAN PEASANT

No. 21b. PORTION NATIONAL COSTUMES SET.

BOHEMIAN.

SCOTCH

SWISS . CANTON BERNE.

FRENCH . COURT OF LOUIS XIV.

NUN . ANNUNCIATION .

No. 21c. Completes National Costumes set.

No. 22. MISS ADELAIDE, 4¼ INCHES. COURTESY MRS. MARGARETT M. DARTT.

Only two paper dolls are known to have been produced by this publisher of Lowell, Massachusetts, and are given in Illustration Number 22a.

At the left is shown a quaint little doll attributed to Hobbs. Through the auspices of Miss Lillian Faffer, and by courtesy of Miss Mathews of The Museum of the City of New York, this unnamed little lady with her four costumes was pictured in the October, 1960 issue of THE TOY TRADER, reproduced here by joint permission of Miss Mathews and Elizabeth Andrews Fisher, publisher of this popular little magazine.

Goody Two Shoes, with but two of her four costumes and only the lower portion of the original envelope, is pictured at the right in the illustration. From the collection of Margarett Dartt of California, the doll measures four inches, has front printing only, costumes executed in various combinations of red, green and yellow.

While a marked similarity in the design of the two dolls is apparent, there is a variation in the costumes. These are two rare and highly prized little paper dolls, date unknown but surely no later than the 1850's. If there are other known Hobbs paper dolls, it would be generous on the part of the owners to share all details.

R. A. Hobbs, paper doll, Lowell, Massachusetts
From collection of the Museum of the City of New York, Fifth Avenue and 103rd Street, New York, N. Y. Through the kindness of Miss Mathews and Miss Faffer.

—25—

Goody Two-Shoes.

No. 22a. L. COLLECTION OF THE MUSEUM OF THE CITY OF NEW YORK.

R. COLLECTION OF MARGARETT M. DARETT, CALIFORNIA.

Presently available records disclose the following listings for the Chromatic Printing Co. of Philadelphia, Pennsylvania, "Publishers of Toy-Books, Games, etc." as perhaps their total paper doll production. If others were published they have not been reported.

PAPER DOLLS, 6 kinds.

3 cents each.

BON TON SERIES.

Emily	Nellie
Clara	Amelia
Florence	Josephine

PAPER DOLLS, 6 kinds.

3 cents each.

LA GRAND SERIES.

Martha	Lucy
Julia	Clarissa
Kate	Minnie

Also, One-Cent Dolls, Soldiers, etc. No. 1, 2, 3 and 4 Series, 6 kinds, 1 cent each.

The following three series of penny folders are presumed to be those mentioned in above schedule. Lacking a listing for the No. 4 Series we assume it to be the "Soldiers, 6 kinds." However, these are not named on the penny folders available to us, and the soldiers are unknown:

ONE-CENT BOOKS & DOLLS

FIRST SERIES—DOLLS.

Our Little Man.	Our Little Sis.
Our Little Kate.	Our Little Charlie.
Our Little Pet.	Our Little Bessie.

SECOND SERIES—DOLLS.

My Dear Coz.	My Dear Aunt.
My Dear Ma.	My Dear Pa.
My Dear Brother.	My Dear Sister

THIRD SERIES—DOLLS.

Dolly.	Annie.
Viola.	Bertie.
Peggie.	Ida.

- - - -

Florence of the Bon Ton Series is reproduced in Illustration 23 by courtesy of Mrs. Orrin E. Daniels of Middletown, Connecticut. The doll and one costume have been cut out, the remainder of the folder still in original condition. An interesting feature is that the doll is printed to give a back view, her hair falling to her waist, her head turned to glance over her shoulder. The cover design also is unusual with *Florence* blind-folded, apparently groping about in a game of Blind Man's Buff. This design is most attractively colored in lively shades of blue and yellow, the doll's vestee and the upholstery on the stool in red.

Illustration 24 gives the folder only for *Nellie* of the Bon Ton Series, doll not available; also included in this illustration is *Viola* of the Third Series of "One-Cent Books & Dolls", the cover design apparently having been cut from the folder and photographed against a plain background.

Of the Second Series of One-Cent Dolls we show an uncut folder of *My Dear Coz,* Illustration 25. This is the usual penny folder approximately 1-3/4 by 3¼ inches. The doll, 2¼ inches in sitting position, further reflects the apparent aim of this publisher to provide the "something different" in his paper dolls, none of the above named specimens conforming to the more conventional pose.

Neither date nor street address appears on the various folders, but an address rundown taken from Godsill's Philadelphia Directory by Mr. Bart Anderson provides the following data:

1874	— Pg. 297	—Chromatic Printing Co., 164 So. 8th.
1876)	— Pg. 308	—Chromatic Press Co., 3514 Spring Garden St.
)		
)	— Pg. 308	Chromatic Printing Co., 3514 Spring Garden St.
1877	— No listing.	
1878	— Pg. 312	—Chromotype Printing Co., 3514 Spring Garden St.
1879	— Pg. 320	—Chromotype Printing Co., S. 16th & Chestnut.

From this record it will be noted that the firm name was changed in 1878 to the *Chromotype* Printing Co., thus proving publication of the Chromatic Printing Co's. paper dolls as prior to that date.

Mrs. Daniels kindly offers the further helpful information that her mother, whose name was Florence and who was born in 1869, received the paper doll *Florence* as a name-gift when she was too young to remember the incident. This further tends to establish publication date of these dolls as in the early or mid-1870's.

A later date of June 11, 1880 is pencilled in old-fashioned penmanship on the inside of the author's folder of *My Dear Coz.* However, since this apparently is a gift-date and also later than directory listings for the Chromatic Printing Co., it is of little significance in our efforts to pinpoint a definite publication date for these paper dolls, all printed fronts only.

Of the three dolls shown in Illus. No. 26, only the one in the lower row has been identified, this as "*Julia*" of the La Grand Series, authenticated by a set having the original envelope bearing likeness of the doll itself.

The other two in this illustration have all the characteristerics of *Julia*—cut from the same textured paper, similarity in costume design, like coloring, with patterns of the three standards printed in the same shade of light blue ink. Presumably these also are of the La Grand Series, names unknown.

Chromatic dolls seem not to be so readily found today as are some others, perhaps because of a more limited production. Whatever the reason, their scarcity at this time tends to add prestige to collections of which they are a part.

No. 23. FLORENCE, 3-11/16 INCHES. COURTESY MRS. ORRIN E. DANIELS.

No. 24. FOLDER FOR NELLIE; VIOLA 2-$\frac{5}{8}$ INCHES.

NO. 25. MY DEAR COZ, 2¼ INCHES. AUTHOR'S COLLECTION.

NO. 26. TOP ROW AND CENTER FIGURE, 3-⅝ INCHES, UNIDENTFIED.

THIRD ROW, JULIA OF LA GRAND SERIES, 3-¾ INCHES. ALL AUTHOR'S COLLECTION.

A handsome boxed set of paper dolls titled *"The American Lady and Her Children in a Variety of the Latest Beautiful Costumes"* was produced by the above famed lithographers of the 1850/1860's. The box cover, illustrated in No. 26a, establishes publishers' address at time of publication as 254 & 256 Canal St., New York. Title appears in four languages, English, German, Spanish, and Dutch.

Pasted on the inside of this box cover is a 5-¾ by 8-⅜ inch advertisement, apparently clipped from a contemporary periodical. Among some 93 printed titles of "Fine Plain and Colored Prints", Chromes and illustrated "Letter Sheets", only two toys are listed, namely, "Book Containing Colored Flags of all Nation, Carried by a soldier in his national uniform. Toy Book for Boys, 75 cts." (Omission of the letter "s" from the word "Nations" probably was a printer's error).

The last of these listings and the one important to collectors is headed in bold type and reads:

"THE AMERICAN LADY AND HER CHILDREN, with various styles of costumes, 25 changes Paper Dolls. We will send to any part of the U.S. and Canada, free for $1 or the two for $1.50." (There is no decimal point in the $1.50, and the offer of "the two" is somewhat confusing).

No date is given, either in the printed advertisement or on the box cover of this set, but it has been tentatively dated circa 1867/70. Heels on the American Lady's shoes identify an after 1860 printing, and a check of New York City Directories establishes that the partners, Christopher Kimmel and Thomas Forster, were listed at 256 Canal Street from the year 1864 into 1871 when there was a change in the partnership though the address remained the same.

Nos, 26b, "c" and "d" are photographic illustrations of the members of this paper doll family including mother, daughter, son, and a tiny girl child. All are lithographed in beautiful colors, both front and back, the American Lady's dresses and mantles especially glamorous. It would have been helpful if backs of her elaborate costumes could have been shown. However, because duplicates of the girl and three of her costumes were available, these backs are shown, as are three of the boy's suits. All costumes have lithographed backgrounds, identifiable in the illustrations.

Noteworthy is the beautiful hairdress of the American Lady, curls at the front and sides; a huge bun covers the crown of her head encircled by what appears to be a braid of hair, while long curls extend well down over her shoulders.

This entire set, said to be complete except for one missing hat, is a very fine example of lithographic art. However, it is not to be confused with a foreign one of similar title, *The American Lady and Her Children in a Variety of Beautiful Costumes,* circa 1850, dolls and costumes hand-colored and coated with protective egg-white. This boxed production is covered in our chapter on Foreign Paper Dolls.

While the similarity of titles may be purely coincidental, it does suggest that Kimmel & Forster may have borrowed the title of the earlier foreign set, making the slight change in wording perhaps to avoid in some measure an appearance of piracy. To our knowledge the above paper doll family comprises the extent of this firm's output in this line since no other specimen has come to light in our extensive research. It does seem strange, however, that an industry with the facilities to produce a boxed set of the quality and beauty of the *American Lady* would not have published other paper dolls, and perhaps further research will in time uncover additional specimens.

No. 26a. Box cover for The American Lady and Her Children. (Kimmel & Forster).

No. 26b. THE AMERICAN LADY, 6⅝". HER BABY 2¼". B & F. (KIMMEL & FORSTER).

No. 26c. THE AMERICAN LADY'S DAUGHTER, 4-1/16, B & F. (KIMMEL & FORSTER).

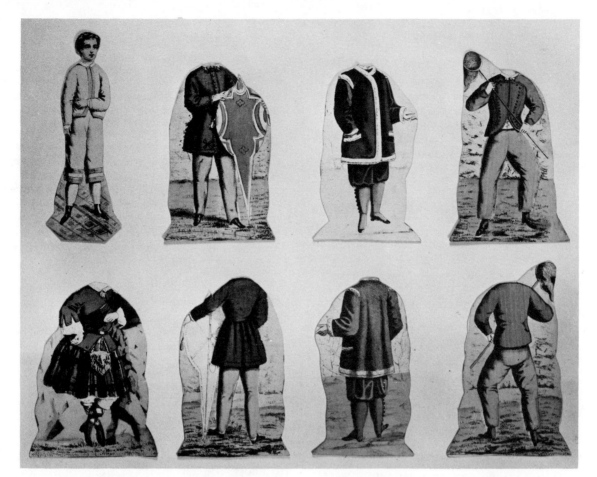

No. 26d. THE AMERICAN LADY'S SON, 4-3/16, B & F. (KIMMEL & FORSTER).

PETER G. THOMSON

One of the lesser known publishers of paper dolls was Peter G. Thomson of Cincinniti, Ohio. None of the Thomson dolls bears a date, but it is noted that while he was listed in a Cincinnati directory as printer and binder among other activities as early as 1875, color printing was not mentioned until 1885. (See the John Greene Chandler Memorial Bulletin, Summer 1952. Information furnished by Mrs. R. W. Jaques). A likely date for the paper dolls, however, would seem to be circa 1889 because of inclusion of one called *Nellie Bly*. (See coverage of Series 3).

Though not of the finest quality these dolls are interesting, and the costumes are nicely styled and colored. The larger dolls are printed both front and back, a helpful feature for fashion students and doll costumers.

Directions for cutting out and pasting the fronts and backs together in such a way that the costumes can be slipped over the doll's head are printed on the back of the Daisy Deane envelope (Number 28), together with the following listing of paper dolls:

NEW PAPER DOLLS

No. 1.	No. 2.	No. 3.
Pansy Blossom	Daisy Deane	Bessie Bright
Flora McFlimsy	Lillie Lane	Nellie Bly
Jessie Jingle	Susie Bell	Flora Frizzle
15 Cents each.	10 Cents each.	8 Cents each.

Flora McFlimsy, Series 1, (Illustration Number 27) bears a name known throughout the country a century ago, made famous by the poem "Nothing to Wear". Composed by a young man who had accompanied his sisters to Paris, the poem apparently was inspired by the tedious hours of waiting while his sisters engaged in a steady whirl of shopping, and fittings by Paris modistes. This satire, appearing first in *Harper's Weekly* in 1857, then published as a 68-page book by Rudd & Carleton, New York, practically swept the country during the Civil War period. Too long to be quoted verbatim, only brief pertinent excerpts are included here. The opening lines immediately engage our attention:

"Miss Flora McFlimsy of Madison Square,
Has made three separate journeys to Paris;
And her father assures me, each time she
    was there,
That she and her friend, Mrs. Harris,

* * * * *

Spent six consecutive weeks without stopping,
In one continuous round of shopping."

- - - - -

The six weeks drew to a close, and the bulk of the ladies' purchases was shipped by the good steamer "Argus" to New York, all excepting a quantity

"Sufficient to fill the largest-sized chest,
Which did not appear on the ship's manifest,
But for which the ladies themselves manifested
Such particular interest that they invested
Their own proper persons in layers and rows
Of muslins, embroideries, worked underclothes,
Gloves, handkerchiefs, scarfs, and such trifles
    as those;

Then, wrapped in great shawls, like Circassian
    beauties,

Gave good-bye to the ship, and good-bye to
    the duties."

- - - - -

Eventually the ship's cargo was unloaded at New York—

"And yet, though scarce three months have
    passed since that day

This merchandise went, on twelve carts, up
    Broadway,

This same Miss McFlimsey, of Madison
    Square,

The last time we met, was in utter despair,

Because she had nothing whatever to wear!"

- - - - -

Children of the day caught the spirit and evolved their own little ditty, "Flora McFlimsey of Madison Square, Has plenty to eat but nothing to wear!" This they chanted over and over, day in and day out as is the way of children.

The surge of popularity which followed publication of "Nothing to Wear" resulted in a doll being named Miss Flora McFlimsey, outfitted with a fabulous trousseau. We are indebted to Mr. R. N. Williams, 2nd, Director of The Historical Society of Pennsylvania, Philadelphia, for the information that this doll, presented to the museum many years ago, has raised money for charitable purposes in every war in which this country has participated from the Civil War on. Her retirement years are now being spent in the museum. Mr. Williams states that her wardrobe was made by the best known dress-makers, corsetieres and milliners of that time. "She has six dresses, riding habit, skating skirt, nine hats ,wrappers, raincoats, parasols, traveling bags, combs, gloves, visiting cards, sewing basket, five pairs of shoes, etc." Yet she, too, it appears soon will have nothing to wear, since Mr. Williams reports that despite the most careful handling, her splendid, century-old wardrobe is beginning to go.

And now we have a contemporary fictitious character called Miss Flora McFlimsey. A lonely little doll who lives in a doll house with her constant companion, a cat called Pookoo, she is featured in a series of attractive little books with charming water-color illustrations. Authored by "Mariana"

and published by Lothrop, Lee & Shepard Co., Inc., New York, these little doll fantasies not only enthrall little girls but will delight doll collectors.

The first book was published in 1949 entitled *Miss Flora McFlimsey's Christmas Eve.* As of this writing, seven volumes of this series have appeared, *Miss Flora McFlimsey's Valentine,* in its second printing in January, 1962, believed to be the latest. And the theme of *Miss Flora McFlimsey's Easter Bonnet,* in its fifth printing in 1960, is suggestive of the theme of the original poem, *Nothing to Wear.* Thus we have three namesakes for the original character. Will there be others to perpetuate the name?

The paper doll called *Flora McFlimsy* (the "e" omitted by the publisher), seems unglamorous by comparison with the earlier museum doll of the same name. She has no such elegant trousseau, her wardrobe consisting of only the four garments shown in Illus. No. 27, but they do have back as well as front views. Her hats have been lost, but even though poor paper Flora McFlimsy hasn't a hat to wear, her status of importance in the paper doll world is firmly established.

Unfortunately, no *Pansy Blossom* doll came in for photographing. However, we are showing, in Number 27a, an envelope, fronts and backs of her four costumes and a rear view of one of her hats. While a doll is pictured on the envelope, it does not necessarily follow that it is a likeness of the doll itself, since differences in other Peter G. Thomson productions have been noted.

In Illustration Number 28 we have an uncut set of *Daisy Deane, Series* No. 2, by courtesy of Mr. Herbert H. Hosmer. Since the writer also has an envelope for this doll, two are pictured, one a rear view to illustrate the printed directions and the doll listings. One of the medium sized dolls, Daisy is 6-⅜ inches tall, and the reproduction of the complete uncut set as published, showing fronts and backs of the costumes and hats, needs no commentary.

Bessie Bright of the No. 3 Series, illustrated in Number 29, is 5½ inches tall, and also has the front and back printing as do all of these three series. Like Flora McFlimsy, Bessie's hats have disappeared over the years.

Nellie Bly of Series 3 (Number 29a), though not necessarily resembling, presumably was named for the real Nellie Bly of around-the-world fame. The name, "Nellie Bly", was adopted as a pseudonym by one Elizabeth Cochrane Seaman (1867/ 1922), a reporter for various New York and Pittsburgh newspapers. She well may have borrowed the name from a ballet dancer of the early 1800's, who, billed as Nellie Bly, is said to have appeared in an operetta, "Vicar of Bray", by Grundy & Solomon.

The Nellie Bly familiar to us, in 1889 at the age of 22, embarked upon a venture to encircle the world, a feat of no small proportions in those days. Her trip by train and steamer, consummated in 72 days, six hours and eleven minutes, fulfilled her ambition of establishing a world record as well as of bettering the time of Phineas Fogg, the fictional character of Jules Verne's novel, "Around the World in Eighty Days".

Two books were authored by Nellie Bly, "Ten Days in a Madhouse" (1888), and "Nellie Bly's Book: Around the World in Seventy-two Days", (1890).

In the light of the above, our paper doll assumes historic status.

Names given to other dolls in these three series may also have been inspired by songs, storybooks, or, as in the case of Flora McFlimsy, by early poems. Wasn't there a song, "My Pretty Susie Bell", perhaps pertinent to the river boats that plied the Ohio River in those earlier, rollicking days of the region?

In addition to the above three series of paper dolls, distributed in envelopes, Thomson also put out a series of six small folders uniformly measuring 2-3/4 by 4½ inches, closed. Each doll has three costumes with matching hats; fronts only are printed in these smaller sets.

Illustration Number 30 shows *Rhoda, Mary Bell* and *Sallie*, while Number 31 gives us *Alice, Louise* and *Ruth*. Mary Bell and Louise measure 3-7/8 inches, the others a full four inches. No prices are given for these small folders which may have been penny ones, and, as no dates are given, it is not known whether they preceded or followed the series of larger dolls. The one clue might be that the large dolls are listed as "new", but without substantiating evidence this cannot be construed as conclusive.

Peter G. Thomson also is credited with having published a set of soldiers listed as the Artillery.

No. 27. Flora McFlimsy, 7-⅜ inches. Author's Collection.

45

No. 27a. ENVELOPE AND COSTUMES FOR PANSY BLOSSOM.

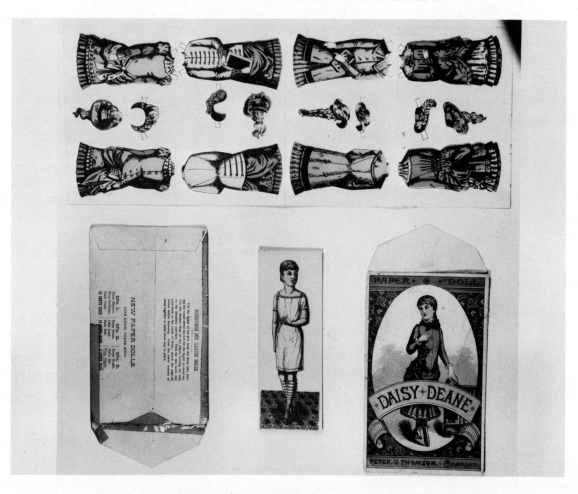

No. 28. DAISY DEANE, 6⅜ INCHES. COURTESY HERBERT H. HOSMER.

No. 29. Bessie Bright, 5½ inches.

No. 30. Rhoda, Mary Bell, Sallie. Author's Collection.

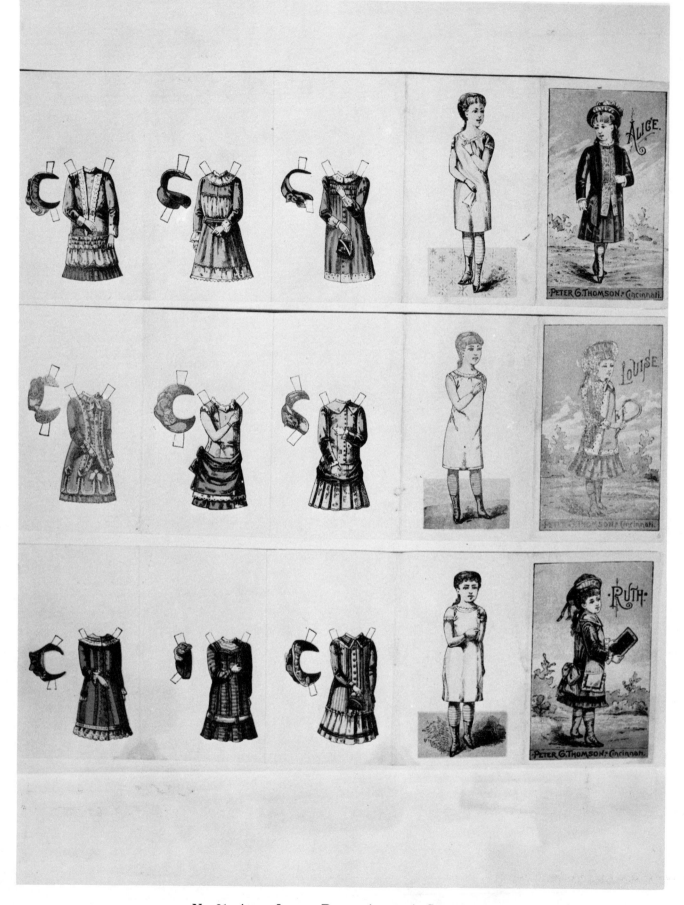

No. 31. ALICE, LOUISE, RUTH. AUTHOR'S COLLECTION.

No. 29a. NELLIE BLY WITH ORIGINAL ENVELOPE.

THE HART WALKING PAPER DOLL

On October 31, 1874 William H. Hart, Jr., of Philadelphia, Pennsylvania, applied for a patent on his "Improvement in Dolls", the improvement constituting mainly a certain walking mechanism for a paper doll. On December 1, 1874 a patent was granted. (For patent copy see Pgs. 140 and 141, PAPER DOLLS — A GUIDE TO COSTUME by Clara Hallard Fawcett). Some time after issuance of the patent Miss Flora and Her Paris Dresses appeared, publisher unknown.

The walking device consists of a pocket of light weight board, narrowed at the middle point to form the shape of a modified hour-glass; this to provide a stop-gap for the doll parts to be inserted as described below.

A lift-flap is cut into one surface of this pocket near the top. When the pocket is slipped into the double skirt the pocket-flap is drawn through a curved slot or track cut into the back of the skirt just below the waist-line, and by moving this little flap backward and forward the pocket itself swings from side to side.

The doll is in two parts, the embossed head and torso in one with a long tab on the back, the feet and legs in one piece tapering to a rounded tip. When the tab on the back of the torso is slipped into the upper part of the inner pocket, and the legs are inserted from below, (the pocket-flap already in place through the skirt slot), it follows that the doll may be moved backward and forward in conjunction with the pocket to give a walking motion. Illustration Number 32 gives back views of the various parts to show the manner in which they function.

The published doll was distributed mounted on a cardboard measuring approximately 13½ inches square, the skirts suspended from thumb-shaped tongues cut into the board. Each skirt is equipped with the walking device; thus to change her dress the two parts of the doll are simply transferred to a different skirt.

The latter are attractively designed with underskirts of white tissue, lace trimmed, and overskirts of tissue in various colors with trimming of embossed floral sprays and gold paper braid. A complete mounted set of this unusual and interesting paper doll is given in Illustration Thirty-three exactly as it was distributed some ninety-odd years ago.

No. 32. Mechanical parts of Hart's Walking Paper Doll.

No. 33. COMPLETE MOUNTED SET, HART'S WALKING PAPER DOLL, APPROX. 6¼ INCHES.

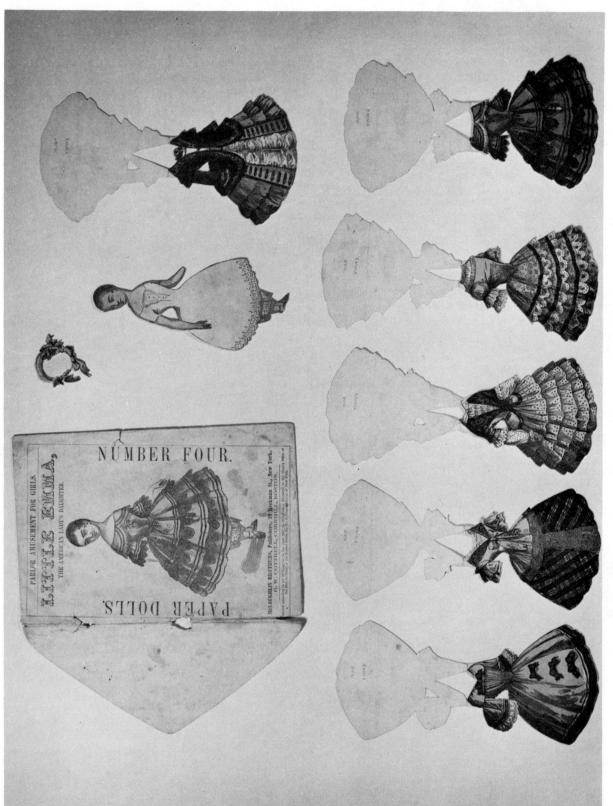

No. 35. Little Emma, the American Lady's Daughter, 5-3/16 inches.

Courtesy Mr. and Mrs. Eugene Van Wye.

Chapter III
McLoughlin Bros.
Section A: Early Series

John McLoughlin, successor to Elton & Co., was the first of the McLoughlins to enter the publishing field. In the year 1828, in a small shop in New York, John founded what was to become an immense enterprise. His first venture was in children's stories, printed in thin paper-covered hand-sewn booklets, usually embodying a moral theme.

By 1857 John had been joined by Edmund McLoughlin to form the partnership, and it is believed that it was in this year that they first produced paper dolls under the firm name of McLoughlin Brothers.

While the production of other United States publishers was more or less limited as was brought out in the preceding chapter, McLoughlin Bros.' output was enormous, perhaps greater than that of all the other early publishers combined. It is safe to say that no one in the year 1857 could have foreseen the continued and vast quantity of paper dolls that would follow those first early ones, intended of course as playthings for children. And certainly no one, the publishers least of all, had even a glimmer of the avidity with which collectors would be searching for these same paper figures a century later. Time has a way of proportioning all things!

Questions continue to arise that we wish could be authoritatively answered, but in an exchange of correspondence with McLoughlin Bros. Inc. in 1950, they advised that when the last of the McLoughlins sold out their interest in the company in 1920, and the business was moved to Springfield, Massachusetts, practically all of the vital statistical records were left behind; further, that such as were taken to Springfield were destroyed in the flood of 1938.

And now it is with a sense of loss that we learn there no longer is a McLoughlin Brothers. A recent letter of inquiry addressed to the Springfield headquarters, with the thought of possibly including in this work something relative to their present activities, was returned through the postoffice, unopened, the envelope rubber-stamped "Out of Business". Subsequent inquiries have revealed that the Springfield Company has been absorbed by Grosset & Dunlap, Inc., Publisher, New York City, who advise that they still retain the company as a division of Grosset & Dunlap, and expect to continue to do so. However, they are publishing only certain types of books under the McLoughlin Bros. imprint—board books for very young children, pop-ups and other toy and activity books. Therefore McLoughlin paper dolls as we know them are products of the past, and those we are so fortunate as to possess are indeed treasures to be preserved.

As stated in the Introduction, no attempt has been made in this work to describe early costumes in detail, as there seems to have been no standard pattern for coloring.

Printing and coloring methods have changed over the years, and it is difficult even for an expert to analyze those of more than a hundred years ago. An effort has been made, however; this writer took one of the dolls in uncut book form, bearing publisher's address of 30 Beekman Street, New York, to an executive of a large printing company, and he quickly demonstrated that the figures were printed, colors added by hand. Moistening his finger he easily rubbed off a small blob of paint which had blurred beyond the figure lines; on a lithographic print the color would have been fast.

Mrs. William Waldron of Wilmington, Delaware, has been of great assistance in this endeavor by making similar contacts, and we find that a diversity of opinion exists among contemporary craftsmen as to the coloring method employed. All agree that the dolls and costumes were for the most part printed from wood engravings over color tint blocks, but their views vary as to the color processes. Some feel colors were stencilled in, which might account for the many instances of marginal blobs of paint found in uncut sets.

One printer is of the opinion that colors were applied by wood blocks.

An eminent engraver expressed the view that possibly the color was added by an engraved block that had been hand-charged with color.

Then again certain envelopes, notably two identical ones for *Grace Lee* of the Early Series, one bearing address of 24 Beekman Street, the other 30 Beekman, bear an inscription in small type on the back, "Stereotyped by Vincent Dill, 24 Beekman Street, New York."

The Students' Standard Dictionary defines this method as follows: "STEREOTYPE: Verb, to make or furnish stereotype plates (for a book, etc.). Noun: A cast or plate taken in stereotype metal from a matrix, as of paper, reproducing the surface from which the matrix was made."

"MATRIX: That which contains and gives shape or form to anything."

This obviously identifies the printing of *Grace Lee* by stereotype-metal plates instead of wood engravings as believed by some to have been, and perhaps were, used in many instances. And the stereotype plates may have been used to print others of the early dolls, but lack of the identifying inscription on containers precludes absolute verification.

As we see it, any one or all of these various processes may have been employed by McLoughlin Bros. in experiments to find the best and perhaps the most economical manfacturing procedure.

It is further noted that on the dolls themselves where no color was applied to the underwear, hand brush work to provide shadows is in evidence, variations occurring in different sets of the same doll.

And when all is said and done, to us the most important point is that no matter which printing method was used, our early paper dolls enjoy the distinction accorded all hand-painted products.

McLoughlin Brothers' (they variously used both the complete noun and the abbreviation "Bros.", sometimes "Bro's."), first known address was 24 Beekman Street, New York. One early advertisement added "upstairs".

Mr. Bart Anderson, Director of the Chester County Historical Society, West Chester, Pennsylvania has generously supplied a painstaking and comprehensive rundown of the changing addresses and personnel of this company, taken from microfilmed copies of New York City directories in the New York Public Library. Mr. Anderson's detailed findings are condensed here to schedule only the company's address changes:

1854/1863—24 Beekman Street.

1864/1870—30 Beekman Street.

1871　　　—52 Greene Street.

1872/1886—71 & 73 Duane Street.

1887/1890—623 Broadway

1891/1892—623 Broadway and 190 Mercer.

1893/1898—874 Broadway

1899/1907—890 Broadway

1908　　　—890 Broadway and 65 S. 11th, Brooklyn.

1909/1919—890 Broadway.

1920　　　—65 S. 11th, Brooklyn.

While no mention is made of paper dolls in the directory listings they presumably came under the general heading of "Publishers". The value of the above schedule of address changes lies in the guide it provides for dating our paper dolls where we have containers showing address from which a given paper doll was published.

One Gregory McLoughlin, listed as Vice President in the years 1918 and 1919, was the last of the family actively connected with the company, and it is to be presumed it was he who negotiated the 1920 sale of the family's interests. We wish we might establish his relationship to the first of the clan.

Following sale of the original company's holdings a representative of the new owner was located at 221 Fourth Avenue, New York, from 1922 to 1925, possibly later; New York directories were not available to Mr. Anderson after 1925.

What well may be the first list of paper dolls to be advertised by McLoughlin Bros. is the so-called EARLY SERIES, published at 24 Beekman Street. This listing was given to the writer some years ago by the late Mrs. H. B. Armstrong, of Austin, Texas, with the information that the sheet had been enclosed in an envelope for *Lucy* of this Early Series. This important listing is given here:

LIST

OF

PAPER DOLLS, ETC.

Manufactured by

McLOUGHLIN BRO'S.

24 Beekman Street, New York

FIRST SIZE

Frank   Jenny

        Lucy

SECOND SIZE

Baby   Fanny

Dolly   Charley

Lizzie   Little Lady

  Willie and His Pony

THIRD SIZE

Bride

American Lady

Emma and Etty

Grace Lee

Susan Lee

Adelaide

PAPER FURNITURE

1. Bed Room Set

2. Parlor Set

3. Drawing Room Set

4. Double Set

SMALL

6. Bedroom Set

7. Parlor Set

— — —

Paper Soldiers for Boys

Two additional paper dolls dated 1857 have come to light, and their omission from above advertisement is somewhat mystifying.

One of these is *Little Mary* (34). She is 3-13-/16 inches tall in black engraving, fronts only, the costumes daintily hand-tinted. This appealing little girl may have been McLoughlin Bros.' No. 3 doll, the designation perhaps inadvertently omitted when the envelope was printed, but we are without proof.

The other unlisted is *Little Emma, the American Lady*'s *Daughter,* the envelope dated 1857 and marked "Paper Dolls. Number 4". This rare doll is reproduced in Illus. 35 by courtesy of Mr. and Mrs. Eugene Van Wye of Johnston, Rhode Island. The envelope is printed in sepia, and the name of G. W. Cottrell, Boston, (said to be a dealer) appears.

Rarely found today, our supposition is that the doll was discontinued almost at once in favor of the twins, *Emma and Etty,* (sometimes listed as *Emma and Her Twin Sister Etty*), brought out in the following year, and printed from the same block as the No. Four doll, but with a different head. Costumes of the two sets are identical as may be seen by comparing illustrations Nos. 35 and 38.

Little Emma, the American Lady's *Daughter* measures approximately 5-3/16 inches including the missing foot, measurement taken by placing the No. 4 doll over a perfect specimen of one of the twins from the author's collection; this also establishes that the No. 4 doll, by reason of her larger head, is about 1/8 inch taller than the twins. We are greatly indebted to Mr. and Mrs. Van Wye for sharing this treasure with our readers.

No. 34. LITTLE MARY, 3-13/16 INCHES.

Of the dolls listed in the Early Series advertisement, we are able to include illustrations of all but one, the exception being *Adelaide* of the Third Size. (Reference to this doll is made further along in this section). Of the Paper Furniture the No. 7 Parlor Set is partially shown, while included are the Paper Soldiers, uncut.

Two of the dolls listed in this flyer are numbered One and Two respectively, evidencing the start of McLoughlin Bros.' publishing of paper dolls.

The question has frequently arisen as to whether or not this company published any paper dolls prior to 1857, and considering that the envelope for *The Bride* of this date was designated as Number One, we would have assumed not, were it not for the tantalizing notation printed beneath the title, "Improved Edition. New Dresses".

This inscription inspired further research which uncovered one specimen only of the bride doll as first issued, the envelope bearing date of 1857, thus seeming to establish that no paper dolls were issued by McLoughlin Brothers prior to this date. The envelope for this first set measures 4-3/4 by 7¼ inches, and is without the controversial inscription. There, however, is an additional line of printing, "Will be published, six kinds", at the top of the envelope just above the heading, "Parlor Amusement for Girls". This must have been the understatement of the century, considering the vast output which followed.

The one difference in the costumes of the two sets seems to be that the elaborate dress with puffed skirt and draped over-dress (lower right in Illus. No. 36), was not included in the first edition. Possibly this lovely costume was substituted for one less attractive in the first printing; also, perhaps the first ones were not perfectly executed.

A direction sheet received with the original edition, not included in the "Improved Edition" as found, mentions ". . . the hat, and head-dresses you will make best by doing in the same manner". These accessories are missing now, unless perhaps the term "head-dresses" was meant to include the bridal veil. We hazard a guess that because of some unsatisfactory workmanship of the first printing, few, if any, reached store counters.

The Bride (36), adopted as Number One, measures 5-1/8 inches, the envelope measuring 4-7/8 by 7-3/8 inches, varying slightly from that of the first edition. Both the lovely doll and her trousseau were printed front and back by wood engravings over tint blocks, colors added to the dresses by hand. The back of the bridal gown, printed on the envelope, points up the beauty of this important costume. It is done in pale pink with sleeve ruffles of white lace and a white diaphanous veil, while the gown itself is in a mellow, creamy shade, high-lighted by touches of blue in the "gathers". This is an exquisite, rarely-acquired paper doll.

The American Lady with Something to Wear (No. 37) is established as the Number Two doll by the printing on the envelope. Like the Bride, this Number Two doll was copyrighted in 1857, and was printed in black ink from wood engravings, with dresses hand-colored. She is the same type doll as Clark, Austin & Smith's *Nellie* (No. 16), and practically a duplicate except Nellie's coiffure includes a red flower, whereas the American Lady's hair is dressed to the nape of her neck. Her wardrobe consists of six beautifully designed costumes, two bonnets, and a gay, frilly hat called a "flat". The amusing last lines of the direction sheet apprized little girls, "You will now have dresses and bonnets quite as tasteful, and ones which will stay on as firmly, and prove just as useful as three-quarters of the *things* which you will meet on Broadway". The American Lady with her "something to wear" is 6¼ inches tall, front printing.

Next in order of listing is *Emma and Her Twin Sister Etty* (No. 38) included by courtesy of Mrs. Margarett M. Dartt of California, the envelope bearing copyright date of 1858. No. 38a provides copy of a Direction sheet showing the manner in which the costumes were printed with fronts and plain backs in one piece to fold at the shoulder line, while in Illustration No. 38b we have these same printed directions combined with a schedule of already published dolls, dated Dec. 10th, 1858. Issuance of these twins well in advance of this date, however, appears to be definitely established, since all indications point to the probability that *Emma and Her Twin Sister Etty* fall into the Number Five position in the parade of McLoughlin Brothers' paper dolls, even though the envelope bears no serial number; indeed, the sequence of listed dolls on this direction sheet leaves little doubt on this point, and the twins well may have been the first dolls issued in 1858.

This pair have been the subject of speculation among collectors for some years. As far as is now known, the two identical dolls have appeared in every set that has come to light, the one difference being that in certain sets one doll wears a red hair ribbon, the other a green one, perhaps intended to differentiate between the two, though other sets have been found with the dolls wearing the same color ribbons. Since little girls might have exchanged dolls among themselves, the matter of hair ribbons may have no significance.

Included in the pictured set are certain duplicate costumes, except they were executed in different colors; however, we cannot safely assume that they were produced in this manner to designate certain ones for a particular doll as there appears to have been no studied pattern to effect this result. Until an authenticated set shows up with two different dolls, if ever one does, we have to conclude that *Emma* and *Etty* were issued as identical twins.

A partial explanation of this unusual feature may have been provided by Miss Faffer who, in the summer of 1960, visited several museums in Germany. She found that in every boxed set published in that country and which she was privileged to examine, where only one character was featured, two dolls exactly alike were included. Perhaps the publishers' reasoning was that two little girls could play with the same toy, and this feature of two like dolls to a set may have inspired McLoughlin Brothers' production of the twins.

Inclusion of a doll named "Mary" in the listing of published dolls on this direction sheet (No. 38b) is presumed to mean "Little Mary" published in 1857, and to our knowledge this is the first mention made of this doll by McLoughlin Brothers in their printed schedules. "Mary" also is listed on other direction sheets bearing date of Dec. 10th, 1858, namely one for *Grace Lee* (No. 40a) and one for *Ida May* (No. 55a). *Little Mary* has already been covered and is pictured in Illustration No. 34.

While *Willie and His Pony* is listed in the Second Size of smaller dolls, we are interjecting here because of a printed notation on the back of the envelope. This bears publishers' address of 24 Beekman Street, New York, with copyright date of 1858, and this enlightening bit of information appears across one end of the back: "Will be published, on June First, SUSAN LEE, a double doll, LITTLE LADY." From this we learn that the unusual little doll, *Willie and His Pony*, was produced prior to June 1st, 1858, and apparently after issuance of *Grace Lee*. Thus our tentative sequence schedule of the dolls in this Early Series seems to be fairly well corroborated by the above printed information in conjunction with the advertisements reproduced in Illustrations Nos. 38b and 40a.

Willie, (No. 39) with front printing, is 2⅞ inches in riding position, and, as shown in the photographic reproduction, his little suits are fashioned accordingly. This paper doll is an important one collectorwise, coveted by serious collectors.

Grace Lee originated at the publishers' 24 Beekman Street headquarters, and was distributed in an envelope as reproduced in Illus. No. 40a. The uncut set pictured in Illus. No. 40 is a later printing in book form. No street address for the publishers is given on this folder, but a duplicate in the writer's collection shows the 30 Beekman Street address. Both folders bear notation, "Stereotyped by Vincent Dill, No. 24 Beekman Street, New York."

The double costumes for *Grace Lee*, comprising a plain dress with apron, three elegant gowns, an ermine-trimmed cloak, a long cape, a bonnet, and a hat, provide a fashion guide for a complete wardrobe for an 1858 period doll.

Susan Lee (No. 41), issued as previously noted on June 1st, 1858, perhaps intended as a sister of Grace Lee, immediately followed *Willie and His Pony* in order of publication.

Susan, a "double doll" (meaning printed front and back), and her six dresses are thought to have been printed from wood engravings over blue and black color blocks, dresses tinted by hand. The label shown on the flap of Susan's envelope and reading "From Wm. N. White, Bookseller, Athens, Geo." provides the name of a dealer-distributor of paper dolls a century ago.

In this text we have covered first the dolls advertised by McLoughlin Brothers as "Third Size" since this series includes the four 1857 dolls. Just when the First and Second Size dolls entered the production line is problematical, but all were originally published at 24 Beekman Street in 1858.

Foregoing text establishes that *Willie and His* Pony, a small doll of the "Second Size," actually preceded publication of *Susan Lee* of the "Third Size," and it is possible others of these small dolls were interspersed as the larger ones were coming through.

Of the three First Size dolls, only prim little *Jenny* (No. 44) is pictured in an original uncut accordion type folder with the envelope. These tiny dolls are printed in black, touches of color used only on the bases. However, the costumes are, as with all of these very early dolls, nicely hand-colored. Backs are plain, cut in one piece with the fronts to fold at the shoulder line for easy slipping over the dolls' heads.

Frank (No. 42) and *Lucy* (No. 43) are later printings, dolls and costumes cut out, the title panel and back fold of the penny strips forming a folder for each. It has not been the author's privilege to see an 1858 envelope for Frank, but Lucy's is identical to Jenny's excepting of course the name change. And Lucy should have a hat with ribbon chin ties, and at least one additional costume. One known set has five costumes.

Baby (No. 45), listed as of the Second Size, while not so identified, is included in this Early Series group by deduction. Regardless of the listing, she has all the characteristics of *Frank* and *Lucy;* she is only 2⅜ inches, printed in black, the only touch of color a faint pinkish red for her socks; the long baby dresses are in color; the small folder is identical to those of Frank and Lucy, even to the listing of certain dolls on the reverse, and like the others, presumably is a reissue.

Dolly (No. 46), also of the Second Size, is 3⅜ inches tall, her slip and the doll in her arms printed in black, flesh tones a very pale, natural pink tint. Costumes have the usual color treatment, the plain backs cut in one with the fronts. The ball, doll, a kitten, and a cornucopia held in the arms of her four dresses emphasize a child's love of her toys and pets. *Dolly* of the Early Series originated at 24 Beekman Street in 1858, distributed in envelopes. The pictured set is a later printing in book form with *Dolly* listed on the back among the five cent dolls.

Lizzie, also an 1858 doll of the Second Size, plain backs, is pictured in No. 47, cut out and incomplete. Her exposed parts are tinted in pale flesh tones, her curly hair and her shoes a darkish brown; the base is a bright green as are the shadows in her slip. The right arm of this particular specimen has been cut free from the body, perhaps to accommodate homemade dresses fashioned by a little owner long ago; for her printed dresses, having arms supplied, such cutting was unnecessary. We have no selling price for the 1858 issue of this doll. However, she is listed among the five cent ones on later folders.

In 47a we have *Fanny* of the Early Series, Second Size. The envelope is printed in blue on deep buff stock, perhaps once white and now discolored by time. It bears the 24 Beekman Street address, copyright date of 1858, no serial number, and across the top is inscribed, "Amusements for Little Girls." Along the left margin is printed "Paper Furniture" and at the right margin "Paper Dolls." Fanny measures 4½ inches, front printing, and with identical costumes was later re-issued as "Fanny Fair," listed in McLoughlin Brothers' 1875/76 catalog under Series 2, 24 kinds, covered in Section C.

Directions for folding the costumes at the shoulders and cutting the plain white backs with the fronts are printed on the flap of Fanny's envelope, and below these instructions the following listing appears: "New Series of Small Dolls—Baby, Dolly, Lizzy, Charley, Fanny, Willie and His Pony, and Little Lady," all Early Series dolls of the Second Size.

The envelope for *Charley* (No. 48) is exactly like that for *Fanny* except for change of title. The same listing of "New Series of Small Dolls" appears on both. Charley's costumes reflect masculine styles for boys of his period, amusing to us but the accepted fashion for young gentlemen of his day.

Little Lady (No. 49), 4-15/16 inches tall, is pictured in an uncut book issued at the publishers' 30 Beekman Street address, another instance of a re-issue of an 1858 doll. This book was compared to an 1858 cut set in the writer's possession at one time, and found to be the same in all details of design but not so mellow as the earlier printing. Possibly the fact that the later uncut book was never played with accounts in part for the difference. Several of these uncut books, all perhaps reprints, were found some time ago in an old store, and therefore are in new condition. Seven of these are owned by the author, and are shown in proper sequence in this work. According to a listing on the back of Little Lady's folder, this later printing sold for ten cents.

Analysis of above statistics reveals that, to our knowledge, with the exception of a set of paper soldiers. (an entirely different type; see Pg. 74), only four paper dolls of a more uniform type were produced by McLoughlin Brothers in 1857. Of these Nos. 1, 2 and 4 have been unquestionably authenticated by existing numbered envelopes, leaving only *Little Mary* to be counted. A condensed table, as we see it, follows:

No. 1. The Bride.

No. 2. The American Lady with Something to Wear.

No. 3. Little Mary. (?)

No. 4. Little Emma, the American Lady's Daughter.

Subsequent envelopes bear no numbers.

PARLOR SET NO. 7 (small) is given in Illus. No. 50. This envelope measures 6-13/16 by 3-5/8 inches and bears copyright date of 1858. Chairs, including the rocker, are a mere 1-3/4 inches high, the table one inch. Frames are brown, chair seats upholstered in red, both seat and back of the rocker tufted. Table top is of simulated marble. According to the Direction sheet which came with this set, inclusion of a sofa and a piano would have been expected; however, later sets having the same set of directions likewise included no piano, and it is conceded that publishers continued use of one set of directions for their various sets of furniture without regard to the specific pieces included in any given set.

— — — —

The **PAPER SOLDIERS** of the Early Series (No. 51) were issued in 1857 according to copyright date on the envelope. The set consists of five uncut sheets of medium weight paper board 7 by 4-5/8 inches, figures arranged horizontally on the sheets. One consists of a General, a fifer and two soldiers; another a drummer and three soldiers, while there are three sheets of five soldiers each, a total of 23 figures. Only one of the five-soldier sheets is shown in the illustration as the three are alike. Uniforms are bright red and lightish blue, some with red trousers and blue jackets, others with the colors reversed as to trousers and jackets. All have gold epaulets. This splendid set is of great historical interest, preserving for posterity an authentic record of the uniforms worn by our American soldiers in 1857.

— — — —

Of the paper dolls listed in the Early Series, only *Grace Lee, Little Lady, Dolly,* and *Fanny* (as "Fanny Fair") were still listed in McLoughlin Brothers' catalog for years 1875 and 1876. Later dolls named the Bride, Baby and Lizzie are listed in the catalog but are not to be confused with those of the Early Series, as comparison of the various illustrations will establish.

Frank, Jenny and *Lucy* are listed as "Old Series" on the backs of the penny folders of the Tom Thumb Series, showing that they were still being offered for sale as late as 1876 even though not included in the catalog.

It seems odd that so many of the lovely early dolls appear to have been discontinued prior to issuance of this catalog. Perhaps paper dolls had not "caught on" sufficiently in those early days to warrant a large production, and new issues were brought up to date in fashion designs. Certain it is that few survivors of certain choice dolls are represented in today's collections. These earliest dolls with their bouffant dresses, lavishly trimmed and befurbelowed, have a distinct charm lacking in many of the later ones, and fortunate indeed are those of us who count one or more among our treasures.

— — — —

No. 36.   THE BRIDE, 5⅛".

No. 37.   THE AMERICAN LADY WITH SOMETHING TO WEAR, 6¼". COLLECTION LATE MRS. H. B. ARMSTRONG

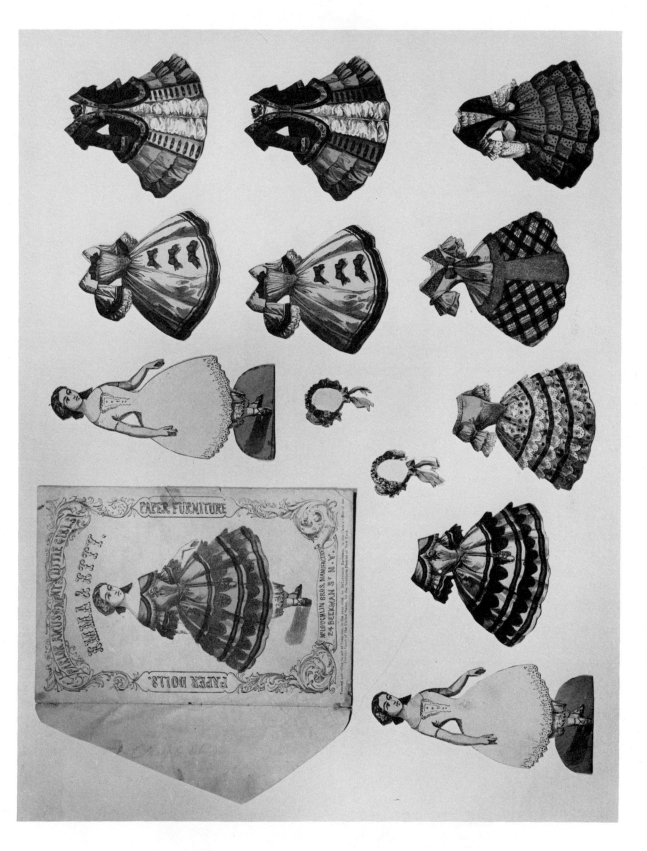

61

DIRECTIONS.

To show how to prepare LITTLE EMMA, AND HER TWIN SISTER ETTY, and their Dresses, in order that they may have a presentable appearance. Cut the paste-board figure very close to the outer line all round. Cut around the right hand and the portion of the arm connected with the body, so that you may bring them in front of the dress when you put it on. Cut out the little piece of white paper between the arms and the waist. When you have done this, she will be all ready for dressing.

We give herewith an example to show how to prepare the dresses. Fold the white paper connected with the dress, over the back at the lines marked A A. Then cut the back and front together close to the outer line of the dress—cut out all the little scollops, where there are any. The closer you cut these dresses, the better they will appear. Leave a little strip uncut at each shoulder, just where those lines marked A A are. On these strips the dress will rest on the shoulder. Cut out that narrow strip between the waist and the left sleeve. With a sharp pen-knife make a little slit just below the right sleeve for the hand and arm to pass through. Follow the edge of the sleeve *exactly* in cutting this slit. Cut out that piece in the back marked C; and when you put on this dress, pass the hand through that little slit below the sleeve *before* putting the dress over the head. You will find a white line on some of the dresses at the sleeves, where the arms should come through.

Now she would like to take a walk, probably, and must have her bonnet. In the first place, cut out the white paper where the face is to come. Then fold over the back at the top of the bonnet, *exactly* on the line of the highest point —rub it down close where you fold it over, then cut all around *close* to the outer edge of the bonnet, excepting a short space at the top, where it is folded; gum the two parts together at the very outside edge, not more than an eighth of an inch, and it is ready for use. To put it on, pass the head between the back and front, so as the face will show right.

You will find among the hats two very pretty flats, these must be gumed close to the head, so as to make them stay on.

No. 38a.   DIRECTION SHEET FOR EMMA & ETTY.

DIRECTIONS.

To show how to prepare LITTLE EMMA, AND HER TWIN SISTER ETTY, and their Dresses, in order that they may have a presentable appearance. Cut out the paste-board figure very close to the outer line all round. Cut around the right-hand and the portion of the arm connected with the body, so that you may bring them in front of the dress when you put it on. Cut out the little piece of white paper between the arms and the waist. When you have done this, she will be all ready for dressing.

We give herewith an example to show how to prepare the dresses. Fold the white paper connected with the dress, over the back at the lines marked A A. Then cut the back and front together close to the outer line of the dress—cut out all the little scollops, where there are any. The closer you cut these dresses, the better they will appear. Leave a little strip uncut at each shoulder, just where those lines marked A A are. On these strips the dress will rest on the shoulder. Cut out that narrow strip between the waist and the left sleeve. With a sharp pen-knife make a little slit just below the right sleeve for the hand and arm to pass through. Follow the edge of the sleeve *exactly* in cutting this slit. Cut out that piece in the back marked c; and when you put on this dress, pass the hand through that little slit below the sleeve *before* putting the dress over the head. You will find a white line on some of the dresses at the sleeves, where the arms should come through.

Now she would like to take a walk, probably, and must have her bonnet. In the first place, cut out the white paper where the face is to come. Then fold over the back at the top of the bonnet, *exactly* on the line of the highest point —rub it down close where you fold it over, then cut all around *close* to the outer edge of the bonnet, excepting a short space at the top, where it is folded ; gum the two parts together at the very outside edge, not more than an eighth of an inch, and it is ready for use. To put it on, pass the head between the back and front, so as the face will show right.

You will find among the hats two very pretty flats, these must be gumed close to the head, so as to make them stay on

---

No. 38b.   COMBINATION DIRECTION AND ADVERTISING SHEET FOR *Emma and Etty.*

No. 39. WILLIE AND HIS PONY, 2-7/8 INCHES. AUTHOR'S COLLECTION.

No. 40.   *Grace Lee*, 5-1/4 INCHES.

65

DIRECTIONS
FOR
GRACE LEE.

This is a very beautiful doll, with both sides of the Figure, Dresses, and Hat, colored; it is so simple as to hardly need any directions; some of my little friends however, may not be able to get along without them.

In the first place you must make the figure right. You will find the front on a piece of card board; this must be very nicely cut out, leaving the green ground about the feet for the figure to stand on. You will now cut out the back very nicely, in the same manner leaving the green ground on this also. The back and front must now put together, the best way will be to paste the paper all over, with good paste, and match it very even to the paste board figure, then put it between the leaves of a large flat book to dry.

In making the dresses, cut all the white paper from the out side, then fold them so that the back and front will match evenly. You will then see how to cut the neck, so as to let the head come through.

If you please you can paste the edge of the dresses together, this will keep them in their place better on the figure. The walking dress trimmed with Ermine, you will notice some dotted lines at the shoulders, do not cut these away, as the neck of the dresses will have to be cut wide enough to let the head slip through.

The hat is made in same way. Cut out the hole for the face before you paste the edges together

ADVERTISEMENT.

The subscribers have recently issued, under the name of "PARLOR AMUSEMENTS FOR LITTLE GIRLS," the following list of PAPER DOLLS, and SETS OF PAPER FURNITURE.

The Bride, a handsome doll, both sides of the dresses colored.
American Lady, a very large doll, beautifully colored.
Emma and **Etty,**
Grace Lee, a splendid doll, both sides of the dresses colored.
SUSAN LEE, "   "   "   "
Just out **IDA MAY,** a beautiful doll, extra large
Also, **LADY GAY,** "   "   "

The following is a list of small dolls.

Dolly,	**Charley.**
Lizzie,	**Mary.**
Baby,	**Fanny,**
Willy and his Pony,	
LUCY,	**JENNY,**
AND FRANK.	

We have also Published, new sets of

PAPER FURNITURE,

No. 1 Bedroom set, contains a French Bedstead, Bureau, Washstand, Table, two Ottomans, and four Chairs.
No. 2 Parlor set, contains a Sofa, Center Table, six Gothic chairs, two Rocking-chairs, and two Ottomans.
No. 3 Drawing-room set, contains Piano-forte Sofa, Table, six Chairs, two Ottomans, and two Rocking-chairs.
No. 4 Drawing-room set Brocatel, contains a handsome imitation Rosewood Piano, two Rocking-chairs, two Tete-a-tete's, six Chairs, and two Ottomans.
No 5 Double set, contains the Bedroom, and the Drawing-room Set.
No. 6 Bedroom set, small,
No. 7 Parlor set, "

ALSO, PAPER SOLDIERS FOR BOYS.
TWO KINDS:
Soldiers on foot containing 28 pieces—Soldiers on horse containing 18 pieces.

PAPER HOUSES.
Something new and beautiful—1st No. will be ready by the 20th of December.

McLOUGHLIN BROTHERS, Manufacturers.
24 Beekman Street, New York.

Dec. 10th, 1858.

No. 40a.   DIRECTIONS FOR GRACE LEE.   DEC. 10TH, 1858 ADVERTISEMENT.

No. 41. *Susan Lee,* 4-7/8 INCHES.

No. 42. *Frank,* 2-11/16 INCHES. AUTHOR'S COLLECTION.

No. 43. *Lucy*, 2-5/16 INCHES. AUTHOR'S COLLECTION.

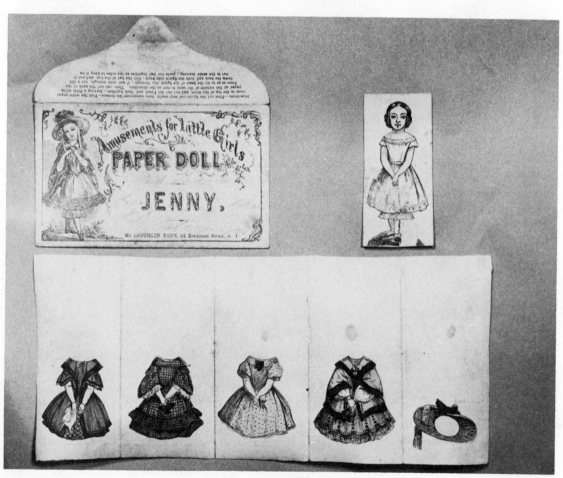

No. 44. *Jenny*, 2⅛ INCHES.

No. 45. *Baby*. 2-3/8 INCHES. AUTHOR'S COLLECTION.

No. 47. *Lizzie*, 4 INCHES.

No. 46.   Dolly.   3-3/8 inches.   Mrs. Ahlstrom Collection.

No. 47a. *Fanny.* 4½ inches. Margarett Dartt Collection.

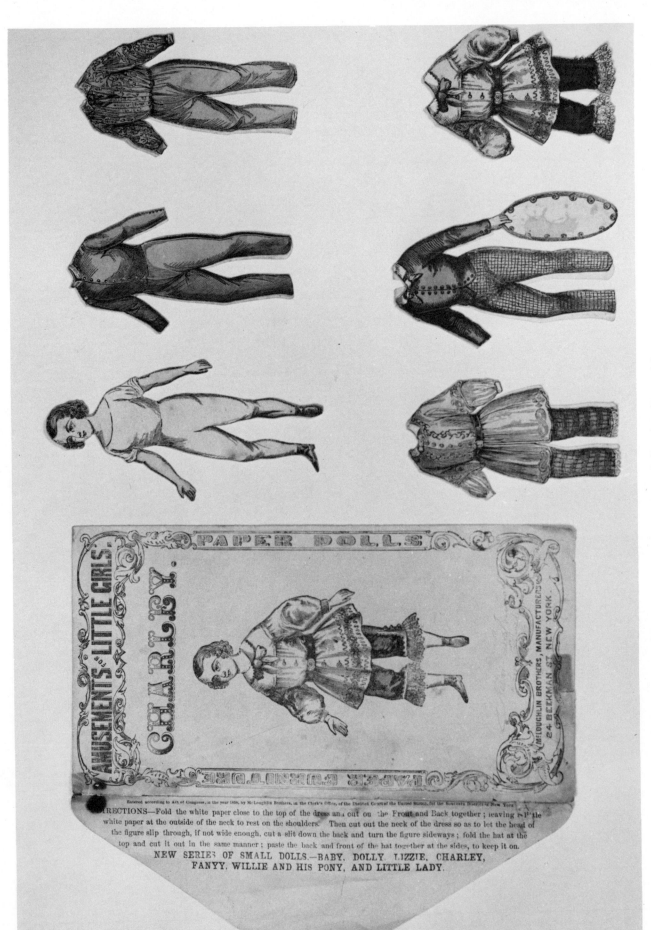

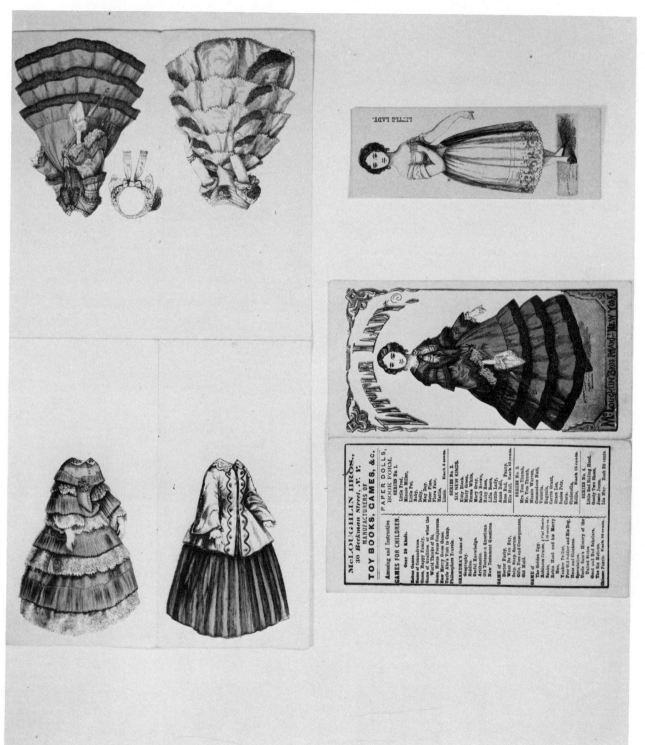

No. 49. *Little Lady.* 4-15/16 INCHES. AUTHOR'S COLLECTION.

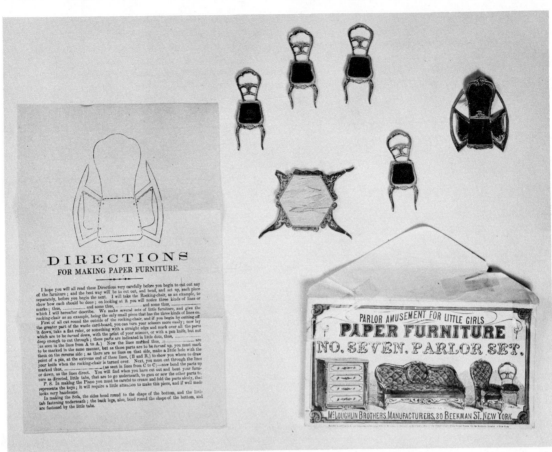

No. 50. *No. Seven Parlor Set,* (SMALL) AUTHOR'S COLLECTION.

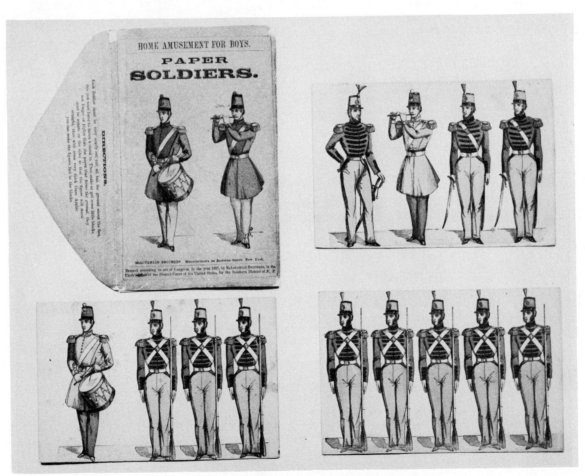

No. 51. *Paper Soldiers* OF 1857.

A curious development occurred in the contribution of Mr. and Mrs. Van Wye of an envelope for a doll named *Adelaide* (52). The heading, "Parlor Amusement for Little Girls" is one of the several variations of similar construction used by McLoughlin Brothers on many of their early containers, but their name does not appear on that for *Adelaide,* nor does that of any other publisher. Measuring 4-15/16 by 7¼ inches, black printing on buff color stock, the envelope bears an inscription across the bottom, "H. Smith & Co., Manufacturers of Envelopes, Dealers in Paper Dolls, Furniture, etc. No. 90 Fulton Street, N. Y."

Accompanying the envelope is a gorgeous fashion figure exactly like that printed on the envelope; this figure is printed front and back, measures 5¼ inches, and the bridal gown she wears is pale pink, visible through the white lace veil; the three flounces are of white lace also. This is exquisitely tinted in softest of shades, the only deep color the ribbon at the back of the head which is a deep rose in contrast to the pale pink of the gown. (We recall that the bridal dress shown on the envelope for the *Bride,* McLoughlin Bros.' No. One Doll, is also pale pink with a white transparent veil).

Just where this fashion figure fitted into the paper doll set of *Adelaide* is not known, but the following directions, copied from the flap of the envelope, substantiate the existence of a regulation paper doll with a wardrobe:

DIRECTIONS

"Cut out the figure first, leave the carpet on, but cut it close to the limbs, as far as the toes of the right foot, and instep of the left, bend back the carpet, and then it will make a stand for the figure. The dresses should be cut back and front in one piece, then fold them even, and when folded, cut out the white strip between the shoulders, to let the head through. In the high neck dresses you can slit the dress behind, which will hardly show, when the dress is on".

Is this McLoughlin Bros.' Adelaide of their Early Series? If so, did the Smith Company choose if from available dolls and purchase exclusive selling rights, with the agreement that McLoughlin's name would not appear? If this fashion figure was used to publicize the paper doll, surely it accounted for a sizeable volume of sales. No little girl, having seen it, could resist wheedling the paper doll from her mother.

An additional point of interest is that the name,

No. 52.   *Adelaide.* 5¼ inches. The Van Wye Collection.

G. Edmonds, S.C., N.Y., presumably the engraver, printed in small letters on the back of the figure where the green carpet flows into the white border, is the same as printed on the base of the Mystery Doll covered in following text.

Can some fortunate owner of the Adelaide paper doll itself supply a photographic reproduction in one of the collector magazines for the edification of less fortunate collectors?

A MYSTERY PAPER DOLL

The interesting doll depicted in Illus. 53 came to this writer some time ago sans container or other identification. A like one, also unidentified, is in the collection of Mrs. Rupert W. Jaques of Marblehead, Massachusetts, a third is owned by Mr. and Mrs. Eugene Van Wye of Johnston, Rhode Island, and there may be others.

Whoever she is she apparently played a part in the advertising program of one "G. Brodie, Mantillas, Cloaks, etc., Canal St." — the inscription on the little card held in the hand of the mantle in the doll's wardrobe.

Traveling cloaks from this establishment are shown in *Godey's Lady's Book,* October, 1856, and mantles much like the doll's are illustrated in *Godey's*

for January, 1858 and in later issues of the same year, captioned "From the establishment of G. Brodie, 51 Canal Street, New York". We have to date this doll as not later than 1858, even though very low heels are barely identified.

She is 5¼ inches tall, printed front and back as are the lovely costumes, delicately tinted. Her hair is done in a huge bun in the back which extends beyond her face at the left side as her head is turned. A ribbon falls from each side of the bun well down over her shoulders in back. Somehow the head appears small in proportion to the voluptuous lines of the body, but she is all original down to her toes; part of one shoe, the base and the hand-painted bonnet were kindly added by Mrs. Jaques, copied from her doll.

The origin of this doll is unknown to us at this time, but studying the figure we find that the tilt of the head, the features and the general pose suggest McLoughlin Bros.' *Emma and Her Twin Sister Etty* of the Early Series, and we offer the surmise that this mystery doll may have been produced by this company as an exclusive advertising medium for G. Brodie. If so, even an original envelope might not carry the firm name, as in case of *Adelaide.* It is to be hoped that these enigmas will some day be solved.

No. 53. *A Mystery Paper Doll.* 5¼ INCHES. AUTHOR'S COLLECTION.

Section B: An Advertising Flyer

In September, 1859, McLoughlin Brothers issued a flyer from their 24 Beekman Street establishment, measuring 7-1/8 by 15¼ inches. Due to the length, this is reproduced in two illustrations, (Nos. 54 and 54a) in order to provide readable copy. This early advertisement, listing paper dolls available as of its date, is of vast importance to collectors today. Certain of the listed dolls, previously covered in Sect. A, Early Series, are not covered here; however, we name them for reference: Emma and Etty (No. 38); Grace Lee (No. 40); Bride (No. 36); Susan Lee (No. 41); American Lady (No. 37); Charley (No. 48); Dolly (No. 46); Willie and His Pony (No. 39); Lizzie (No. 47); Little Lady (No. 49); Baby (No. 45); Jenny (No. 44), and Frank (No. 42).

Presenting the other dolls in order as listed, we start with lovely *Ida May*, illustrated in No. 55, in which two sets are combined in order to include back views.

Illustration No. 55a shows a Direction sheet for this doll, dated Dec. 10th, 1858, and it will be noted that the printed schedule of published dolls and other toys is identical to those· of the two direction sheets of same date previously reproduced (Nos. 38b and 40a).

The instructions for cutting out dolls and costumes printed on these sheets, together with the uncut dolls illustrated, establish that all of these early dolls were issued in sheet form, none die-cut. The notation on the subject sheet, "Just out", dates *Ida May* as of December or possibly November in the year 1858. She measures 7-5/8 inches, and is the "sweet young girl" type, with a wardrobe designed in the styling for young women of the pre-civil war period. The set is believed to have been printed over engraved wood color blocks, and is hand-tinted. The ornately embellished envelope appears to have been printed over black, orange and green color blocks, a printer's work of art in itself. Indeed, the entire production exemplifies the excellent quality of this company's earlier paper dolls.

Lady Gay (No. 56), "same size as Ida May but a lady with long dresses", followed Ida May as noted on various flyers dated December 10th, 1858, and is a beautiful specimen of the publisher's skill. All parts have both front and back printing, and are delicately tinted. An unusual feature of the costume shown at lower left in the illustration is the panel of real lace applied under the paper overdress, a dressy touch not often found in other paper dolls. Laces do appear on some of the early handmades. One of the less frequently found early paper dolls, *Lady Gay* was distributed in an envelope which unfortunately failed to survive the years which sit so lightly upon the lady herself.

Susie of *Susie's Pets* (No. 57) is an especially appealing little girl 6½ inches tall, published in 1858. Her pouting expression belies her apparently affectionate nature, evidenced by the close cuddling of her various pets when she wears certain of her pretty dresses. Her under-slip is more lavishly embroidered than those worn by many of the dolls, and her pantalettes are lace-edged. The dress with the little puppy shown in the upper left hand corner of the illustration was cut from the container, balance of the design, including Susie's head, folded over to provide a back for the extra costume wanted by some little girl who played with Susie; this explains duplication of this dress at lower right in the photographic illustration.

It is indeed disappointing that with most of the cut sets the backs of the double costumes are pasted to the fronts, either at the side edges, or by the fold-back tabs, of course so little girls could dress and undress their paper dolls. But for this we could show the backs of Susie's costumes and her gay hat. And if she herself were not pasted double, we could show her long, natural curls held in place just below the crown of her head by what appears to be a circle-comb.

In the section of Chapter II devoted to Clark, Austin & Smith's output, we raised the question as to which of these two companies preceded the other. The number of duplicated dolls cited in the following text, coupled with the unquestionable evidence that certain of these were still being marketed by McLoughlin Brothers as late as 1875 and '76, seems to substantiate our opinion that this firm in some manner acquired paper doll publication rights from Clark, Austin & Smith, further strengthened by our coverage of *Master Frank* (No. 59).

With *Clara*, the next doll for consideration, we have an unique problem. Inquiries have failed to disclose as to whether or not McLoughlin Brothers at first exactly duplicated Clark, Austin & Smith's No. 5 doll of the same name, or if their *Clara West*, listed in the 1875/76 catalog, was originally produced as Clara, the surname added later, perhaps to follow a policy of giving their dolls surnames in certain of their series. *Clara West*, of Series No. 3, Twelve Kinds, has a body identical to that of Clark, Austin & Smith's *Clara*, but with a different head. With one exception, the costumes of both sets are alike. Comparison of Illustrations No. 17, Chapter II, and No. 90 in Section C of this chapter, will plainly evidence these points. As to the one variation in costumes only uncut specimens would serve to verify correct wardrobes. The puzzling question which collectors would like to have answered still stands: Was McLoughlin's 1859 *Clara* like the Clark, Austin & Smith's number 5 doll, or was she actually *Clara West?*

Nellie of the 1859 listing, poses a problem similar to that of Clara. The only McLoughlin Bros.' Nellie we can identify is *Nellie North*, listed in the later catalog, and a duplicate of Clark, Austin & Smith's Nellie, but having an additional costume as may be seen by comparing Illustrations Nos. 16 in Chapter II and 95 in Section C, this chapter. Was *Nellie North* originally published as *Nellie?*

McLoughlin Bros.' *Cinderella* (No. 58) is a duplicate of C. A. & S's. No. 6 doll of same name shown in Illus. 18, Chapter II, with the exception of an additional costume in the McLoughlin set; this latter has been verified as correct by comparison with an uncut set in the collection of Mrs. Jaques. *Cinderella* is 4-5/8 inches tall, dresses have plain backs cut in one piece with the fronts, folded at the shoulder line to be slipped over the doll's head. Cinderella's wardrobe is based on the popular fairy tale, running the gamut from her plain work dress with apron to her beautiful ball gown. The dress at lower right hand corner of the illustration, white with red roses as trim, furnished the design for the container cover, though the latter was executed in the combined colors of red and yellow.

Ella of the flyer listing has not been authenticated by an original envelope. However there is no question that the doll is a duplicate of Clark, Austin & Smith's *Ella* No. 8, since McLoughlin Bros.' *Ella Hall* (No. 99) is like the C.A. & S. doll.

Master Frank, 4-1/8 inches tall, is shown in No. 59 by courtesy of Mrs. Margarett M. Dartt of California, with a direction sheet in 59a. Reference was made in Chapter II to Clark, Austin & Smith's doll of the same name, and it is interesting to note that McLoughlin Bros.' envelope for their doll appears to be an exact copy of a C. A. & S. type envelope with their heading, *The Girl's Delight,* rather than McLoughlin's usual one, except, of course, for the firm name change. Included in doll listings on the McLoughlin 1859 flyer for the first time seems almost to verify the concensus that McLoughlin Bros. did acquire rights from Clark, Austin & Smith.

Publishers indulged in extravagant flights of fancy in the stories they printed on the envelopes of some of their earliest paper dolls. *Master Frank's*'s is no exception, and his story, which appears to explain the paradox of a girl's picture adorning the envelope, is quoted verbatim:

> "Our young friend appears in a variety of characters. Sometimes as a school-boy;
> Sometimes as a '*Young Gent*'.
> "Being an ardent admirer of '*The Land o'Cakes*' and its people, he has supplied his wardrobe with a suit in exact imitation of that worn by *Malcolm McGregor.* He is a patriot of the stamp of '76, and when his country calls to arms to defend her rights and her liberties, he, of course appears armed and equipped as the law directs.
> "Frank has an acquaintance living in East Twenty-seventh St.; a young lady just turned of sweet sixt—thirteen,—a—a—a cousin of his, as he says, on whom he frequently calls, and when he does so, he of course dresses in a style suited to the occasion".

The cousinly relationship is doubtful, as to all appearances Master Frank was romantically interested in his young lady acquaintance.

Lillie Beers ("Lilly" on the container) (No. 60), is presumed to be a copy of Clark, Austin & Smith's Number 9 doll but without an envelope of the latter this remains supposition. McLoughlin Bros.' *Lilly Beers* stands 3-15/16 inches, front printing. The address on the folder, 71 & 73 Duane Street, New York, indicates this particular set to be a re-run during the years 1872/76 when the company was located at the Duane Street address. The flyer offers ample proof that the doll was originally published in or prior to 1859.

Miss Florence is unknown to us. Is this perhaps a further instance of a duplicated Clark, Austin & Smith doll?

Illustration No. 61 shows *Minnie Miller,* a 3-3/16 inch little lady of slender lines with a disproportionately small head, offering interesting contrast to some of the other McLoughlin paper dolls. Fronts only are printed, and while we cannot call Minnie Miller pretty as to features, dressed in any one of her lovely costumes she presents a very attractive appearance. We have no date for Minnie Miller other than that she is listed on the 1859 advertising flyer.

Nancy Fancy (No. 62), front printing, was designed on the slender lines of Minnie Miller, though she measures about five inches as against Minnie's mere 3-3/16, and has a head even smaller in proportion to her other body lines. While Nancy is a rather plain young woman, her features appear to be finely chiseled, and costumed, she assumes the fancy role attributed to her by name. The envelope for this number bears publisher's address of 24 Beekman Street, New York, measures approximately 4-13/16 by six inches, is lavishly decorated and flamboyantly colored; against a background of pale blue, Nancy's bright reddish-orange dress with white ruff and a white apron trimmed in green presents a striking contrast. The one cut costume in this otherwise uncut set, (excepting only the doll itself), matches the envelope design, though is colored in different, more subdued tones.

With the advent of *Little Pet* (No. 63), the publishers produced an entirely different type of doll from the former ones, a toddler with babyish features and stance. 3-1/8 inches tall, fronts only printed, McLoughlin Brothers apparently again either copied a Clark, Austin & Smith doll, or perhaps had acquired and used the latter company's original printing blocks. *Little Pet* is an exact duplicate of Clark, Austin & Smith's No. 7 doll which they called *The Little Pet,* Illus. No. 19, Chapter II, except for a fifth costume lacking in the latter firm's production; this may or may not have been originally included in Clark, Austin & Smith's printing.

Fanny, (No. 47a, Section A), also appears as "Fanny Fair" in Section C to follow, (Illus. No. 97).

Miss Hattie was not available for photographing, but it is plausible to assume she may be the same as Clark, Austin & Smith's doll of the same name, (Illus. No. 15, Chapter II).

Little Fred (No. 64) stands 3-1/4 inches, front printing, and his fanciful wardrobe is adequately depicted in the photographic illustration, which pictures an early doll with costumes combined with a later folder issued from 30 Beekman Street. The plain backs of the hand-tinted suits appear to have been cut in one piece with the fronts, folded at the shoulders and with vertical slits cut from the neck line to allow easier slipping on and off the doll. Only one of the pictured costumes retains this original fold. Collectors who are familiar with the paper dolls published in GODEY'S LADY'S BOOK, November, 1859, issue, will readily recognize the similarity of the effeminate styling of the boys' costumes to those of Little Fred, boys at the time frequently dressed much like little girls.

We have no information on a McLoughlin Brothers' doll named simply "Susy", as listed on the flyer. Might she be Susie's Pets? Or is there a specimen of "Susy" extant?

Emma is familiar to us, but unavailable for illustrating. She is a tiny girl of same general proportions as *Willie* shown in an incomplete set in Illus. No. 65, and they comprise an appealing pair of small dolls. They were printed in horizontal strips and folded in the manner of other one-cent dolls.

DIRECTIONS
FOR MAKING
DOUBLE PAPER DOLLS.

This is a very beautiful doll, with both sides of the Figure, Dresses, and Hat colored; it is so simple as to hardly need any directions; some of my little friends, however, may not be able to get along without them.

In the first place, you must make the figure right. You will find the figure on a piece of card board, printed on both sides. This must be very nicely cut out, leaving the green ground about the feet, for the figure to stand on.

In making the dresses, cut all the white paper from the outside, then fold them so that the back and front will match evenly. You will then see how to cut the neck, so as to let the head come through.

If you please, you can paste the edge of the dresses together, this will keep them in their place better on the figure.

The hat is made in the same way. Cut out the hole for the face before you paste the edges together.

McLoughlins' Toys for Girls and Boys!

Over 50 kinds of Paper Dolls, Soldiers, Furniture, Animals, Houses, &c., and new kinds constantly adding.

No. 54.   McLoughlin Brothers' 1859 Flyer, 7-1/8 by 15-3/4 inches.

PAPER DOLLS.

IDA MAY,		LADY GAY,

SUSIE'S PETS,	GRACE LEE,	SUSAN LEE,
EMMA & ETTY,	BRIDE,	AMERICAN LADY,
CLARA,	NELLIE,	CINDERELLA,

ELLA,	MASTER FRANK,	LILLIE BEERS,	MISS FLORENCE,

MINNIE MILLER,	LITTLE PET,	LIZZIE,
CHARLEY,	FANNY,	LITTLE LADY,
DOLLY,	MISS HATTIE,	BABY,
NANCY FANCY,	WILLIE & HIS PONY,	LITTLE FRED.

Twelve Kinds,

JENNY,	SUSY,	FRANK,	EMMA & WILLIE,

PAPER FURNITURE.

PARLOR FURNITURE,—No. 1,	PARLOR FURNITURE,—No. 6,
BED-ROOM " —No. 2,	BED-ROOM " —No. 7,

DRAWING-ROOM FURNITURE,—No. 3,
BEAUTIFUL PLAY HOUSE,—1 Room, Parlor,
"   "   "   1 "   "   and outside,
"   "   "   2 · "   Parlor and bed-room,
FURNITURE, PARLOR, TO MATCH HOUSE,—No. 4,
"   BED-ROOM.   "   "   —No. 5,
·PAPER COTTAGE,—No. 1,

PAPER SOLDIERS.

SOLDIERS,—FOOT, SOLDIERS,—HORSE,—large size,

CONTINENTALS,	MONTGOMERY GUARD,	LIGHT GUARD,
UNION RIFLES,	BRASS BAND,	HIGHLANDERS,
FIREMEN & HOSE CARRIAGE,		FIREMEN & ENGINE.

Eight Kinds.

ANIMALS,

SEPTEMBER, 1859.
McLOUGHLIN BROTHERS, Manufacturers,
No. 24 Beekman Street, New York.

No. 54a. LOWER PORTION 1859 FLYER.

No. 55. *Ida May.* 7-5/8 INCHES.

DIRECTIONS

FOR

This is a very beautiful doll, with both sides of the Figure, Dresses, and Hat colored; it is so simple as to hardly need any directions; some of my little friends, however, may not be able to get along without them.

In the first place, you must make the figure right. You will find the figure on a piece of card board, printed on both sides. This must be very nicely cut out, leaving the green ground about the for the figure to stand on.

In making the dresses, cut all the white paper from the outside, then fold them so that the back and front will match evenly. You will then see how to cut the neck, so as to let the head come through.

If you please, you can paste the edge of the dresses together, this will keep them in their place better on the figure

The hat is made in the same way. Cut out the hole for the face before you paste the edges together.

ADVERTISEMENT.

The subscribers have recently issued, under the name of "PARLOR AMUSEMENTS FOR LITTLE GIRLS," the following list of PAPER DOLLS, and SETS OF PAPER FURNITURE.

The Bride, a handsome doll, both sides of the dresses colored.
American Lady, a very large doll, beautifully colored.
Emma and **Etty,**
Grace Lee, a splendid doll, both sides of the dresses colored.
SUSAN LEE. " " "
Just out **IDA MAY,** a beautiful doll, extra large.
Also, **LADY GAY,** " "

The following is a list of small dolls.

Dolly, **Charley.**
Lizzie, **Mary.**
Baby, **Fanny,**
Willy and his Pony,
LUCY, **JENNY,**
AND FRANK.

We have also Published, new sets of

PAPER FURNITURE,

No. 1 **Bedroom set,** contains a French Bedstead, Bureau, Washstand, Table, two Ottomans, and four Chairs.
No. 2 **Parlor set,** contains a Sofa, Center Table, six Gothic chairs, two Rocking-chairs, and two Ottomans.
No. 3 **Drawing-room set,** contains Piano-forte Sofa, Table, six Chairs, two Ottomans, and two Rocking-chairs.
No. 4 **Drawing-room set Brocatel,** contains a handsome imitation Rosewood Piano, two Rocking-chairs, two Tete-a-tete's, six Chairs, and two Ottomans.
No 5 **Double set,** contains the Bedroom, and the Drawing-room Set.

No. 6 **Bedroom set, small,**
No. 7 **Parlor set,** "

ALSO, PAPER SOLDIERS FOR BOYS.
TWO KINDS:
Soldiers on foot containing 28 pieces—Soldiers on horse containing 18 pieces.

PAPER HOUSES.
Something new and beautiful—1st No. will be ready by the 20th of December.

McLOUGHLIN BROTHERS, Manufacturers,
Dec. 10th, 1858. 24 Beekman Street, New York.

No. 55a.

82

No. 56. *Lady Gay.* 7-5/8 INCHES.

No. 57. *Susie's Pets.* SUSIE 6½ INCHES AUTHOR'S COLLECTION.

No. 58. *Cinderella.* 4-5/8 INCHES. AUTHOR'S COLLECTION.

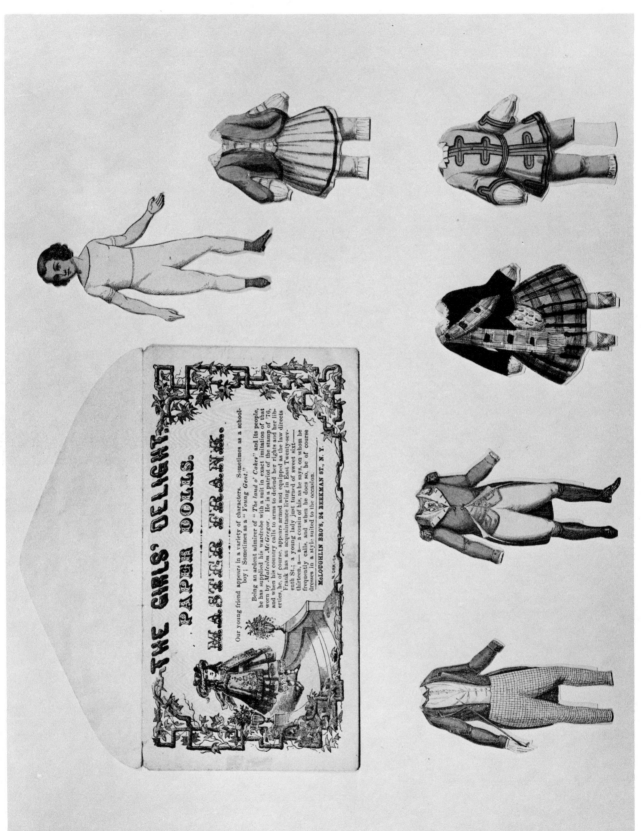

THE GIRLS' DELIGHT.

PAPER DOLLS.

MASTER FRANK.

Our young friend appears in a variety of characters. Sometimes as a school-boy; Sometimes as a "Young Gent."

Being an ardent admirer of "The land o' Cakes" and its people, he has supplied his wardrobe with a suit in exact imitation of that worn by Malcolm McGregor. He is a patriot of the stamp of '76, and when his country calls to arms to defend her rights and her liberties, he, of course appears armed and equipped as the law directs

Frank has an acquaintance living in East Twenty-seventh St., a young lady just turned of sweet sixteen, or thirteen, a— a cousin of his, as he says, on whom he frequently calls, and when he does so, he of course dresses in a style suited to the occasion.

McLOUGHLIN BRO'S, 24 BEEKMAN ST, N. Y.

No. 59.   Master Frank. 4-1/8 inches.   Margarett Dartt Collection.

DIRECTIONS FOR MASTER FRANK.

THE best and fullest directions how to prepare Paper Dolls and their dresses for use are contained in an elegant little book called "PAPER DOLLS AND HOW TO MAKE THEM," which also comprises a variety of beautiful patterns. But for the guidance of those who have not got that book, we herewith give a single example, which is amply sufficient to show how to prepare them all.

Cut out the figure carefully close to the outside line; cut out also the white piece between the arms and the body, and that between the lower limbs.

To prepare the clothes for use—first, double the white paper over back at the black lines marked A A; then cut with a small pair of scissors both parts of the paper close to the outer edge of the clothes, leaving only a short space uncut just where those black lines are. This will be the point where the whole will rest on the shoulders of the figure. Cut out the strip between the legs of the pantaloons. The closer you cut the better. You will see that if you do as above directed, the back will have been cut just about where the dotted lines are. In order that you may put on the clothes more easily, cut out of the back that little piece marked B. This will give you a large space to pass the head through sidewise, and you will be less likely to tear the clothes in putting them on. You can then turn them around to their proper position. Of course you will understand that the neck is to be cut out in the same way as other parts of the dress, leaving a narrow strip uncut, as mentioned above.

The Hats and Caps are to be prepared in a similar manner. Double the white paper over back at the highest point of the Hat or Cap, rub it down close where it folds, then cut all around the outside *excepting* a very small space where it is folded over at the top. Gum or paste the back to the front at the top a very little, just enough to prevent their coming over the face too far; also gum the sides a little at the point where widest.

No. 59a. DIRECTIONS FOR ASSEMBLING *Master Frank* AND HIS WARDROBE.

No. 60. *Lilly Beers.* 3-15/16 INCHES.

No. 61. *Minnie Miller.* 3-3/16 INCHES.

No. 62. *Nancy Fancy.* 5 inches. The Van Wye Collection.

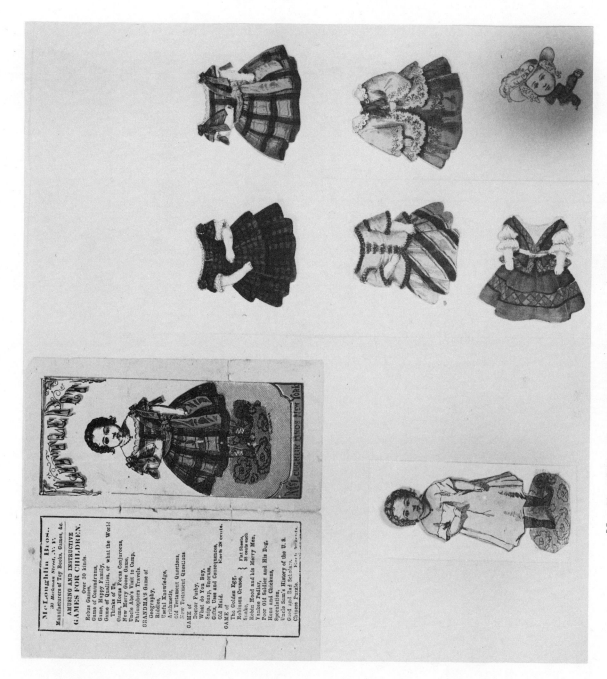

No. 63. *Little Pet.* 3-1/8 inches. F. Author's Collection.

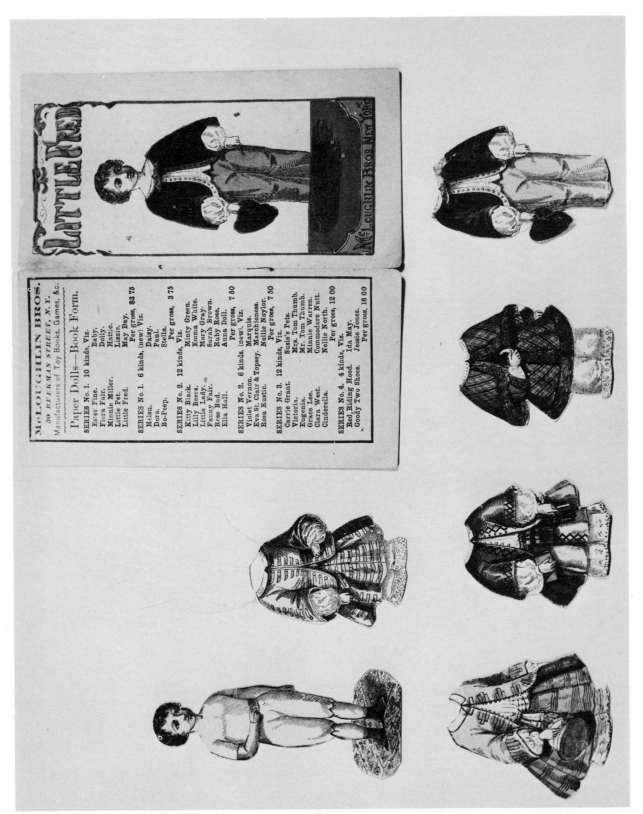

No. 64. *Little Fred.* 3¼ INCHES.

No. 65.   *Willie.* 2-15/16 INCHES.   AUTHOR'S COLLECTION.

Note

The status of McLoughlin Bros.' *Nellie* was left in doubt as covered on Pg. 77. This now has been clarified by courtesy of Mrs. R. C. Wildman, of Medina, Ohio.

Mrs. Wildman advises that she and her daughter, in their joint collection, have McLoughlin Bros.' *Nellie* with the envelope, a direction sheet, and costumes exactly like those of Clark, Austin & Smith's doll Nellie, illustrated on pg. 23.

The McLoughlin direction sheet measures 11 by 5½ inches, with, oddly, a Flora McFlimsey poem printed at the end.

In the design on the white envelope, Nellie wears the ruffled dress shown in upper row, center, Illus. No. 16. A red streamer across the top of the envelope is inscribed, "Paper Dolls & Paper Furniture." An inscription across the bottom reads, "McLoughlin Brothers, Manufacturers, 30 Beekman Street, New York". Since the name "Nellie," no surname, appears on several of our McLoughlin Bros. folders, and, according to Mrs. Wildman, on at least one direction sheet bearing inscription, "Entered according to Act of Congress, 1858", as well as on the September, 1859 flyer (Pg. 80), it is presumed that the doll had been in circulation for some time before the surname "North" was added; also that subject *Nellie,* issued from 30 Beekman Street address, is a rerun of the original doll.

Mrs. Wildman's contribution definitely establishes that the listed *Nellie* is a duplicate of Clark, Austin & Smith's doll of the same name, possibly printed from the same plates, the surname added later as brought out in Section C of this chapter.

Section C: 1875-1876 Catalog

The cover of this interesting catalog is shown in Illus. 66. As will be noted, the catalog contains five sections of detailed listings, one covering paper dolls, and it is this that we are quoting here. It is to be presumed that listings cover the total inventory of paper dolls available through 1875 and into 1876.

Frequently, names allotted by little girls in their play are found on the backs of paper dolls in a childish scrawl. In other instances, however, the publisher's name for a doll has been carefully inscribed on the back by an adult, and in such cases the printed record and descriptions contained in this early catalog may often verify these pencilled appellations as well as making possible positive identification of certain of our unknowns.

While the catalog does not provide specific publishing dates for individual dolls, it does serve to establish that the listed ones actually were produced during or prior to these years. Costume styling then furnishes additional aid to our approximate datings.

Further information is provided by a catalog of this company for years 1876—'77 in the collection of the late Nellie MacLachlan. Careful checking of the two disclosed identical listings with but one exception; the later issue adds one series, namely the "Centennial Belles", described as "Dressed Paper Dolls, three and one-half and five and one-half inches high. Twelve styles of dresses. Trimmed with imitation lace, with pretty overskirt. Very perfect representations of the fashionable ladies of the present day. Size No. 1—Per Gross, $9.00. Size No. 2—Per Gross, $15.00."

These dolls apparently were brought out in 1876 to commemorate the Centennial International Ex-

position held in Philadelphia, Pennsylvania, in that year. It is regrettable that this set is not available for illustrating.

Certain of the paper dolls already covered in the Early Series and in the 1859 flyer sections of this chapter still are listed in these catalogs, attesting their popularity with little girls over a period of some eighteen years or more.

Bear in mind that the prices given are wholesale; however, in many cases retail prices are established by the printing on certain of the dolls' containers. Even these arouse a touch of envy when we consider the prices we pay today for these same dolls, and we wail, "Why *didn't* I save my paper dolls!"

It will be noted that the publisher gave one overall measurement for all dolls of a given catalogued series. We have established that these printed sizes are only approximate, as measurements vary among the different dolls. Therefore, to provide a convenient reference, we have included individual measurements, carefully taken and substantially correct, measured from the top of the head to the tip of the lower shoe.

While with one exception no specimens of the first eight listed series were available for photographing, the balance of the catalogued dolls are largely represented by photographic reproductions of actual dolls. Certain sets are somewhat incomplete, but the parts shown may be helpful to our readers in identifying their unknowns, and in correctly assigning a portion of their accessories from accumulations of "odds." And of course the uncut sets provide unquestionable authentication. Quotation marks designate verbatim catalog copy, commentaries following.

- - - - -

"McLOUGHLIN BROS.' CATALOGUE

For 1875—'76.

"DRESSED PAPER DOLLS

"These are a new feature in the Doll Line, and make attractive and salable gifts. In the different series, the figures vary in size, and in the style and beauty of the toilets. These are made of fine imported papers, in imitation of moire-antique and corded silks, elaborately trimmed in imitation with lace, and are only excelled by the original fabrics. The dresses have full plaited skirts with slight trains.

DOLLS WITH TISSUE DRESSES

"SERIES No. 1..Per Gross, $24.00.

Three kinds: *Baby — Brunette — Blonde*

"The figures are eleven inches in height, made of pasteboard, and give front and back views. The dresses are made of tissue paper tastefully trimmed, with sash. Put up in pasteboard boxes containing one dozen each, and packed six dozen in a package."

None of these three ready-dressed dolls was available to show, but identical dolls with a given or a sur-

name, and with *printed* costumes appear in this chapter under the heading of DOLLY VARDEN DOLLS.

CATALOGUE

OF

TOY BOOKS,

PAPER DOLLS,

A B C BLOCKS,

GAMES,

VALENTINES, &c.

FOR 1875—'76.

MANUFACTURED BY

McLOUGHLIN BROS.,

73 Duane Street,

NEW YORK.

No. 66. Catalog Cover. Author's Collection.

"DOLLS WITH SILK DRESSES

"SERIES NO. O...Per Gross, $12.00.

"Each box contains twelve dolls, same in size and toilet as No. 1. This series is assorted, and enables dealers to meet the demand for single dolls."

(Regret no illustrations possible. Author).

- - - - -

"SERIES No. 1—Three kinds...Per Gross, $24.00.

"House No. 1 contains...Rosie and Charlie.
House No. 2 contains...Lillie and Harrie.
House No. 3 contains...Susie and Willie.

"Each box contains two dolls, a girl and a boy, mounted upon separate standards. They represent two well-dressed children about ten years old. The dresses of the girls vary with each figure, and are in imitation of silk, trimmed with lace, and in the latest style. Each set is put up in a pasteboard box, presenting the appearance of a three-story brick English basement house. Put up in pasteboard boxes containing one dozen sets each, and packed assorted gross cases."

Of the above Series No. 1 we are able to include only one illustration (67) showing the box for *Lillie and Harrie,* ("Lilly" and "Harry" on the box cover). We are indebted to Miss Maude E. Willand of Manchester, New Hampshire, for the loan of this box for photographing, and to Kimport Dolls of Independence, Missouri, for permission to include a copy of Miss Willand's letter to them, published in DOLL TALK, October, 1948:

"I do not have any McLoughlin dolls, but I do have a box which contained some. It measures 6x3x2 inches in depth. The outside is covered with paper imitating brick. The cover pictures steps leading from the front walk to an interesting old door, either side of which is a window with lace curtains. The three upstairs windows have like curtains while the attic windows have only shades. The small portion of fence resembles fences on old Beacon Street in Boston. A label reads—DRESSED PAPER DOLLS—No. 1, LILLY AND HARRY,—McLoughlin Bros., Manfs., N. Y. I wrote the firm in 1943 and received a reply saying, 'We assure you, you have a really valuable antique. It was one put out by this company

first in 1865 and sold through 1873 at which time it was discontinued.'."

The above information from the publisher authoritatively dates the paper dolls distributed in the boxes representing brick English basement houses, and we are especially grateful to Miss Willand and to Kimport Dolls for the privilege of sharing this data with our readers. We note that the manufacture of this series ceased in 1873, and gather that the listing in the later catalog represented close-out stock.

From the box measurements we know *Lilly and Harry* were small figures. Measurements of the boxes for the larger dolls are given in the catalog copy. The label referred to in Miss Willand's letter is pasted at one end of the box, the "No. 1" at variance with the No. 2 of the catalog listing. The variation of the spelling of the dolls' names from that given in the catalog is but one of several such instances. The two ten-year-olds are long gone, their little house vacant, but we should like to feel that the brother and sister are safely housed in the collection of some fortunate owner.

"SERIES No. 2 — Three kinds . . . . Per Gross, $72.00.

House No. 1 contains   . . .   Mademoiselles Madeliene and Jeannette.
House No. 2 contains   . . .   Mademoiselles Fanchon and Louise.
House No. 3 contains   . . .   Mademoiselles Nannette and Hortense.

"Each box contains two fashionably dressed dolls, seven and one-half inches high, drawing-room dresses, full plaited, with a slight train, made in imitation of moire-antique and corded silks, trimmed with lace; also handsome sash. Put up in three-story brick English basement houses, seven and one-half inches high by three wide. Each set packed in quarter dozen packages."

"SERIES No. 3 — Four Kinds . . . . Per Gross, $90.00.

House No. 1 contains   . . .   Le Marquis et La Marchioness.
House No. 2 contains   . . .   Le Comte et La Comtesse
House No. 3 contains   . . .   Le Monsieur et La Madame.
House No. 4 contains   . . .   Le Duc et La Duchesse.

"Each box contains two figures, a lady and gentleman nine inches in height, differing in style from the foregoing. Dresses with full-trained skirt in moire-antique and corded silks of different shades. Apron overskirt, with handsome lace sash. Full evening or party dress in the height of the fashion. Put up in three-story brick English basement houses nine inches by four and one-half wide. Each set packed in one-quarter dozen packages."

No. 67.   Box 6 x 3 x 2 inches, for Lilly and Harry, Courtesy Miss Maude E. Willand.

"SERIES No. 4 — Three kinds . . . . Per Gross, $108.00.

House No. 1 contains . . . Mademoiselles Blanche et Elenore.
House No. 2 contains . . . Mademoiselles Laure et Levinee.
House No. 3 contains . . . Mademoiselles Irene et Isidore.

"Each box contains two figures of ladies ten and one-half inches in height. These are elegantly dressed figures in reception toilets. The dresses are in moire-antique and corded silks, with full trained skirts richly trimmed with lace. Handsome silk overskirt with lace trimming and lace sash, or lace apron overskirt. Put up in three-story brick English basement houses, ten and one-half inches high by five wide. Each set packed in one-quarter dozen packages."

These descriptions fire our imagination, and we deeply regret that the fine ladies could not be shown with their ravishing wardrobes.

"DOLL FAMILY — Six Kinds . . . . Per Gross, $72.00.

These dolls are all girls, the same in size and toilet as No. 1, and make a very fine assortment. Put up on cards containing six each, and packed twelve cards in a box."

"DOLL PARTY — Six kinds . . . . Per Gross, $72.00.

Contains three boys and three girls mounted upon cards. In size and toilets they correspond also with No. 1. Put up on cards containing six each, and packed twelve cards in a box."

While it is disappointing that illustrations could not be included for all of the above, we believe that those shown in the following constitute the most frequently found paper dolls, and therefore that the coverage is of greater importance and value to the average collector.

"PAPER DOLLS IN ENVELOPES.

"SERIES No. 1 — Large Sized Dolls . . . . Per Gross, $12.00.

Dotty Dimple	Bride
Susie Simple	Bridesmaid
Bertie Bright	Groom and Groomsman

The figures are seven and one-half inches in height, cut out of pasteboard, printed in colors upon both sides, giving front and back views. They are accompanied by four toilets suitable for a young lady, and are put in envelopes, with full directions. The toilets are rich and elaborate, and in the latest fashion. Packed in pasteboard boxes containing one gross of each kind."

As will be noted these are all large dolls, and are believed to have been lithographed in color on stones. The uncut set of *Dottie Dimple* ("Dotty" in the catalog), Illus. No. 68, is from the collection of the late Mrs. Armstrong of Texas. The sheet of costumes measures 8-15/16 by 21-3/16 inches, and folds for enclosure in the 5-3/4 by 9-5/16 inch envelope.

Susie Simple, likewise uncut, is shown in No. 69 by courtesy of Mrs. Wm. M. Ahlstrom of Mentor, Ohio. *Bertie Bright* (70) still has her four costumes, but the hats failed to survive childish hands.

As described in the catalog, these three sets are printed front and back, the features executed in deep flesh tones, while the costumes are in dark, almost somber shades.

THE PAPER DOLL BRIDAL PARTY from the author's collection is given in Illustrations No. 71 through 73a. The envelope for the Bride is shown in 71 while the Bride herself appears in 71a, the Bridesmaid in 72. Costumes for the Bride are executed in soft pastels with the exception of the opera cloak which is in bright red; the bridal gown is a luscious pink with white veil, a combination which appears to have been popular with McLoughlin Bros. for wedding dresses in the early and mid-nineteenth century.

Pictured costumes for the Bridesmaid also are in soft pastels; however a set of the Bridal Party has been reported as executed in vivid, garish colors similar to the dolls in the Dolly Varden Series, imparting a decidedly changed appearance to the Bridal Party.

The Bridegroom and Groomsman were distributed in one envelope (No. 73), which plainly identifies the bridegroom as the mustached gentleman. These figures are permanently dressed in formal attire, the balance of their wardrobes as shown in No. 73a. These four suits appear to be interchangeable, and while perhaps an uncut set would disclose additional apparel, the wardrobe as shown is believed to be complete with the exception of hats which presumably accompanied the gentlemen as published.

Listings on the backs of the two envelopes shown opened flat, (the flaps having disappeared), give a schedule of retail prices for many McLoughlin Bros.' paper dolls, and it is hoped that they will be legible in the illustrations; they are envy provoking!

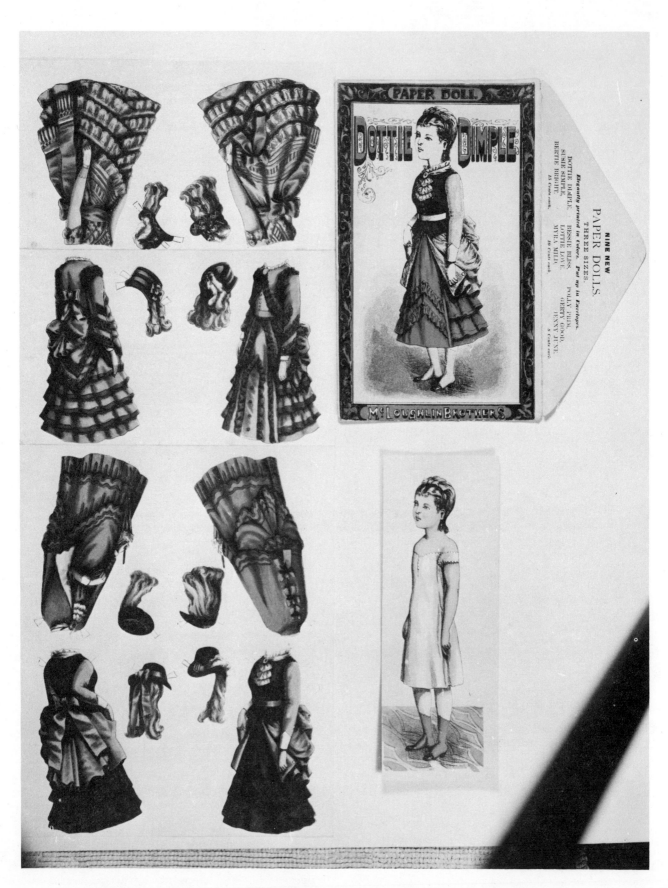

No. 68. Dottie Dimple, 7-3/4 inches. Collection late Mrs. H. B. Armstrong.

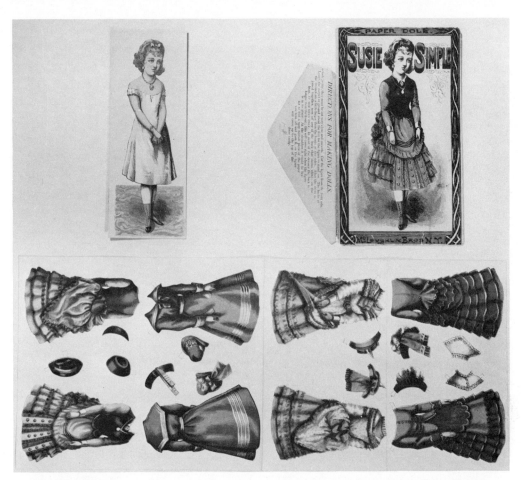

No. 69. Susie Simple, 8¼ inches, uncut. Mrs. Wm. M. Ahlstrom Collection.

No. 70.   Bertie Bright, 7¼″.

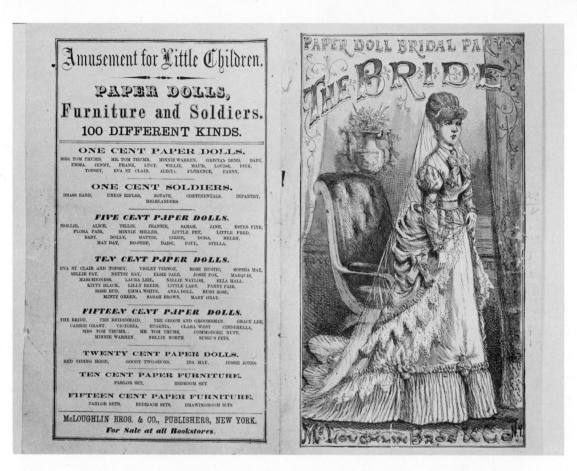

No. 71.   Envelope for The Bride of The Paper Doll Bridal Party. Author's Collection.

No. 71a.   The Bride, 7-7/8 inches. Author's Collection.

No. 72. The Bridesmaid, 7-5/8 inches. Author's Collection.

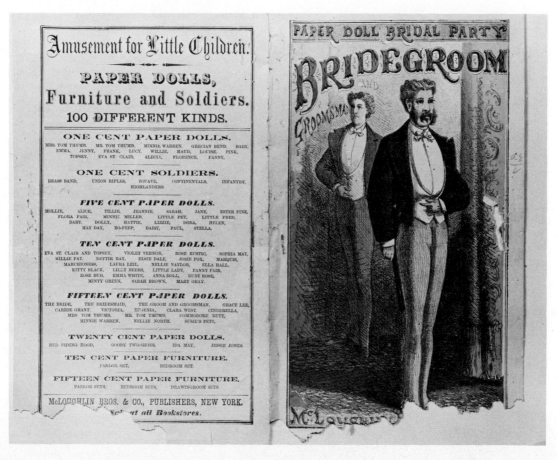

No. 73. Envelope for The Bridegroom and Groomsman. Author's Collection.

No. 73a.   The Bridegroom and Groomsman.   Author's Collection.

"SERIES No. 2 — Medium Sized Dolls . . . . Per Gross, $9.00.

Bessie Bliss   Lottie Love   Myra Mild

"The figures are six and one-half inches in height, and are printed in colors. They have four toilets suitable for a girl, and are put up in envelopes with full directions. The toilets are of the latest fashion, in good taste, and adapted to a variety of occasions. Packed in pasteboard boxes containing one gross of each kind."

These medium sized dolls are somewhat smaller than those in Series No. 1. However, they were executed by the same process and have the same general characteristics, features in deep flesh tones, costumes in the darker, duller shades.

Bessie Bliss (No. 74) is in original uncut condition except that the doll herself has been cut from the card on which she was printed. Costumes shown with both front and back views provide a perfect fashion plate for doll dressmakers and students of costume.

In No. 75 we have *Lottie Love* also in uncut condition, by courtesy of Mrs. Ahlstrom, with *Myra Mild* from the author's collection pictured in No. 76 but without the hats which failed to accompany the doll when received. Her costumes unfortunately are pasted at the sides for slipping over the doll's head, precluding our showing the back views. This is an attractive series of dolls with wardrobes in the fashion of the day.

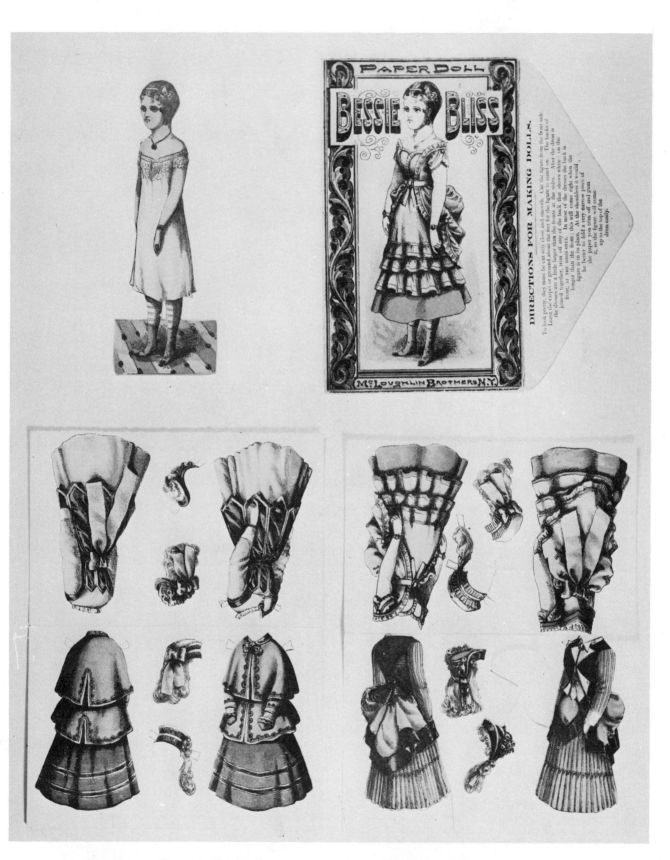

No. 74.   Bessie Bliss, 6-3/8 inches.   Author's Collection.

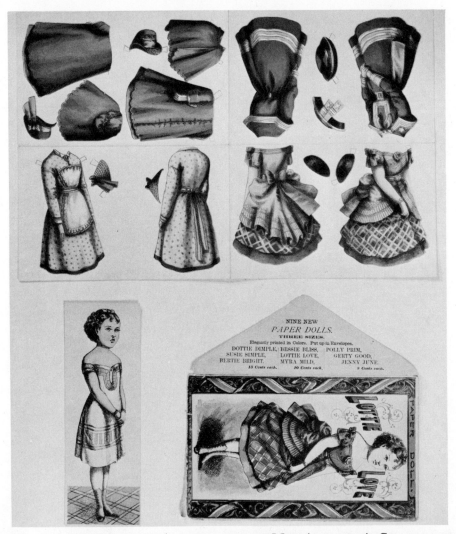

No. 75.   LOTTIE LOVE, 6-7/8 INCHES, UNCUT. MRS. AHLSTROM'S COLLECTION.

No. 76.   MYRA MILD, 6-3/8 INCHES. AUTHOR'S COLLECTION.

"SERIES No. 3 — Small Sized Dolls . . . . Per Gross, $6.00.

Gerty Good   Jenny June   Polly Prim

"The figures are five and one-half inches in height, and give front and back views in colors. They have four neat and stylish toilets suitable for a young girl—all in the latest fashion. Put up in envelopes with full directions. Packed in pasteboard boxes containing one gross of each kind."

This third series of smaller dolls (Nos. 77, 78 and 79) was executed by the same process as the larger ones in the two preceding series, and in the same combination of deep flesh tones and darker costumes. Only *Girty Good* ("Gerty" in the catalog) is uncut to allow showing both front and back views of the costumes. Those in the two cut sets are pasted in the usual manner for play.

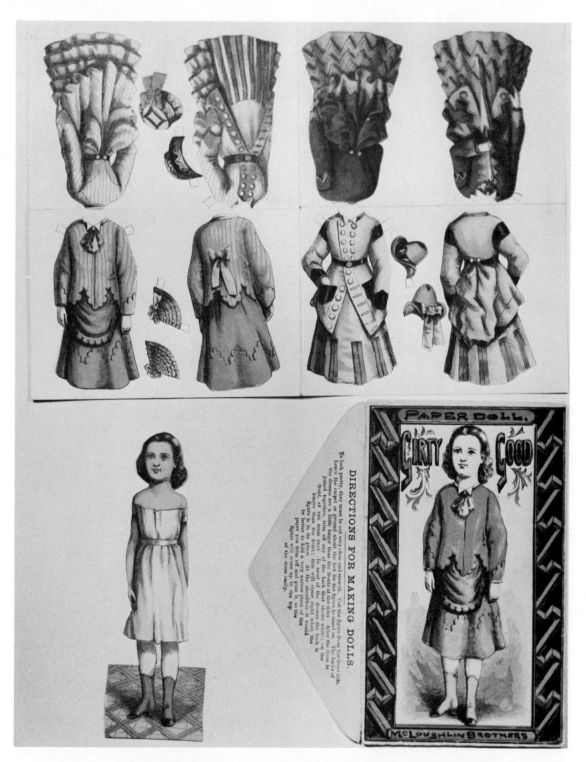

No. 77. Girty Good, 5-5/8 inches. Courtesy Mrs. H. B. Armstrong Estate.

No. 78.   JENNIE JUNE, 5-5/8 INCHES. AUTHOR'S COLLECTION.

No. 79.   POLLY PRIM, 5-5/8 INCHES.

"DOLLY VARDEN DOLLS . . . . Per Gross, $24.00.

Baby Blue   Bertha Blonde   Betsey Brunette

"The figures are eleven inches in height, cut out of pasteboard, and give front and back views in colors. Each doll has three elegant toilets in colors. Put up in fine envelopes with full directions. Packed in pasteboard boxes containing one-half gross of each kind."

As mentioned in the text covering Series No. 1, "Dolls with Tissue Dresses", the three large Dolly Varden dolls are exact duplicates of the Series No. 1 figures, except they are provided with removable costumes, printed, rather than the readymade tissue dresses.

In this Dolly Varden Series, colors have undergone a drastic change, costumes executed in gaudy, flamboyant hues, thus presenting a less attractive appearance, despite which the dolls have an important place in any well rounded-out collection.

In Illus. No. 80 we have *Baby Blue* with her three costumes and one cap; two caps are believed to be missing from this set.

In No. 81 we show the face of the 7-3/4 by 11-15/16 inch envelope for *Bertha Blonde,* while 81a gives us the back of this envelope containing printed listings with retail selling prices for many of the catalogued dolls.

Bertha Blonde herself appears in No. 82, with *Betsey Brunette* in 83 to complete the trio.

Was this series named for the famous circus aerialist, Dolly Varden, who is said to have earned the fabulous sum of $10,000 a week at the height of her career, was toasted throughout America and Europe, and who had various products named for her as had been done for Jenny Lind in the early 1850's?

It is recorded that Dolly Varden performed with "Buffalo Bill" (William F. Cody), presumably in his "Wild West" show which he started in 1883, touring both continents. Unless Dolly exercised her woman's prerogative of under-stating her age, which is unlikely, she was born in 1871, and would have been twelve years of age when Buffalo Bill's show was organized, and only four years old when McLoughlin Bros.' 1875 catalog was printed. Was her name becoming known at that early age? With two series of paper dolls listed under this uncommon name, the second one the "Little Dolly Varden Series", to be covered in a later section of this chapter, it appears that Dolly Varden's fame was already established, providing the inspiration for the naming of paper dolls in her honor, though not necessarily resembling her.

During Dolly's career she amassed a fortune which was dissipated in luxurious living and over-generosity toward those less fortunate than herself. She died in poverty in 1955 at the stated age of 84.

NO. 80. BABY BLUE, 10-5/8 INCHES. AUTHOR'S COLLECTION.

No. 81. Envelope for Bertha Blonde. Author's Collection.

No. 81a. Back of the Bertha Blonde Envelope.

No. 82. Bertha Blonde, 11-1/16 inches. Author's Collection.

No. 83. Betsey Brunette, 11-1/16 inches. Author's Collection.

For some reason known only to the publishers at the time, the next four series were catalogued in reverse numerical order. Headed "Paper Dolls in Book Form", a brief description of what is meant by "book form" may be helpful.

By referring to various illustrations of uncut books, it will be noted costumes are printed on long sheets of paper folded horizontally at the center, then vertically to provide two double sheets with one costume to a page where fronts only are printed. Where both fronts and backs are given, they are arranged in a manner to conserve space. Frequently, too, the horizontal fold has been cut so that four single sheets result. In turn these are folded, enclosed between the covers, and hand-sewn at the back fold. A set where the sheets have been cut into singles may be seen in Illustration No. 92, *Mrs. Tom Thumb*. The first illustration then in next following Series 2, Twenty-four kinds, *Kitty Black*, No. 96, will provide an example of the full-length costume sheet, the horizontal fold-line visible in the photograph. In the latter, as with other uncut books in Series 2, the finished one measures 3½ by 7 inches.

The dolls are printed on fairly heavy white cardboard for sturdiness when cut out for play, and are secured to the first page of the book by just a touch of paste at the "spine" or fold, to allow easy removal without disfiguring either the doll or the costumes. When this has been accomplished, and the costumes have been cut out, the book covers provide a folder in which to store the doll and her wardrobe.

"PAPER DOLLS IN BOOK FORM.

"These dolls are not as elaborate as the foregoing, and differ from them in style of their toilets. They are essential to variety, and with the others make the household complete. Four toilets in colors accompany each figure. The prices of these dolls have been reduced since July 1st.

"SERIES 4 — Four kinds . . . . Per Gross, $12.00.

Red Riding Hood   Ida May
Goody Two Shoes   Jessie Jones

Contrary to the publishers' comment that "these dolls are not as elaborate as the foregoing", those in Series 4 are very lovely and certainly as fine as any of those previously listed. The two storybook sets are outstanding, the costumes and appurtenances bringing the stories to life, and these dolls are avidly sought by collectors today.

Order of publication of these four listed dolls is established as follows: *Ida May* was produced in 1858 as was revealed in Sect. B of this chapter (Illus. 55).

Goody Two Shoes preceded *Little Red Riding Hood*, evidenced by a notation printed on the back of the folder for Minnie Warren, circa 1863/64, "Will be ready on the 1st of Sept., *Goody Two Shoes*, a Splendid Doll with Story."

Then at the bottom of an early folder for *Goody Two Shoes*, bearing publishers' address of 30 Beekman Street, (1864/1870 bracket), we read "Will be ready about the 1st of November, *Little Red Riding Hood*." Omission of the year from these printings is disappointing, but the 30 Beekman Street address approximately dates the two storybook sets.

Taking up the dolls in order of the catalog grouping, the folder for *Little Red Riding Hood* (No. 84) shows 30 Beekman Street, N.Y. as publishers' address at time of publication. The doll and appurtenances are given in No. 84a. All parts except the bed are printed front and back; two hoods are missing, the pictured set believed to be otherwise complete. While the general heading for this series stated each doll had four toilets, apparently the wardrobe for Little Red Riding Hood was reduced to two garments to allow space for the more interesting storybook figures. The story is printed on the folder, and directions admonish children to consult it "so they can carry the little figures through all the scenes portrayed in it."

A child playing with this fascinating paper doll would first cut a slit underneath the pillows on the bed, tucking Grandmother cozily in place beneath the gayly hued coverlet. Red Riding Hood then would be dressed in her flower-sprigged dress with its apron, a hood would cover her pretty curls; she would don her red cloak (called a "cardinal" in the early part of the preceding century), her bouquet of wild flowers would be slipped through a tiny slit carefully cut in the hand of the cloak, and she would be started on her way to Grandmother's with her basket of goodies.

Sadly she would arrive only to find the ferocious wolf which she had encountered on her way through the wood, reclining in the bed, brazenly wearing terrified Grandmother's night-cap.

The story ending is well known, and in imagination we can sense the enthrallment of little girls privileged, some one hundred years ago, to re-enact this exciting story in stage-play form.

For *Goody Two Shoes* we show covers of two different editions, one (No. 85), an early one carrying publishers' address of 30 Beekman Street, the other, (85a), apparently a later printing, having a different cover design, bearing only the inscription "McLoughlin Bros., New York" as used on many of their later productions. The two printings are alike in all respects excepting the covers. No. 85a shows both front and back views of an uncut doll, while 85b gives us the costumes, the wig, and various accessories, all in original uncut condition. Goody's wedding dress is said to be the fancy one at left. All parts are printed double except the A.B.C. cards, the card case and the two little shoes.

Among the unusual appurtenances are the shoes, the A.B.C. cards and card case, a dog, lamb, crow, dove, and a blue bird, (called a "skylark" in the story), all to allow enactment of the popular tale which is printed on both of these folders.

Directions tell us that in play the wedge shaped tabs of the A.B.C. cards and case would be inserted in slits cut between the thumb and first finger of each hand on the figured dress. The birds would be cut entirely out and "gumed" or pasted together, except the feet of the crow ("raven" in the story) would be left open to straddle the shoulder of the doll. The dove, called a "pigeon" in the story, also would be affixed to a shoulder by inserting the wedge between the back and front of the dress so that the dove's bill would appear to be in Goody's mouth.

The shoes would be placed on the front of the doll's feet by cutting slits at the ankles where the lacing crosses, and at the toes, to admit the tabs provided at the top and bottom of the shoes.

This must have been an exciting toy for children a century ago, and at the present time acquiring a set is an exciting adventure to any collector.

Incidentally, McLoughlin Bros. published a little story book of Goody Two Shoes in 1888, beautifully illustrated and colored, but differing in certain episodes from the story printed on the paper doll folders. The essentials, however, remain the same— Goody's rescue and care of the little mis-treated wild creatures, her marriage to Sir Charles Jones, and her brother Tom's return from overseas, now a wealthy, influential man. No mention is made in the book, however, that Goody Two Shoes' death was "the greatest calamity that ever was felt in the neighborhood."

McLoughlin Bros.' propensity to alter their doll listings, sometimes causing confusion, is evident in the various printed series on the back of the earlier Goody Two Shoes' folder. Here the early dolls are broken down into four series of different price ranges, but the same series numbers are applied to later listings in the 1875/76 catalog as above set out. And the catalogued dolls are likewise divided into different series on the backs of many of the folders. Thus one cannot refer to a specific series number for a given doll unless the source of the information also is provided.

Available information on *Jessie Jones* (No. 86) is somewhat meager. However, we do know there were two different printings, but we have no specific publication dates.

On the back of the early Goody Two Shoes folder (No. 85) is printed, "Ida May and Jessie Jones have only to be seen to be admired". Since Jessie Jones was not mentioned in any of the earlier listings we adhere to the opinion, not official, that the first edition came out perhaps at 30 Beekman Street and just prior to Series No. 3, Twelve kinds, which includes the Tom Thumb group.

The writer was privileged some years ago to examine one of the later printings of Jessie Jones with container and at least one precious bonnet, neither of which is included in the pictured set, and we regret not having had it photographed at the time.

Unlike the other three dolls in this Series 4, Four kinds, *Jessie Jones* and her wardrobe of four garments have front printing only. Was this number originally printed double, the backs of the pictured set lost over the years? Except for this feature, Jessie ranks with other early dolls in nice execution of all details. Not frequently found today, acquisition of this doll in either of the two known printings is of importance to present day collectors.

No. 84.   Book Covers for Little Red Riding Hood.

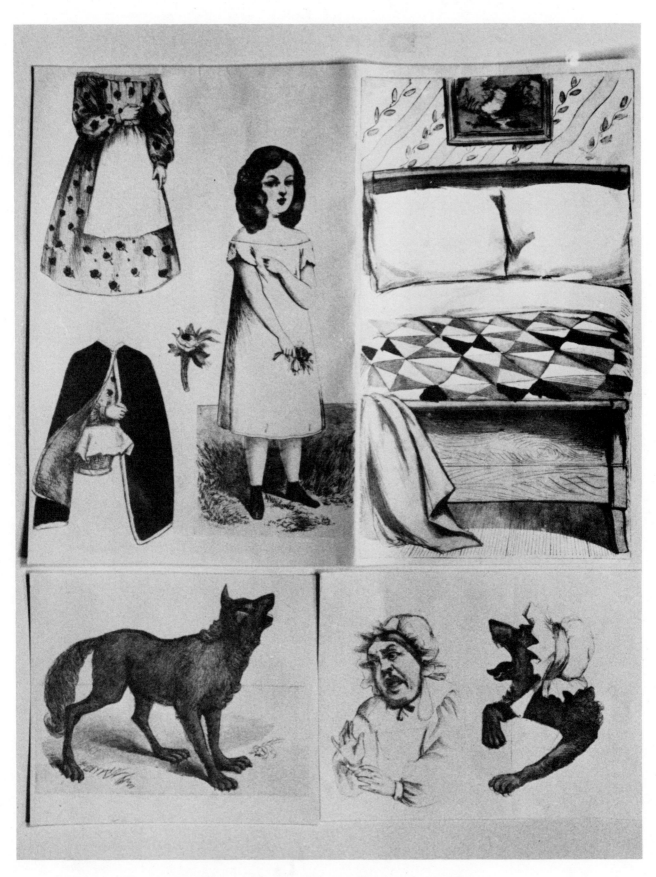

No. 84a. LITTLE RED RIDING HOOD, 7-5/16 INCHES

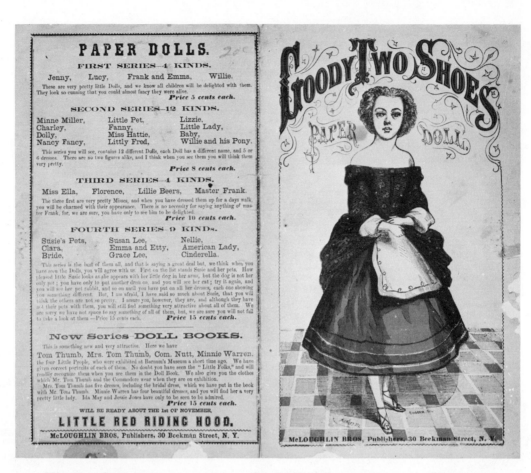

No. 85. COVERS OF EARLY BOOK FOR GOODY TWO SHOES. AUTHOR'S COLLECTION.

No. 85a. COVER OF LATER BOOK FOR GOODY TWO SHOES WITH DOLL, UNCUT. COURTESY NEW YORK PUBLIC LIBRARY.

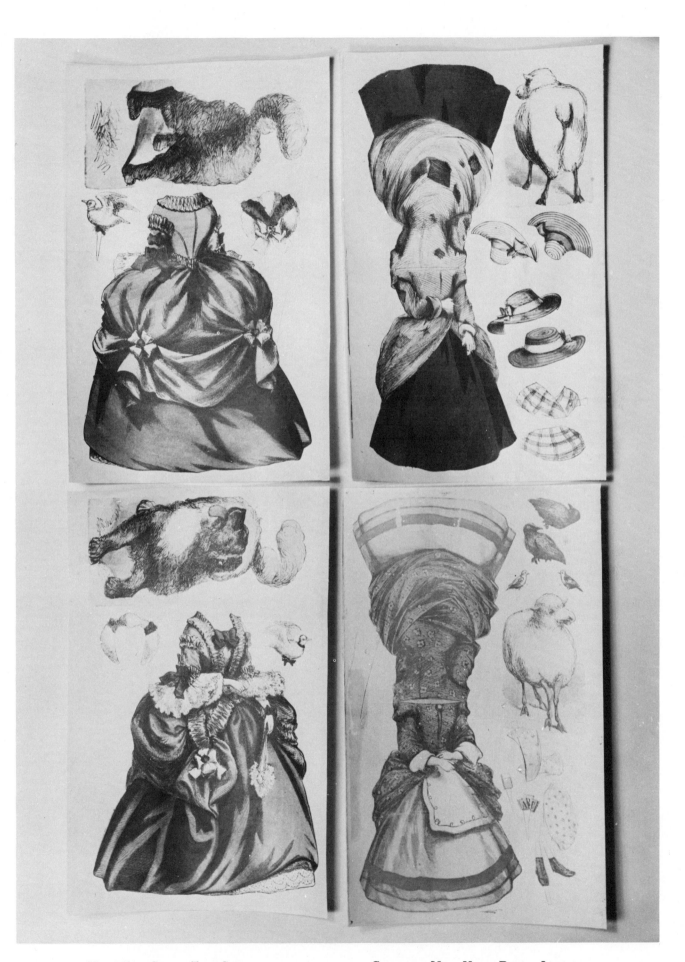

No. 85b.   GOODY TWO SHOES COSTUMES, UNCUT. COURTESY NEW YORK PUBLIC LIBRARY.

No. 86. JESSIE JONES, 7-5/8 INCHES.

118

Dolls in this series are of diversified types, all well designed and nicely colored.

Carrie Grant (No 87), *Victoria* (No. 88) and *Eugenia* (No. 89) are included in original book form by courtesy of The Newark Museum, Newark, New Jersey. A certain similarity in the general characteristics is evident. Costume coloring, while less somber than in Series 2 and 3 in envelopes, still leans to the darker shades. Costumes are double, and hair bands, perhaps intended as combs, confine the luxurious locks of the dolls, Carrie Grant's and Victoria's extending across the back of the head from ear to ear, while Eugenia's long curls are held in place by only a short band or comb just beneath the crown of her head.

For *Grace Lee* reference is made to Sect. A of this chapter, Illustration No. 40.

Clara West (No. 90) has front printing only, and as was noted in the coverage of Clark, Austin & Smith's No. 5 doll called "Clara" (Chapt. II, Illus. No. 17), the bodies of the two dolls are alike, McLoughlin Bros. having adopted an entirely different head for *Clara West*. Since only the name "Clara" appears in the doll listings on the back of the Clara West cover, our supposition is that Clara West is the "Clara" of McLoughlin Bros.' listing on their 1859 flyer covered in Sect. B, this opinion borne out by the styling of Clara West's wardrobe, which dates it as of the 1858/59 period. Book covers of the pictured set bear no street address for the publishers, evidencing it to be a later printing of a previously published number, a further indication that the original printing presumably was titled "Clara."

Cinderella and *Susie's Pets* may be seen in Sect. B, Illustrations Nos. 58 and 57 respectively.

And now come the "little people." Of the many portrait paper dolls valued by today's collectors, probably none is so prized as those representing the four famous midgets.

Publication of this group was announced on the book cover for Mrs. Tom Thumb, a fragment of which appears in Illus. No. 91 with General Tom Thumb. This establishes that Mrs. Tom Thumb was the first of the four to be issued, followed by her sister, Minnie Warren, with the little General and Commodore Nutt following almost immediately. The series originated at the Publishers' 30 Beekman Street headquarters, and while, as previously disclosed, Mrs. Tom Thumb preceded Goody Two Shoes of Series No. 4, an announcement on the latter's folder proclaims:

"This is something new and very attractive. Here we have TOM THUMB, MRS. TOM THUMB, COM. NUTT, MINNIE WARREN, the four Little People, who were exhibited at Barnum's Museum a short time ago. We have given correct portraits of each of them. No doubt you have seen the 'Little Folks', and will readily recognize them when you see them in the Doll Book. We also give you the clothes which Mr. Tom Thumb and the Commodore wear when they are on exhibition.

"Mrs. Tom Thumb has five dresses, including the bridal dress which we have put in the book with Mr. Tom Thumb. Minnie Warren has four beautiful dresses, and we know you will find her a very pretty little lady . . . Price 15 cents, each."

These dual notices appear to confirm a close publication sequence for the foregoing Series No. 4 dolls and the midget group.

While the suits for Mr. Tom Thumb and the Commodore were publicized as copies of those actually worn by the little gentlemen when on exhibition, it is noted no such claim was made for the ladies' wardrobes. Certainly, the dress believed to have been included as Mrs. Tom Thumb's wedding dress bears no relation to the elaborate gown with its long tulle veil trailing the floor in which she and her bridegroom posed with their attendants, Com. Nutt and Minnie Warren, for their wedding photo- graph, reproduced in Illus. No. 92b—1 from HOBBIES Magazine by courtesy of the publishers.

Illustration 92b—2 is a reproduction of a commercial photograph from the author's collection, the caption of which reads: "GENERAL TOM THUMB AND WIFE. In the identical costumes worn before Emperor Louis Napoleon and the Empress Eugenie, at the Palace of the Tuilleries, Nov. 13, ...", the year illegible. History records that Empress Eugenie, well disguised, fled from the Tuilleries on the afternoon of September 4, 1870, following the abdication of the Emperor; since the midgets' appearance pre-dated this event, it probably took place in or shortly after 1863.

Tom Thumb, (legally Charles S. Stratton), was born on January 4, 1838 at Bridgeport, Connecticut, apparently normal until he was a year and a half old, when his growth was retarded, his height reaching only 40 inches at maturity. His marriage to Mercy Lavinia Warren Bumpus took place in Grace Church, New York, on February 10, 1863. No children were born of this union which was terminated by the General's death on July 15, 1883.

Exploited by the great showman, P. T. Barnum, the little General was first exhibited to the public at the age of six years at a starting wage of $3.00 per week plus room and board, and traveling expenses. From this small beginning Tom Thumb ran his holdings into the millions during his career.

Illus. No. 91 shows four of the eight costumes worn by the General during his appearances, this identified as a complete paper doll set by printed notation on the cover listing included in this illustration. Only the dress suit is uncut, but all four give front and back views. An uncut, or even an incomplete set of this important paper doll comprises a greatly valued rarity today.

"Lavinia Warren" was adopted as a stage name by Mercy Lavinia Warren Bumpus for exhibition purposes until her marriage to Gen. Tom Thumb approximately a year following her discovery by Barnum. Slightly shorter than the General, they presented a doll-like appearance in their many public exhibitions, emphasized by a poster used by Barnum and reproduced here in No. 91a from HOBBIES Magazine with the kind permission of the publishers.

The uncut set of *Mrs. Tom Thumb* (No. 92) furnishes a perfect record of this choice paper doll book. This particular folder, bearing the publishers' address of 71 & 73 Duane Street, New York, (1872/1886 bracket), proves the set to be a reissue of the original printing at 30 Beekman Street.

As stated on Goody Two Shoes' folder, Mrs. Tom Thumb's bridal dress was included in the book of the General, presumably due to space limitations in her own book of bouffant gowns. The cut dress shown off-side in the photographic illustration, is thought to be the so-called bridal dress, since it has been included in the several cut sets known to us, and does not appear in the uncut book of the little lady. However, we should have liked the evidence of an uncut book of the General.

At the time the pictured fragment of the early book cover for Mrs. Tom Thumb was printed, (No. 91), the publishers announced the staggering sale of 10,000 sets of the paper doll, indicating several printings at 30 Beekman Street. A discouragingly small proportion of this vast distribution has survived.

Mrs. Tom Thumb out-lived the General by some 36 years, her death occurring in 1919 when she was 78 years of age.

Illustration No. 92a gives the directions for "making" the Tom Thumb paper dolls, together with a reproduction of the chair from the back cover of Mrs. Tom Thumb's book which bears this notation: "This is an ordinary sized chair, compared with this little family. When you have them dressed up, you will realize how small they are if you will place them along side of it".

Tiny *Minnie Warren* (No. 93) stood only two-thirds the height of her sister, Lavinia, this difference plainly apparent in the bridal party photograph.

The dress in the upper left of Illustration No. 93 shows both front and back views, impossible with the others due to their having been pasted double in the usual manner for dressing the dolls.

Contrary to a rumor which persisted among collectors for some time, Minnie Warren did not marry Commodore Nutt. An early biography of the midgets discloses her marriage to an English skater, and records that she lost her life in the birth of a baby girl who also failed to survive.

Commodore Nutt (No. 94), a mere 29 inches tall, joined the midget group in 1861 at the age of 18 years. Included in the photographic illustration are the eight costumes believed to comprise a complete paper doll set. Again it is impossible to show the back views of these pasted costumes.

The folder for the Commodore, a tiny man saddled with the ponderous name of George Washington Morrison Nutt, carries McLoughlin Bros.' address of 71 & 73 Duane Street, another instance of a reissue of the earlier book, and attesting the many required printings to accommodate an adoring public. The same directions and chair that appeared on the cover of Mrs. Tom Thumb's book are duplicated on the cover of the Commodore's book. A point of interest also is a notation at the bottom of the outside book cover of the latter, stating, "Electrotyped by Vincent Dill, 25 & 27 New Chambers Street, New York." It will be recalled that Mr. Dill, at the time located at 24 Beekman Street, *stereotyped* certain earlier paper doll sets, using an apparently different method for the Commodore Nutt set. It is stated that electrotyping consists of a bath solution for making metallic plates.

It would be interesting to know the combined total distribution figure of all editions of the midget paper dolls. Judging by the publishers' claim that 10,000 sets of the early issue of Mrs. Tom Thumb were sold, (always supposing this to be a true figure, not a publicity gimmick), the final total for the group must have been enormous.

The identity of *Nellie North* is established by accompanying addenda to Sec. B, this chapter. However, a fifth costume, the tailored street dress lower center in Illus. No. 95, will be noted, but by comparing the position of the doll's left arm to the corresponding sleeve of the dress, we have to assume that this does not belong to *Nellie North*.

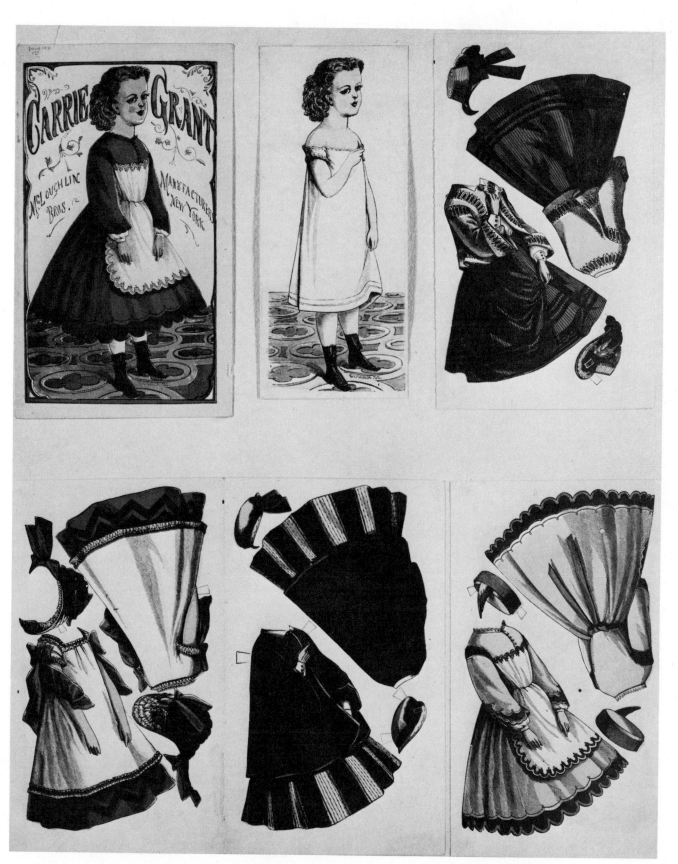

No. 87.   Carrie Grant, 7¼ inches, uncut. Collection The Newark Museum.

No. 88.   VICTORIA, 5-7/8 INCHES, UNCUT. COLLECTION THE NEWARK MUSEUM.

No. 89.   EUGENIA, 6¼ INCHES, UNCUT. COLLECTION THE NEWARK MUSEUM.

No. 90.   Clara West, 5-5/8 inches.   Author's Collection.

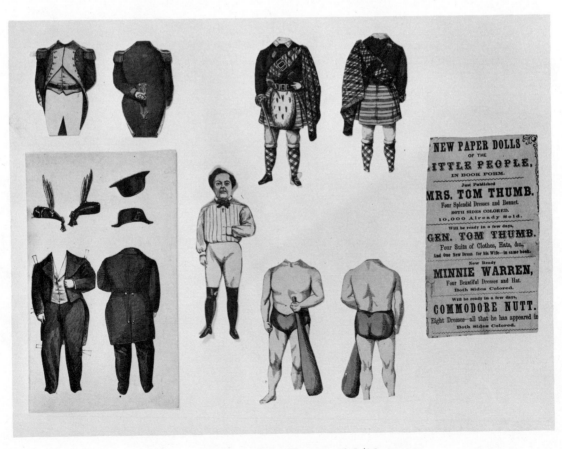

No. 91.   General Tom Thumb, 5-3/16 inches.

No. 91a. P. T. Barnum Poster, publicizing Gen. Tom Thumb and Wife. Courtesy HOBBIES.

No. 92. Mrs. Tom Thumb, 4-11/16 inches, uncut.

MRS. TOM THUMB.

DIRECTIONS FOR MAKING.

Cut the stitch and open the book, before you begin to cut out the dresses.

This is a very beautiful Little Lady, with both sides of the Figure, Dresses, and Hat colored; it is so simple as to hardly need any directions; some of my little friends, however, may not be able to get along without them.

In the first place, you must make the figure right. You will find the figure on a piece of card board, printed on both sides. This must be very nicely cut out, leaving the ground or carpet about the feet, for the figure to stand on.

In making the dresses, cut all the white paper from the outside, then fold them so that the back and front will match evenly. You will then see how to cut the neck, so as to let the head come through. Leave a little paper at the outside of the shoulders uncut, so as to keep the dress in its place.

If you please, you can paste the edge of the dresses together; this will keep them in their place better on the figure.

The Hat is made in the same way. Cut out the hole for the face before you gum the edges together. P. S.—Use Gum Arabic. Have it thick. You can get it powdered at the druggists', and it will dissolve in a few minutes.

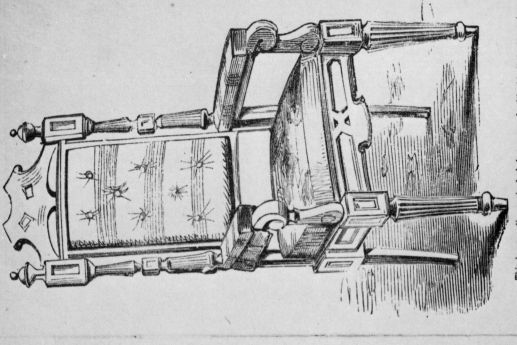

This is an ordinary sized chair, compared with this little family. When you have them dressed up, you will realize how small they are, if you place them along side of it.

No. 92a.   Inside Covers of the Mrs. Tom Thumb Book.

No. 92b. 1. Wedding Photograph of Gen. Tom Thumb and Wife. Courtesy HOBBIES.

No. 92b. 2. APPEARANCE OF GEN. TOM THUMB AND WIFE BEFORE EMPEROR NAPOLEON AND THE
EMPRESS EUGENIE, FROM PHOTOGRAPH IN AUTHOR'S COLLECTION.

No. 93.   MINNIE WARREN, 4-5/16 INCHES.

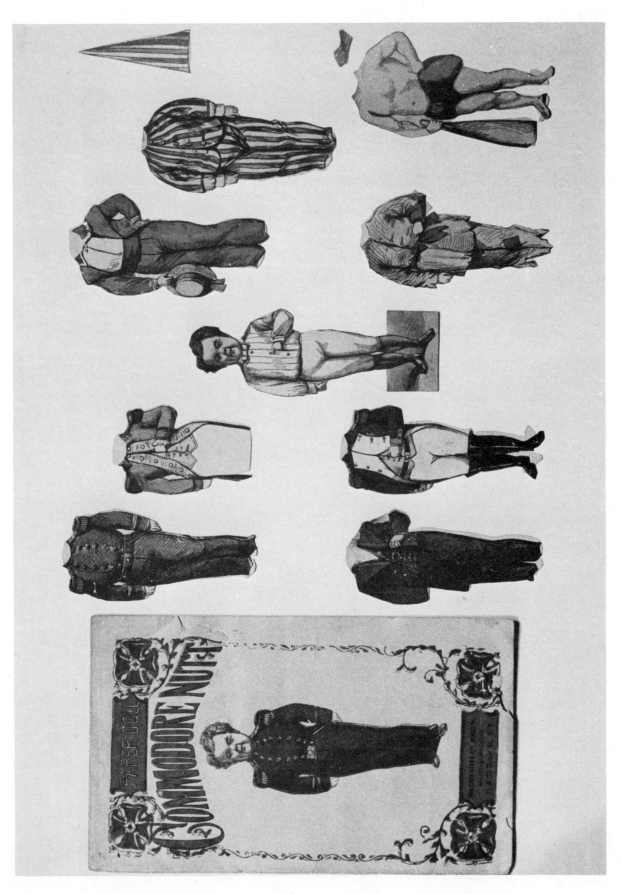

131

"SERIES No. 2 — Twenty-four kinds ....Per Gross, $4.50

Kitty Black	Violet Vernon	Minty Green	Marquis
Lilly Beers	Eva St. Claire & Topsy	Emma White	Marchioness
Little Lady	Rose Rustic	Mary Gray	Nellie Naylor
Fanny Fair	Millie Fay	Sarah Brown	Elsie Dale
Rose Bud	Nettie Ray	Ruby Rose	Josie Fox
Ella Hall	Sophie May	Anna Doll	Laura Leil."

- - - - -

Analysis of the 24 dolls listed in the above series discloses that, with the exception of four carry-overs of earlier dolls, a similarity of execution and general characteristics exists. Exceptions comprise the following:

Fanny Fair (No. 97) is a later printing of *Fanny* of 1858 (Illus. No. 47-a, Sect. A).

Little Lady and *Lillie Beers* ("Lilly" in the catalog) may be seen in illustrations No. 49, Sect. A, and No. 60, Sect. B respectively.

Ella Hall (No. 99): Folder of the illustrated set carries McLoughlin Bros.' address of 30 Beekman Street, New York, evidencing a re-issue of *Ella,* listed on the 1859 advertising flyer, the surname added as in later printings of other early dolls.

Variations in pose and costume details of the remaining 20 dolls in this series provide variety, clearly evident in the photographic illustrations, captions providing doll sizes with designations "F" for front printing, "F & B" for front and back views.

Printing and coloring methods were covered in Sect. A, and it is felt that this coverage, in conjunction with the illustrations, amply defines these dolls, that to include individual descriptions would result in repetitious and boresome reading.

Each doll should be outfitted with four costumes, but there is no uniformity to the number of hats provided. Mention also is made that while the uncut reprints made of certain dolls might vary from the original printings in minor details, they are substantially correct; those that were checked against earlier specimens correspond.

Cut sets of *Topsey* (No. 102). *Minty Green* (No. 107) and *Sarah Brown* (No. 110) are pictured with only the three costumes available, the fourth in each set unfortunately missing. Those shown, however, can be helpful for identification purposes.

Differences in the spelling of "Nellie Naylor" as given in the catalog, "Nailor" on the folder, and "Laura Leil" of the catalog becoming "Laura Neil" on the folder, are noted.

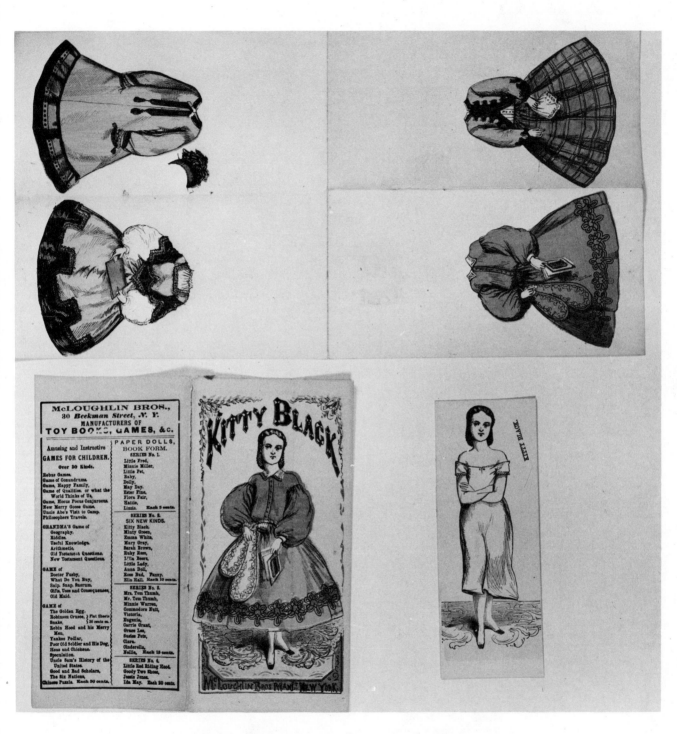

No. 96.   Kitty Black. 5″. F. Author's collection.

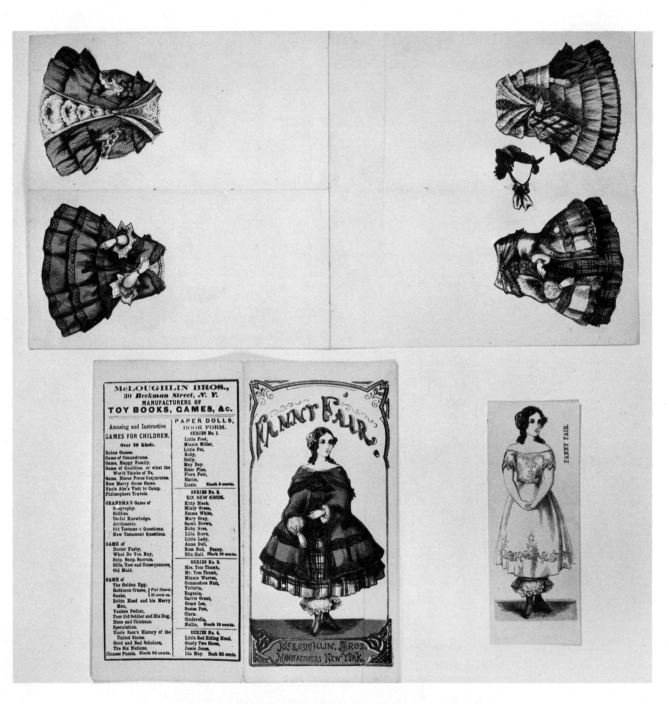

No. 97. FANNY FAIR. 4½". F. AUTHOR'S COLLECTION.

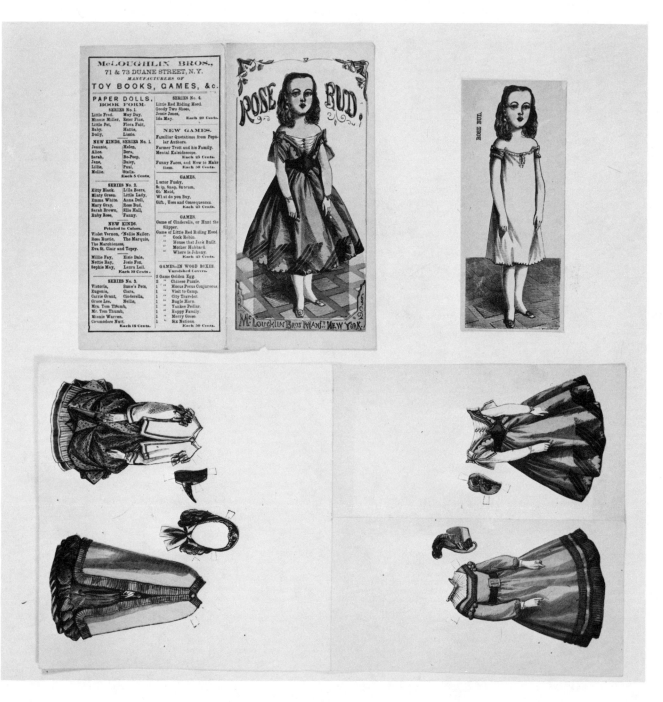

No. 98.   Rose Bud. 5½″. F. Author's collection.

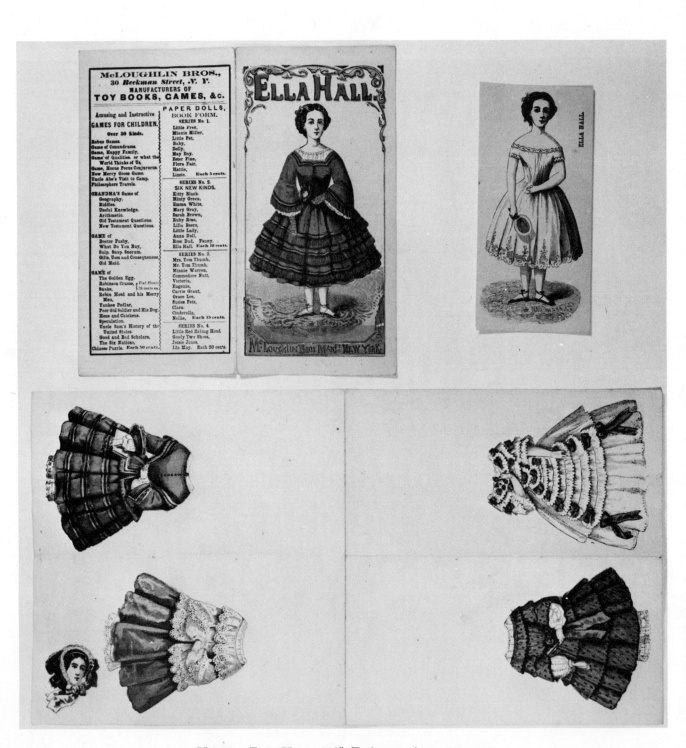

No. 99.   ELLA HALL. 4½". F. AUTHOR'S COLLECTION.

No. 100.   VIOLET VERNON. 5½". F & B.

No. 101.   EVA ST. CLAIRE. 3¾". F & B. AUTHOR'S COLLECTION.

No. 102. TOPSEY. 4$\frac{11}{16}$″. F & B. AUTHOR'S COLLECTION.

No. 103. ROSE RUSTIC. 5¼″. F & B. AUTHOR'S COLLECTION.

No. 104. Millie Fay. 6″. F & B.

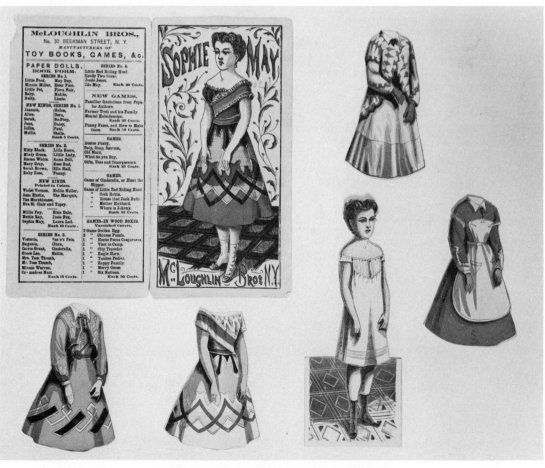

No. 106.   Sophie May. 5-13/16″. F & B.

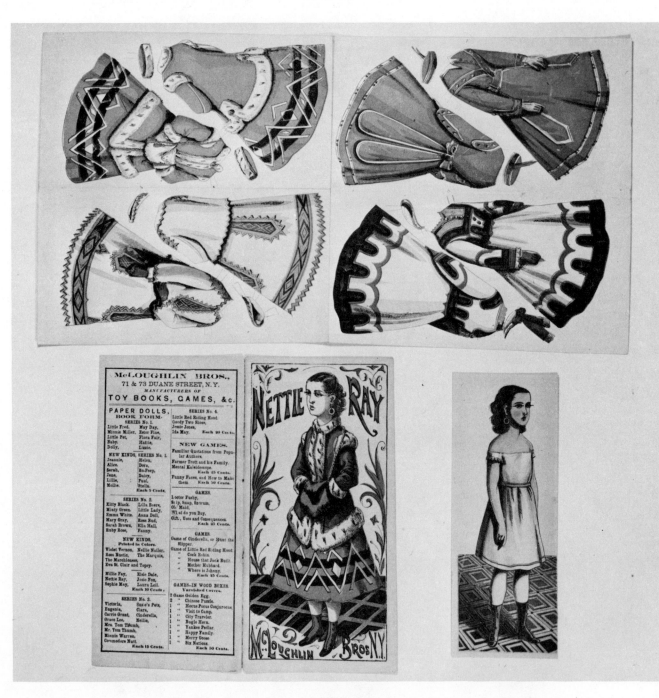

No. 105. NETTIE RAY. 5-5/8". F & B. AUTHOR'S COLLECTION.

No. 107. MINTY GREEN. 5-1/8". F & B.

No. 108. EMMA WHITE. 5". F & B. AUTHOR'S COLLECTION.

141

No. 109.   MARY GRAY. 5". F & B. MRS. W. M. AHLSTROM COLLECTION.

No. 110.   SARAH BROWN. 4-5/16". F & B. AUTHOR'S COLLECTION.

No. 111. Ruby Rose. 3⅝". F & B. Author's collection.

No. 112. Anna Doll. 4⅞". F & B. Author's collection.

143

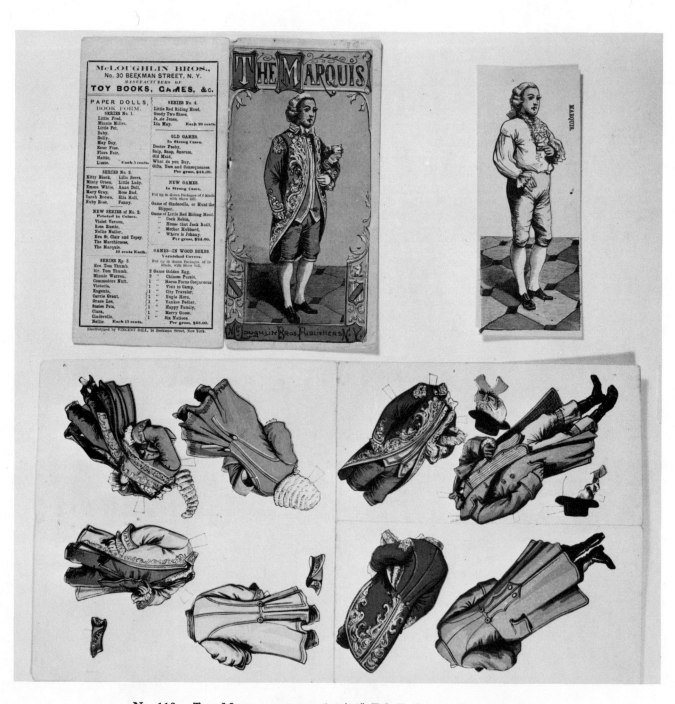

No. 113. THE MARQUIS, UNCUT. 5-1/16". F & B. AUTHOR'S COLLECTION.

No. 114. THE MARCHIONESS. 5⅜″. F & B. AUTHOR'S COLLECTION.

No. 115. NELLIE NAILOR. 5⅝″. F & B. AUTHOR'S COLLECTION.

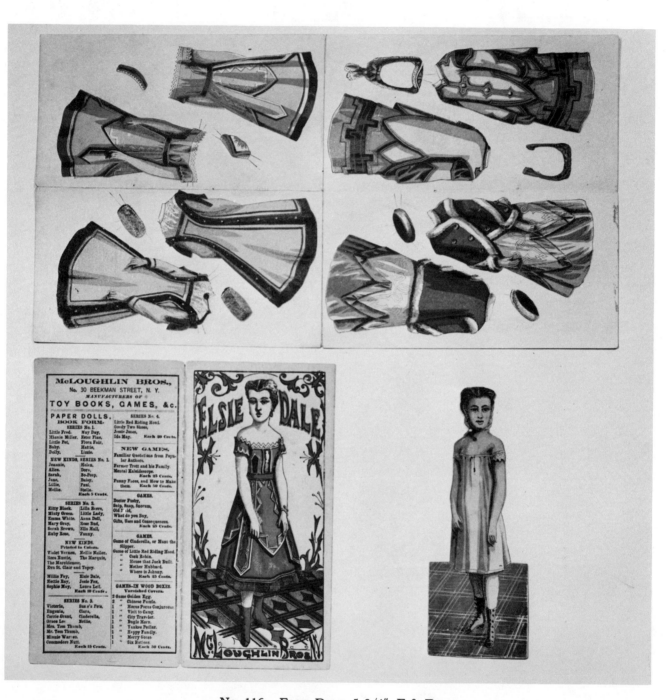

No. 116. ELSIE DALE. 5-3/4″. F & B.

No. 117.   JOSIE FOX. 5-15/16″. F & B. AUTHOR'S COLLECTION.

No. 118. Laura Neil. 5-3/4". F & B. Author's collection.

"SERIES No. 1 — Twenty-two kinds..Per Gross, $2.25

Minnie Miller	Ester Fine	Daisy	Dolly	Sarah
Flora Fair	Little Pet	Jeannie	Helen	Lizzie
Little Fred	Baby	Mollie	Paul	Dora
Bo-Peep	Hattie	May Day	Tillie	Alice"
	Stella		Jane	

- - - - -

Of the above listed dolls only *Mollie* is missing. Four carry-overs not illustrated here may be seen in preceding sections of this chapter, namely *Minnie Miller* (No. 61), *Little Fred* (No. 64), and *Little Pet* (No. 63), all pictured in Sect. B. *Dolly* of the Early Series is shown in Sect. A, Illus. No. 46. Remaining listed dolls, with the exception of *Baby,* are included, and even though a certain number are incomplete, the illustrations serve to make individual descriptions unnecessary.

Only two *Baby* dolls are known to this writer. One tiny one is shown on pg. 69, Illus. No. 45, and, as explained in the accompanying text, this was included by deduction in coverage of the Early Series because of its obvious like characteristics of other dolls of the First Size, even though listed as of the Second Size. Perhaps an error in making the layout of the Early Series advertisement.

No *Baby* has been identified as belonging to this Series 1, 22 kinds, unless possibly the tiny one of the Early Series was included as were the other earlier dolls noted in the foregoing text. Other than this tiny Baby, the only one known to us has been included in the Mulligan Guard Series of Penny Paper Dolls because of matching characteristics; this series is covered further along in this chapter. We stress possible erroneous inclusion of these Baby dolls in the two sections noted above, since no definite authentication is at hand.

All parts of the sets listed in this Series 1, 22 kinds, have front printing only, as captioned. Dolls are presented in different ages and with variations in pose, features and costume details, perhaps with intent to furnish some degree of variety in a sizeable series.

148

Checking publishers' various addresses as they appear on the folders against the schedule of address changes contained in Sect. A makes it possible to establish approximate publication dates for those particular dolls.

Mention is again made of certain dolls having been listed in more than one numbered series, suggesting the possibility that publishers continued printing the best-sellers, reshuffling them into newly created series carrying varying prices. As previously noted, this causes confusion where reference is made to a certain doll in a given series if source of the reference is omitted. Sharply visible in the photographs, these listings should be readable in the book reproductions.

A point not previously mentioned in this work is that, with the few specific exceptions, McLoughlin Bros.' paper dolls do not represent portraits of living persons. Names appearing in these listings, except where otherwise stated, are fictitious, assigned by the publishers, probably as an added feature to interest children.

While these catalogued paper dolls of McLoughlin Brothers are more widely represented in present-day collections than those of the "Early Series", they still are coveted collectors' items, avidly sought by paper doll enthusiasts as well as by collectors of "real" dolls, the latter for their authentic costume value.

No. 119. FLORA FAIR. 4-5/16". F. AUTHOR'S COLLECTION.

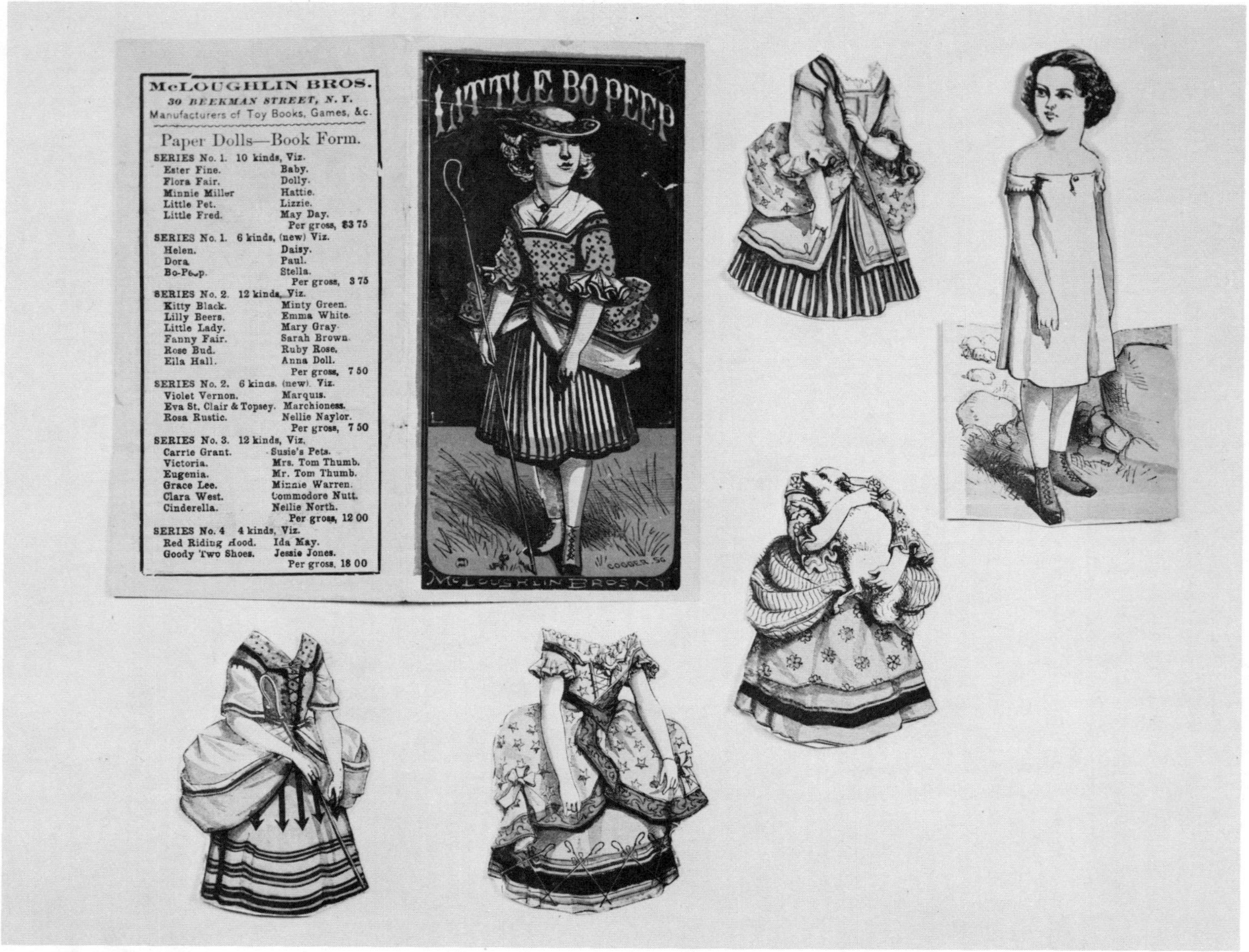

The paper doll booklet shown contains the following text:

McLOUGHLIN BROS.

30 *BEEKMAN STREET*, N.Y.

Manufacturers of Toy Books, Games, &c.

Paper Dolls—Book Form.

SERIES No. 1. 10 kinds, viz.

Ester Fine.	Baby.
Flora Fair.	Dolly.
Minnie Miller	Hattie.
Little Pet.	Lizzie.
Little Fred.	May Day.

Per gross, $3 75

SERIES No. 1. 6 kinds, (new) viz.

Helen.	Daisy.
Dora.	Pearl.
Bo-Peep.	Stella.

Per gross, 3 75

SERIES No. 2. 12 kinds, viz.

Kitty Black.	Minny Green.
Lilly Breen.	Emma White.
Little Lady.	Mary Gray.
Fanny Fair.	Sarah Brown.
Rose Bud.	Ruby Rose.
Ella Hall.	Anna Doll.

Per gross, 7 50

SERIES No. 2. 6 kinds, (new) viz.

Violet Vernon.	Marquis.
Eva St. Clair & Topsey.	Marchioness.
Rosa Rustic.	Nellie Naylor.

Per gross, 7 50

SERIES No. 3. 12 kinds, viz.

Carrie Grant.	Susie's Pets.
Victoria.	Mrs. Tom Thumb.
Eugenia.	Mr. Tom Thumb.
Grace Lee.	Minnie Warren.
Clara West.	Commodore Nutt.
Cinderella.	Nellie North.

Per gross, 12 00

SERIES No. 4. 4 kinds, viz.

Red Riding Hood.	Ida May.
Goody Two Shoes.	Jessie Jones.

Per gross, 18 00

LITTLE BO PEEP

McLOUGHLIN BROS N.Y.

No. 120.   LITTLE BoPEEP. 4-9/16″. F. AUTHOR'S COLLECTION.

150

No. 121.   ESTER FINE. 4⁵⁄₁₆". F.

No. 122.   HATTIE. 4". F. AUTHOR'S COLLECTION.

No. 123.   DAISY. 4-5/8″. F.

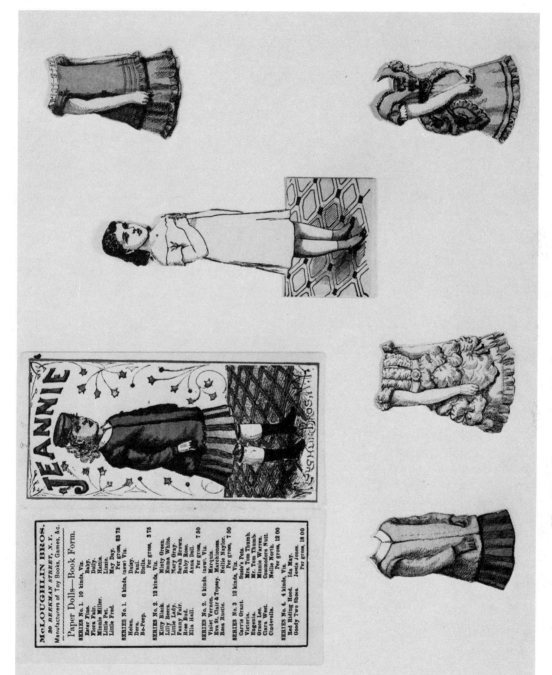

No. 124.   Jeannie. 4-11/16″. F.   H. H. Hosmer Collection.

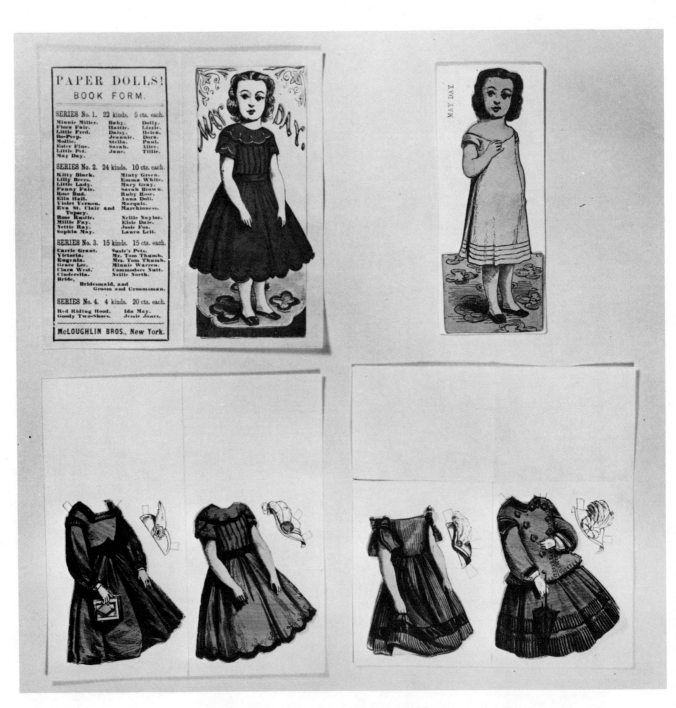

No. 125. MAY DAY. 4-9/16". F. UNCUT.

No. 126.   HELEN. 4½". F. UNCUT.

No. 127.   PAUL. 4½″. F.

Cut the stitch and open the sheet before you commence to cut out the dresses; leave an equal proportion of paper for each dress.

DIRECTIONS FOR MAKING.

Cut the figure out close to the edge down to the ground—leave the ground square at the bottom for the figure to stand on.

Fold the white paper at the top of the dresses over back exactly on the highest point of the shoulder, cut all around both parts together close to the dress, leaving uncut a small space at each shoulder on which the dress will rest upon the figure. Gum the two parts together at the outer edge near the bottom. Prepare the hats by bending over the paper at the top of it, and then cutting away all around, as in the case of the dresses. It will be better if you gum the two parts together slightly at the sides, where it is the widest.

No. 128.   TILLIE. F. NEW YORK LIBRARY COLLECTION.

157

* No. 129.   Envelope for Sarah.

*No. 129a.   Sarah. 45/8″. F. Author's collection.

No. 130.   Lizzie. 4″. F.

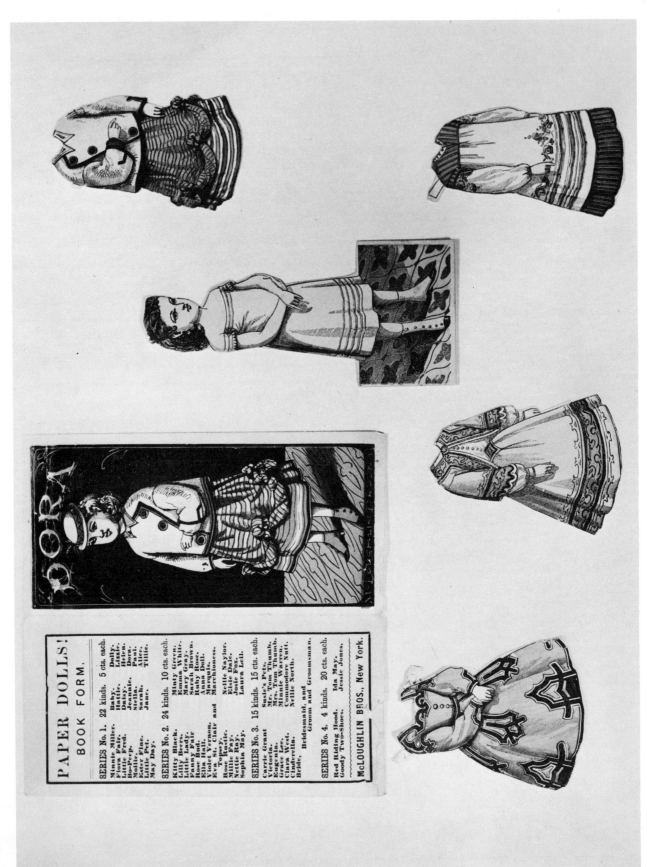

PAPER DOLLS!
BOOK FORM.

SERIES No. 1. 22 kinds. 5 cts. each.

Minnie Miller.   Baby.
Flora Fair.   Dolly.
Little Fred.   Hattie.   Lizzie.
Bo-Peep.   Daisy.   Helen.
Mollie.   Jeannie.   Dora.
Katie Fine.   Stella.   Paul.
Little Pet.   Sarah.   Alice.
May Day.   Jane.   Tillie.

SERIES No. 2. 24 kinds. 10 cts. each.

Kitty Black.   Minty Green.
Lilly Berry.   Emma White.
Little Lady.   Mary Gray.
Fanny Fair.   Sarah Brown.
Rose Bud.   Ruby Rose.
Ella Fine.   Anna Doll.
Violet Vernon.   Marquis.
Eva. St. Clair and Marchioness.
   Towsy.
Rosie Battle.   Nellie Naylor.
Millie Fay.   Elsie Dale.
Nettie Ray.   Josie Fox.
Sophia May.   Laura Leli.

SERIES No. 3. 15 kinds. 15 cts. each.

Carrie Grant   Susie's Pet.
Victoria.   Mr. Tom Thumb.
Eugenia.   Mrs. Tom Thumb.
Grace Lee.   Minnie Warren.
Clara West.   Commodore Nutt.
Cinderella.   Nellie North.
Bride,
   Bridesmaid, and
      Groom and Groomsman.

SERIES No. 4. 4 kinds. 20 cts. each.

Red Riding Hood.   Ida May.
Goody Two-Shoes.   Jessie Jones.

McLOUGHLIN BROS., New York.

No. 131. DORA. 4-5/8". F.

No. 132.   Alice. 4-3/4". F. Collection of the Newark Museum.

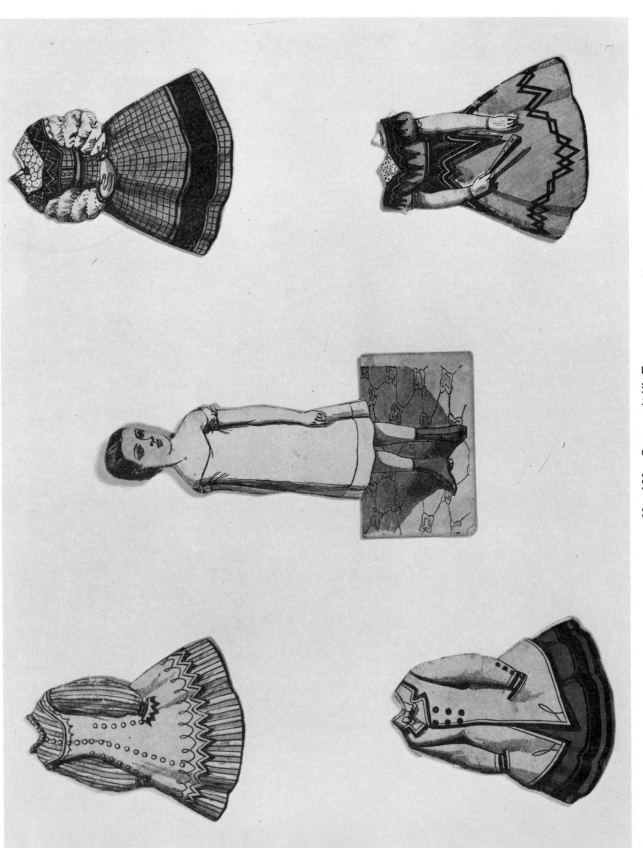

No. 133. STELLA. 4½". F.

No. 134. JANE. 4-3/4". F.

"PENNY PAPER DOLLS.

"These are about four inches in height, and consist of a figure with three suits, printed in colors upon stiff paper. They embrace a variety of subjects, with dresses suited to each kind, and are folded and put up in pasteboard boxes containing one assorted gross each. Packed in twelve gross packages.

MULLIGAN GUARD SERIES (New)

"Three kinds ....Per Gross, $1.00

Mulligan Guard.   Madame Pompadour.   The Baby".

This series introduces a run of penny folders with dolls and costumes printed in horizontal strips which fold, accordion fashion, to approximately $2\frac{1}{2}$ by 4-3/4 inches. Not so glamorous as the fashionable ladies with their elaborate wardrobes, they presumably served to supply a market for the more slender purse, making paper dolls available to many children who otherwise might have been deprived of one of childhood's most pleasureable pastimes.

Identity of a possible character named Mulligan Guard from which this paper doll stemmed is unknown to this writer, unless perhaps it was inspired by a storybook character. In the book section of subject catalog, under the heading, AUNT LOUISA'S BIG PICTURE BOOKS, listing 50 different titles, one is given as "Ten Little Mulligan Guards", perhaps the inspiration for this unlovely paper doll, pictured in No. 135a.

Madame Pompadour of this Series (No. 135b), is a very nice doll. Attractively posed, her beautifully designed costumes vividly colored, she is quite the loveliest of this oddly assorted trio.

Conversely, *The Baby,* 136a, is the ugliest, one whom only a mother could love. The title assigned to him here, *The Baby,* may be questioned, as no uncut set or even a folder was available. However, we feel justified in assigning him to the Mulligan Guard Series. Both the doll and the two costumes shown embrace all of the characteristics of the other dolls of the series. The paper on which they were printed appears to be of the same texture, the Baby measures the prescribed four inches, features are of a deep, tanned shade, costumes brightly colored. Added to the above is the fact that it was termed Baby by an advanced collector. We stand open to correction if inclusion of this set in subject series cannot be supported by fact.

Incidentally, a third costume came with this doll, but it is not pictured because we question its belonging. However, since there may be doubt we describe it as a brown cape outfit for a toddler, quite lavishly "embroidered", one side front thrown back. The size is correct, but it has a full-length plain back with a neck opening too small to allow slipping over the doll's head, whereas the two costumes shown in the illustration are equipped with stay-on tabs. Consideration of the above points leads to the conclusion that it cannot belong.

No. 135a.   MULLIGAN GUARD. 4″. F. UNCUT.

No. 135b.   MADAME POMPADOUR. 4″. F. UNCUT.

"HUMPTY DUMPTY SERIES (New) — Three kinds.............Per Gross, $1.00

Humpty Dumpty.   Dame Trot.   Little BoPeep."

- - - - -

Uncut folders of the three dolls contained in this series are of uniform size, approximately 2-3/4 by 4-7/8 inches, the title doll pictured in No. 136b with The Baby of preceding series. Printed on one side only, these folders are of the accordion-folding type usual to penny folders, and dolls and costumes are brightly colored as others in these various series of penny dolls.

Dame Trot and *Little BoPeep* may be seen in Illustrations 137a and b respectively.

With Little BoPeep, only the costume with the sheep and the crook has an attached hat, while for Dame Trot both hats and her bonnet, the latter with

her red cape, are attached to the costumes themselves. The mob-cap, shown with the costume at right of Dame Trot in the illustration, attests the publishers' careful attention to detail. Intended to be worn with the high-crown hat accompanying it, in the manner of early pedlar women, it is as worn by Dame Trot in all illustrations contained in a small paper-covered hand-sewn booklet, "Dame Trot and her Comical Cat", published by McLoughlin Bros. at their 24 Beekman Street house, much earlier than the paper doll. The story is in verse, the hand-tinted illustrations depicting the various episodes in the Comical Cat's eventful but highly improbable life. It is quite fitting, therefore, that he appear with Dame Trot on the folder of the paper doll.

No. 136a.   THE BABY. 4″. F. CUT. AUTHOR'S COLLECTION.

No. 136b.   HUMPTY DUMPTY. 4″. F. UNCUT. SARAH VAUGHAN COLLECTION.

No. 137a. Dame Trot. 4-3/8". F. Uncut. Author's collection.
No. 137b. Little BoPeep. 4-5/16". F. Uncut. Author's collection.

"LITTLE DOLLY VARDEN SERIES — Six kinds...................Per Gross, 75¢

"Pompey Varden (Colored).   Charley Varden (White).
Dinah Varden (Colored).   Tom Thumb's Baby (White).
Little Dolly Varden (?).   Clara Louise Kellog" (White).

(Parentheses added by author).

Regrettably, no specimen of the title doll, *Little Dolly Varden*, was available for illustrating. Reference was made to her, however, in foregoing coverage of DOLLY VARDEN SERIES in this section. We assume she may have been issued as a sister of Charley Varden (139a), and that the two colored dolls, bearing the same surname as Charley, were intended to represent servants of the Varden paper doll family. As with others of this series, the dolls are in penny folder form, printed on one side only. Pompey and Dinah Varden are paired in No. 138a and b.

The folder of Clara Louisa Kellog (Clara Louise Kellogg in the catalog), No. 139b, depicts this operatic soprano of an earlier era against a theater billboard background, stage boards forming the base for the doll itself, further emphasizing the artiste's career. Born in South Carolina in 1842, she acquired her musical education in New York, singing her first operatic role in that city in 1861. It is said that while she later sang in London, the major portion of her appearances was in America.

In 1874 she organized her own opera company, retiring in 1887 when she married Carl Strakosch. In 1913 she published "Memoirs of an American Prima Donna", and died in Hartford, Connecticut, in 1916. This doll joins the ranks of prized portrait paper dolls.

Illustration No. 140a, *Tom Thumb's Baby*, represents a composite photograph of actual costumes from the author's collection, and a reproduction of the baby and the folder-cover from HOBBIES Magazine, April, 1955, by courtesy of the publishers and of Clara Hallard Fawcett, author-artist of the interesting article with her drawings, contained in that issue. As brought out by Mrs. Fawcett and other chroniclers of Tom Thumb lore, also noted in our own earlier coverage of the little General (Pg. 120), Mr. and Mrs. Tom Thumb did not have a baby of their own, the so-called Tom Thumb's Baby a brainchild of the sagacious P. T. Barnum for its publicity value. This is one of the harder-to-find paper dolls even though not honestly titled.

And now, in 140b, we have one of the oddities of the paper doll world, *Grecian Bend*. This uncut penny folder serves as a bonafide record of a ridiculous style in women's attire which seems to have been injected into the fashion parade of 1868. Fashion notes tell of the ridicule directed at women who assumed the distorted posture necessary to "do justice" to this exaggerated styling, and while we acclaim McLoughlin Brothers for having preserved for us even so absurd a fashion, we should welcome assurance that, as we suspect, the ludicrous mode enjoyed a short and not very popular life. One wonders why it came into being at all except that perhaps some out-of-ideas designer had a misguided inspiration. Consider the similarity in pose to that of *Tabby* of the Comic Series, No. 144a....

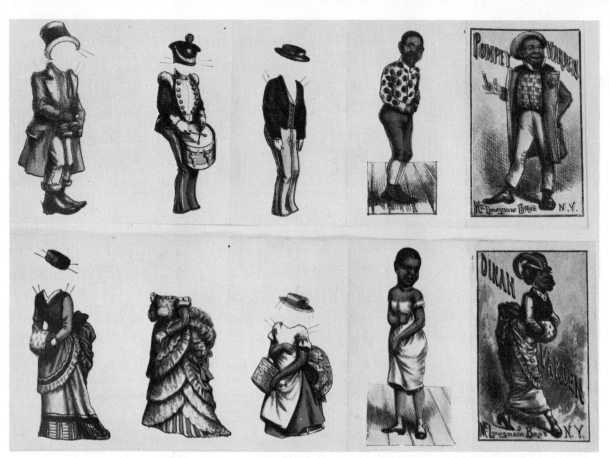

No. 138a. POMPEY VARDEN. 4¾". F. UNCUT. MARGARETT DARTT COLLECTION.
No. 138b. DINAH VARDEN. 4⅛". F. UNCUT. MARGARETT DARTT COLLECTION.

No. 139a. CHARLEY VARDEN. 4½". F. CUT. AUTHOR'S COLLECTION.
No. 139b. CLARA LOUISE KELLOG. 4⁵⁄₁₆". F. UNCUT. AUTHOR'S COLLECTION.

No. 140a.   Tom Thumb's Baby. 2-3/8". F. Cut. Assembled set.

No. 140b.   Grecian Bend. 2-5/16". F. Uncut. Author's collection.

"GEM SERIES — Six kinds..Per Gross, 75¢

Amelia	Julia
Emily	Martha
Isabella.	Josie."

- - - - -

A notation on the reverse of the envelope for Bertha Blonde of the Dolly Varden Series (Illus. No. 81a) apprises that these six dolls were printed in oil colors, to our knowledge the first instance of the publishers' supplying definite information as to their color processes.

As in certain foregoing sections, these dolls show a marked conformity in general characteristics; however, an unusual feature in McLoughlin Bros.' paper dolls is that none of the cover dolls wears a dress fashioned in the design of any one costume included in her separate wardrobe, (a peculiarity also of the two Little BoPeeps, Nos. 120 and 137b). And *Julia,* as a cover girl, appears dressed in the exaggerated "Grecian Bend" style of circa 1868, though

the doll and her costumes are executed in the usual conservative manner. Does this date this series of penny folders?

Amelia appears on an original uncut folder in No. 141a, *Emily,* a mounted cut set in 141b, one hat missing. *Isabella,* a cut set, hats missing, is paired with *Julia* uncut, in 142a and b respectively, with *Martha* uncut, and *Josey* cut in 143a and b. The variation in the spelling of Josey's name, (Josie in the catalog) is another instance of similar differences.

Certain it is that many little girls were made happy with these various penny dolls, presumably allowed to cut them out themselves, and to play with them to their hearts' content. The surprising element is that there are any survivors.

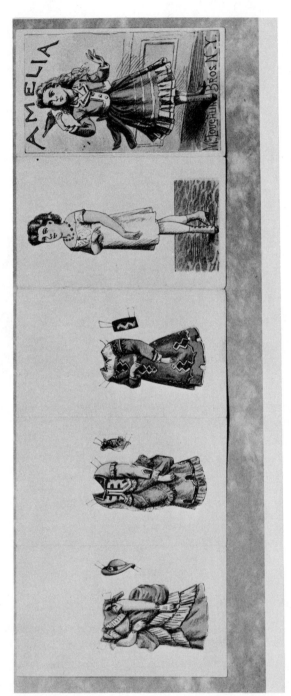

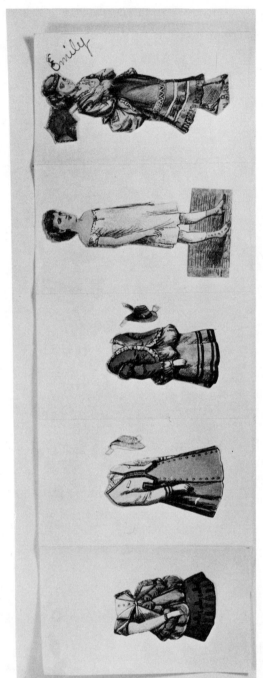

No. 141a. AMELIA. 4". F. UNCUT. AUTHOR'S COLLECTION.

No. 141b. EMILY. 4". F. CUT. AUTHOR'S COLLECTION.

No. 142a.   ISABELLA. 4″. F. CUT. AUTHOR'S COLLECTION.
No. 142b.   JULIA. 4⅜″. F. UNCUT. MRS. WM. M. AHLSTROM COLLECTION.

No. 143a.   MARTHA. 4³⁄₁₆″. F. UNCUT.
No. 143b.   JOSEY. 4¹⁄₁₆″. F. CUT, MOUNTED. AUTHOR'S COLLECTION.

"COMIC SERIES — Three kinds...Per Gross, 75¢
Tabby   Fido   Jocko."

- - - - -

Little can be said for the above trio, though pets with removable costumes probably had strong appeal for early-day children who associated them with the dressed-up animals woven into the texture of many popular stories read aloud by doting parents.

Tabby with three costumes and one bonnet, cut and mounted, appears with *Fido* with his four of each, in 144a and b. It is assumed that Tabby was as well outfitted when published.

The missing *Jocko,* in common with all monkeys, would have been an amusing finale to our coverage of this small group of dressed pets.

No. 144a.   Tabby. 3-1/8″. F. Cut, mounted.

No. 144b.   Fido. 3″. F. Uncut.

Minnie Warren and Willie	Florence and Alecia
Mr. and Mrs. Tom Thumb	Maud and Louise
Eva St. Claire and Topsey	Fanny and Pink."

- - - - -

The penny paper dolls in this interesting series were printed in oil colors, and two different types of folders are represented. One, with the cover design in horizontal position and measuring 4-3/8 by 2-11/16 inches closed, contains two dolls as paired in the above schedule. The other type folder, a 2 by 3¼ inch vertical one, contains a single doll. Both are accordion type, and both are represented in our illustrations.

Confusion might arise from the fact that while the catalog lists the above twelve dolls in the one series of six pairs as set out, the same dolls are also broken down into three separate series of single dolls as listed on the backs of the penny folders, namely, "Old Dolls—Dolls" containing Willie among others of the earlier productions. "Topsey Series—Dolls" lists Topsey, Eva St. Claire, Fanny, Alecia, Florence, and Grecian Bend, the last named not included in the catalog. The remaining dolls are listed on the folders as "Little Tom Thumb Series". In our coverage we are adhering to the catalog designation, "Tom Thumb Series—Six kinds", the dolls illustrated in pairs in accordance with this schedule.

A cut set of *Mr. and Mrs. Tom Thumb* (No. 145), is a mounted set, laid out in the form of the horizontal folder with which it came, but not necessarily in the same order as the original set. It is noteworthy that these tiny paper dolls representing the Tom Thumb group, printed in vivid oil colors, represent actual portraits of the famous midgets. To our knowledge the fourth member of this quartet, Commodore Nutt, was not produced in a penny folder.

Illustration No. 146a shows the vertical folder cover for *Miss Minnie Warren* with two of her three costumes, and two hats; there should be a yellow dress, the printed hand holding a handkerchief, and presumably a third hat or bonnet.

Willie (146b), paired with Minnie, also should have a third costume and probably one or more bonnets. These wee accessories were easily lost, and uncut folders were not at hand for comparison. (It will be noted that this is Willie's second appearance, having been included in coverage of the 1859 advertising flyer, Sect. B, Pg. 98, Illus. 65).

Eva St. Claire and *Topsey* are shown in 147a and b, *Florence* and *Alecia,* also uncut, in 148a and b, all small vertical folders, while *Maud* and *Louise* (149a) and *Fanny* and *Pink* (149b) are shown in original horizontal folders as published.

In addition to the four above uncut vertical folders, the author's collection includes the Little General, Mrs. Tom Thumb, and Fanny, of Fanny and Pink, in the 2 by 3¼ inch vertical folders. It appears from the various and varied listings that the entire Tom Thumb Series may have been published in both types of folders.

No. 145. MR. AND MRS. TOM THUMB. 2-15/16" & 2¼". CUT. MRS. AHLSTROM COLLECTION.

No. 146a. Miss Minnie Warren. 2-5/16″. F. Cut. Author's collection.
No. 146b. Willie. 2⅛″. F. Cut. Author's collection.

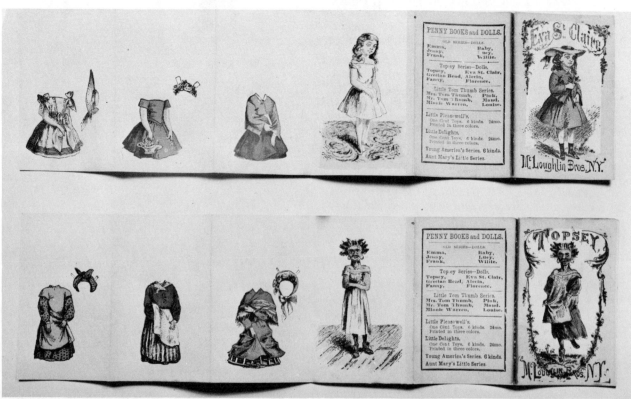

No. 147a. Eva St. Claire. 2-5/16″. F. Uncut. Author's collection.
No. 147b. Topsey. 2-5/16″. F. Uncut. Author's collection.

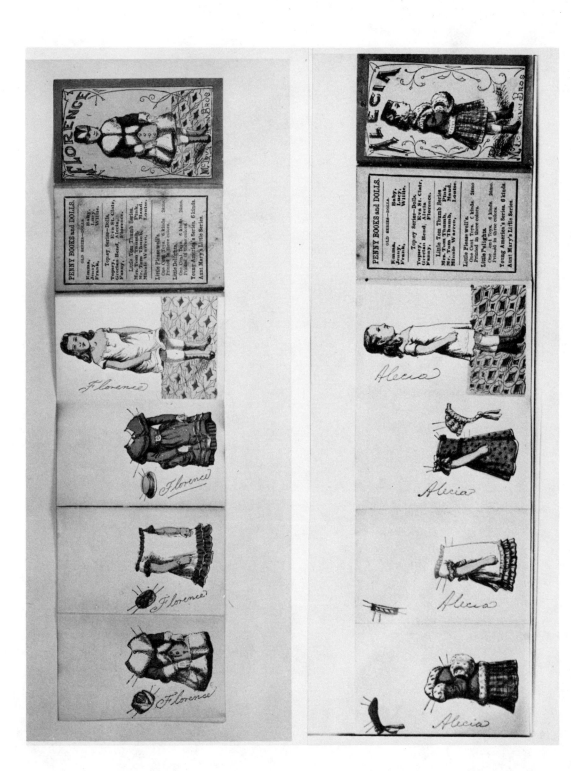

No. 148a.   FLORENCE. 2-15/16″. F. UNCUT. AUTHOR'S COLLECTION.

No. 148b.   ALECIA. 2-15/16″. F. UNCUT. AUTHOR'S COLLECTION.

No. 149a. MAUD AND LOUISE. EACH 2-7/8″. F. UNCUT. MAXINE WALDRON COLLECTION.

No. 149b. FANNY AIND PINK. EACH 2-15/16″. F. UNCUT. ANNA CAPPALONGA COLLECTION.

176

"PAPER SOLDIERS — Six kinds ....Per Gross, $1.00.

Continentals.	Highlanders.	Zouaves.
Union Rifles.	Brass Band.	Infantry.

"Each set consists of a company of twelve soldiers, printed in colors upon stiff paper. Put up in gross boxes, and twelve gross packages."

- - - - -

These sets of paper soldiers, headed "Amusement for boys to cut out", were published in regulation type penny folders, measuring 2-7/8 by 4½ inches closed, printed in oil colors. The illustrated sets are printed in combinations of brilliant colors, but it has been learned that McLoughlin Brothers issued the sets in different color arrangements; whether these were supposed to follow Government regulations, which may have prescribed different combinations for the many regiments outfitted with the same general uniform is uncertain, but regardless of whether or not absolute accuracy prevailed in all minor details of army uniforms of the periods represented, these paper cutouts provided educational toys for young boys, and may have aroused their first patriotic emotions.

Illustration No. 150 shows eight Continental soldiers with an officer, cut from one of these folders. They have been defined as soldiers of the regular forces under the control of Congress in the Revolutionary War, (also known as the War of Independence), 1775-83.

The *Continentals* illustrated are four inches tall, and the late Mr. Lloyd Eastwood-Seibold, formerly curator of The Valley Forge Historical Society, Pennsylvania, kindly supplied interesting items of history. The white cross-belts crossed both back and front, and were worn on the entire assembled uniform, both by privates in the Light Infantry and the Artillery Division of the Continental Army. These belts crossed midway between the shoulders and the hips, terminating on the sides in a narrow pointed "V" with attachment provisions to which the knapsack could be fastened on the right side, and on the left a canteen if the latter was not already equipped with a shoulder strap. We note that these accoutrements are not included in the uniforms of these penny paper soldiers.

In the latter years of the Revolutionary War, when funds were low and war equipment scarce, General George Washington issued orders prohibiting seasonal change of uniforms, that, instead, the soldiers, as an economy measure, would wear light or heavy underwear according to the season.

A further historical item of interest is that the Continentals pioneered the rifle in the wars of our country. A precision weapon, the rifle had been known in Europe for some years prior to the Revolutionary War, and it is reported that British soldiers were in constant fear of the deadly weapon in the hands of skilled American riflemen.

The *Highlanders*, (No. 151a), measure only 3-1/16 inches in height. The two figures shown next to the title panel had been cut apart from the strip,

though not cut to form; these were laid in place for photographing.

"Highland Regiments" are defined as Scottish regiments belonging to the British Army, their uniforms the kilt and plaid known as "Highland Dress". Certain of these regiments were organized in the late eighteenth and early nineteenth centuries, and obviously were engaged in the Revolutionary War.

Illustration No. 151b portrays *Zouaves*, soldiers of the Union Army engaged in the Civil War. The figures are four inches in height, uniforms adopted from French dress. All are very colorful and of historical significance. Other sets of paper Zouaves have been reported in which the soldiers are portrayed as charging, lending a quality of action. What fun young boys must have had, playing their paper war games.

Nos. 152a and b show the *Union Rifles* and the *Infantry,* both uncut folders. All figures are four inches in height, printed in oil colors, two to each folder panel. While the catalog states that each set consists of a company of twelve soldiers, those included in our photographic reproductions show only ten to a company. As discrepancies between publishers' descriptions and their published products have been previously noted, it is probable such a situation exists with the soldiers; they have every appearance of having been printed only ten to a folder, apparent by the finished edge of the extreme left-hand panel, bearing no mark of having been cut.

The uniforms of the Union Rifles in the illustrated company are brightly colored, equipped with regulation white cross-belts, and what appear to be blanket rolls carried across their shoulders.

The Infantry represent a company of well-drilled foot soldiers of the Union Army engaged in the Civil War, 1861-65.

The nine 4-5/8 inch bandsmen (No. 153) were cut from a folder, probably also consisting of ten members. These have been identified from a partly uncut penny folder titled *Brass Band,* listed under the heading of "Paper Soldier Series" in subject catalog. The term "Brass Band" has been generally applied to organized groups of marching musicians employing wind instruments, drums and the like, as differentiated from orchestral groups playing string instruments.

The pictured bandsmen wear gray trousers with blue jackets, the instruments executed in gold. We have no specific war record for this particular band other than that inclusion in this catalog of 1875/76 seemingly identifies it as a military band of the Civil War.

No. 150. CONTINENTALS. 4″. F. CUT.

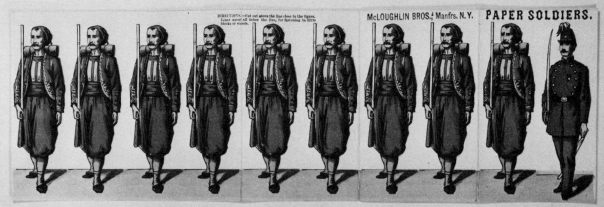

No. 151a.   Highlanders. 3-1/16". F. Partially cut.
No. 151b.   Zouaves. 4". F. Uncut.

No. 152a.   Union Rifles. F. Uncut.
No. 152b.   Infantry. F.Uncut.

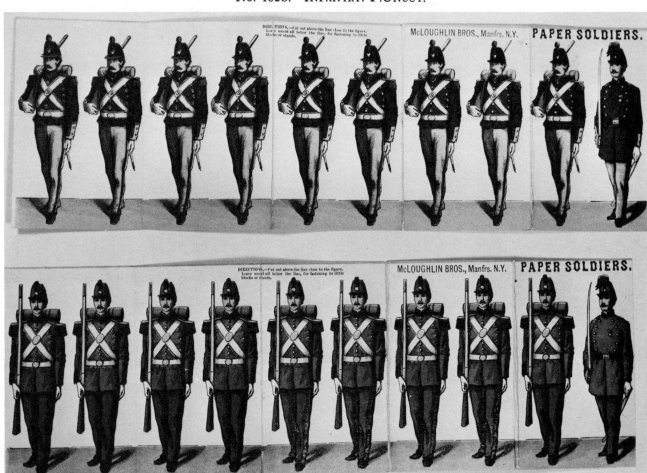

No. 153.   BRASS BAND. 4-5/8". F. CUT.

- - - - -

"PAPER DOLL HOUSES.

Per Dozen, $24.00.

"These are two-story wooden houses eighteen inches high, and eleven inches wide, made in imitation of brick with slanting tile roof, chimney, etc. The floor of each story is furnished with a pattern carpet, and the walls are handsomely papered. The upper story is designed for a bedroom, and the lower story for a parlor. The separate parts of the house are compactly put up in a neat box, with full directions for putting together."

- - - - -

"PAPER FURNITURE.

"PARLOR SET No. 1 — Eleven pieces ....Per Gross, $12.00

"It contains six chairs, two fancy rockers, two sofas in maroon damask, and one marble-top table. Put up in fine envelopes with full directions. Packed in pasteboard boxes containing six dozen each."

"PARLOR SET NO. 2 ....Per Gross, $7.50.

"Same as No. 1 except in size. Packed in the same manner also."

"DRAWING ROOM SET — Nine pieces ....Per Gross, $12.00

"It contains four chairs, two fancy rockers, one sofa in maroon brocatelle, one marble-top table, and one piano, with furnishings. Put up in fine envelopes with full directions. Packed in pasteboard boxes containing six dozen each."

BED ROOM SET NO. 1 — Ten pieces ....Per Gross, $12.00

"Contains four chairs, two ottomans, one marble-top washstand, bureau, table, and one bedstead, 'cottage style'. Put up in fine envelopes with full directions. Packed in pasteboard boxes containing six dozen each."

"BED ROOM SET NO. 2 ....Per Gross, $7.50

"Same as foregoing except in size. Packed also in same manner."

- - - - -

The No. 2 Parlor Set shown in No. 154 is believed to be the set listed, even though neither date nor street address for publishers appears on the envelope. Our opinion is based solely upon the early design of the envelope, inclusion of the same direction sheet as was used for the 1858 "Parlor Set No. 7," Pg. 74, Illus. No. 50, and further, that it conforms to the publishers' printed description. While this is a complete set, only three of the straight chairs, one rocker and one sofa are illustrated in order to provide sharp reproductions.

Mention is made, however, that a "No. 2 Parlor Set" is listed in McLoughlin Bros.' July, 1890, catalog, for which we have no identified specimen. To add to the confusion, in a children's magazine, THE DOLL'S DRESSMAKER, February, 1892, the same sofa, rocker and table as shown in Illus. No. 154 were pictured. A chest which appears to be of the same design as the one pictured on the envelope, was pictured in the August issue of this same magazine, a matching bed in the November issue, all of these with accompanying instructions for children to make their own paper dolls' furniture. So, while it seems plausible to assume that our illustrated set was listed in the 1875/76 catalog, this is not conclusive. It well may be that the publishers re-issued the same set in 1892.

Continued use of the 1858 design on envelopes for furniture of a later date apparently was an economy policy of the publishers, giving rise to doubt as to the authenticity of the contents. Too, the inclusion of a piano on these envelopes is misleading, since pianos seem to have been reserved for drawing rooms.

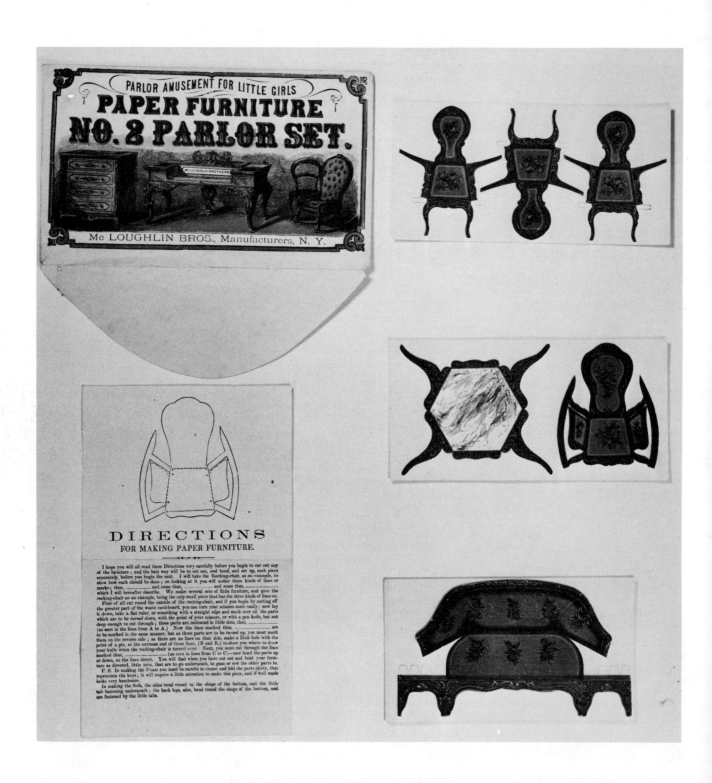

No. 154.   No. 2 Parlor Set. Uncut.

No. 155. PLAY-HOUSE DOLL FIGURES. 4-3/4" TO 5".

"PLAY-HOUSE DOLL FIGURES.

"Six kinds ....Per Gross, $9.00

"These are embossed figures of girls and boys, four and one-half inches high, mounted upon maple standards. Each figure has a flower base, and is cut out with great nicety. The costumes are varied and handsome, and printed in bright, rich colors. Put up in pasteboard boxes, containing an assorted dozen each.

FLORA — The Flower-girl.

HARRY — The Butterfly-catcher.

POLLY — and her pet Parrot.

ROSEY — The Garden-flower.

FREDDY — Which? the dog or the ball.

CHERRY — Who'll have a Cherry?

Not all of the six dolls, shown in the Illustration (No. 155), conform to the above printed descriptions, though all are of the same construction.

The girls' bodies are in two parts, the lower lithographed in one piece with the base, and with printed long, lace-trimmed drawers, striped stockings and red shoes. Wrap-around pleated skirts of early "watered" paper in various shades with lace bottom ruffles are then added, providing a foundation to which the beautifully embossed heads, arms and waists (in one piece) are pasted. Scalloped oval wafers of the same shade of watered paper as the skirts cover the joining of the parts on the backs of the dolls.

Boys also are constructed in two parts, the embossed uppers pasted to the lithographed lower parts. There are no added paper costumes for the boys.

The second doll from the left in our photographic illustration carries a plate of flowers, which seems to identify her as "Flora—the Flower-girl". The next little girl is readily identified as "Cherry", dangling cherries forming her earrings, her scooped-up skirt filled with the same luscious fruit.

"Freddy" with his snow-balls, and "Harry — the Butterfly-catcher", are next in line, while identity of the little girl at extreme right, with a shoulder bag slung over her shoulder, has not been established, nor has the little boy, trudging along with his book, been identified. "Polly — and her pet Parrot" are conspicuous by their absence. These variations from the printed descriptions suggest the possibility of two or more sets of Play-House Doll Figures having been produced. The four dolls shown with the triangular maple standards, which are 2-1/8 inches long, 3/4 inches wide at the base, with full-length slits at the apex, allowing the lithographed bases of the dolls to be inserted for firm standing, are from the writer's collection. The other two from another collection have only the lithographed bases, the maple standards having been lost over the years.

It is hoped and felt that this virtually illustrated catalog of McLoughlin Brothers' early paper doll output will serve as a valuable reference source in the building up of collections of correctly assembled paper doll sets.

No. 156. Alice, 5″, uncut. Author's collection.

No. 157. Bertha, 4-15/16″, uncut. Author's collection.

Section D: 1890's-1900's

The following excerpts from McLoughlin Brothers' catalog dated July, 1894 were contributed by Miss Faffer, formerly Curator of Dolls and Toys, Brooklyn Children's Museum, included here by authorization of Miss Helen V. Fisher, formerly Director of the Museum.

"No. 247½ — New Series—Penny Dolls; The figures in this series are over 5" high, with four dresses in the latest styles. Very handsomely printed in colors."

"No. 247 — French Paper Dolls; In Envelopes 10¢; in sheets 6¢; 6 kinds— Elegantly printed in colors. Envelopes in color and gold. Some of these have two figures. The dresses are perfectly beautiful.

MARIE LOUISE AND HENRI.	VIRGINIE.
ANTOINETTE AND IRENE.	PAULINE, BABY AND ANNETTE.
DIANE, THE BRIDE.	EUGENIA AND HORTENSE."

"No. 248 — New Paper Dolls — Size 1 — In envelopes—10¢; Envelopes 6" by 11", printed in colors. Figures 7" high, all cut out of heavy cardboard. 5 dresses in the modern style, with hats, etc. to match."

"No. 249 — New Paper Dolls — Size 2 — In envelopes—10¢; envelopes 7½" by 11", printed in color. Figures 9½" tall, already cut out of cardboard; 6 dresses and 6 hats."

Lacking names for the penny dolls, catalog Item No. 247½, it is impossible to establish definite identification of any that may by chance be included in our collections. However, at considered risk, we offer the suggestion that dolls named Alice, Bertha, Clara, and Dora, circa 1892, may belong in this group. Illustrations Nos. 156 to and including 159 show the four in uncut sheets.

Named in alphabetical sequence, they are printed on light weight board, inexpensive stock at the time, sheet dimensions 12¾ by 8½ inches. Following our adopted method of measuring dolls to the tip of the lower shoe, these measure five inches or slightly under.

With the bases included, as presumably measured by the manufacturer, they would be "over 5 inches high," placing them in the size range of the catalog listing. Each has four costumes, and they are "handsomely printed in colors" with both front and back views. Interesting accessories are the separate wig of long hair and the numerous hats for each doll. With the larger die-cut figures supplied with more costumes, and distributed in decorated envelopes selling at 10 cents, it seems logical to suppose these sheets of lesser quality were sold for a penny. We shall gratefully stand corrected if definite information on this one cent group disproves our supposition.

No. 158. CLARA, 4⅞″, UNCUT. AUTHOR'S COLLECTION.

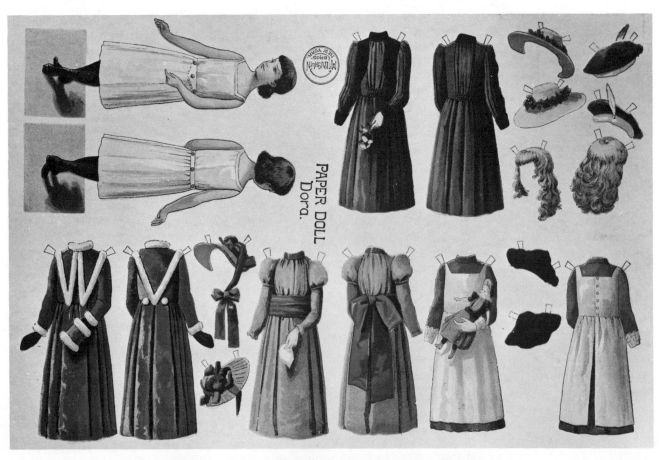

No. 159. DORA, 4-15/16″, UNCUT. AUTHOR'S COLLECTION.

Group No. 247 provides specific names, and of the six listings we can illustrate four, the exceptions being *Virginie,* and *Antoinette and Irene* named as a pair. Authenticated specimens of these are lacking, but the elegant dresses with lavish trim and sweeping trains of wardrobes for the many dolls in the author's collection similar to those shown in Illustrations Nos. 163, 164 and 166 suggest that these two sets of unknowns may be among them.

The dolls in this group are glamorous indeed, but though called "French," in reality they originated in Germany. Printed on large sheets of good quality board, many are embossed, others lithographed. Those of one company, identity unknown, bear a trademark of W & S/B enclosed within an artist's palette, a sheet number printed below this mark. This same trademark appears on both embossed and lithographed sheets. Other numbered sheets have a trademark of "J S" within a tiny rolling pin, while many have no trademark at all. One embossed sheet in the author's collection, showing the W & S over B trademark, has the added inscription, "Made in Germany." While this evidences a printing of 1891 or later, those without such inscription are believed to have preceded this date.

While it is safe to assert that all of these embossed sheets originated in Germany, this is not true of all lithographed ones, this medium having been employed by both European producers and McLoughlin Brothers of New York, the latter apparently having copied many of the German figures to bring out their series of "French Paper Dolls," the French designation applied apparently as a clever sales device, prompted by the elaborate dresses of the grand ladies. These dolls were produced in two sizes, the larger die-cut and distributed in envelopes at 10 cents, the smaller in sheets at 6 cents each, both included in our illustrations.

The trio, *Marie Louise and Henri,* (No. 160) assuredly were first produced in Germany as evidenced by illustrated embossed sets. And while listed in McLoughlin Brothers' 1894 catalog, there is no proof that this company was the first to publish them in the United States, since lithographed sets, designated as "French Dolls", were being distributed in New York at least ten years prior to the catalog date.

In the publication referred to in Chapter II, THE PRESBYTERIAN of Dec. 20, 1884, there appears an advertisement of one Frank G. Wehoskey, Providence, Rhode Island, headed, "Only 12 Cents for 3 French Dolls, with an Elegant Wardrobe of 32 Pieces." Henri, Louise and Marie are pictured in that order, the advertisement reading in part:

"Consisting of Reception Dresses, Evening Dresses, Street Costumes, Morning Dresses, Cloaks, Hats and Bonnets, Hand-Satchels, Sun Umbrellas, Music Portfolios, Overcoats, Sailor Suits, Military Suits and Drums, Street Jackets and Dress Suits, Watering-Place Suits, Travelling Costumes, etc. These Dresses and Suits in this Elegant Wardrobe represent nine different colors, and they are lovely beyond description, several of them being from designs by Worth, of Paris. There is one little Boy and two Girls in each set. . . ."

Potent sales appeal follows, directed to mothers on behalf of their children, the copy then ending—

"Sample Set, consisting of 3 Dolls, with their Wardrobe of 32 pieces, by mail postpaid, for 12 cents. Two Sets, 6 Dolls, 64 pieces, for 20 cents. 13 Sets for $1. If you send for one or two sets, we will send our Secret Method and Full Directions how you can make more than One Hundred Dollars a month out of these Dolls. This is an opportunity too valuable for you to lose."

Frank G. Wehoskey, Providence, R. I."

☆ ☆ ☆

This advertisement serves not only to prove that these dolls were issued in or prior to the year 1884, but also the existence of three dolls in the set, absence of a comma following the name "Marie" in the catalog listing having suggested to certain collectors that "Marie Louise" signified one doll.

This trio must have been very popular with children. Mrs. Philip Cappalonga of Spring City, Pennsylvania, reports having in her collection four approximately six by seven inch uncut sheets of these dolls in lithographed medium and marked "Copyright applied for by L. Ray," (No. 161). It is quite apparent that the four were originally published as a single sheet, deduced by the inscription at the bottom having been cut through. Neither a date nor an address is given, but there is a sheet of directions for cutting and dressing the three "French" dolls which also includes *Directions to Agents How to Sell These Dolls.* This is reproduced in Illustration No. 162, and the directions to agents offer a study in pressure salesmanship.

The pictorial illustration on this sheet of directions is an exact duplicate of the one in Mr. Wehoskey's advertisement in the 1884 issue of THE PRESBYTERIAN, and the entire content of his advertising copy suggests that he may have been an agent-customer of Mr. Ray.

It also is quite possible that The Willimantic Thread Co. purchased from Mr. Ray, the right to use Henri and Louise as separate entities on individual folding cards, with different toys, in their advertising program.

And just where did McLoughlin Brothers come into the picture? If available, a catalog for some year between 1876 and 1884 possibly might establish McLoughlin Brothers as the original United States publisher. One wonders, too, whether or not Mr. Ray obtained the copyright for which he had applied. The answer might be the key to a solution.

No. 160. TOP TO BOTTOM: MARIE, 5″. LOUISE, 3⅞″. HENRI, 4¼″. AUTHOR'S COLLECTION.

No. 161. MARIE, LOUISE, HENRI; UNCUT SHEET. PATENT APPLIED FOR BY L. RAY. ANNA CAPPALONGA COLLECTION.

DIRECTIONS
For Cutting and Dressing the
3 FRENCH DOLLS.

Use a scissors in Cutting out the Dolls and the 32 Different Dresses and other articles that belong to the Wardrobe. Follow closely the Outside Edge of each Article. Be Careful NEVER TO CUT OFF THE SMALL TABS that have the Light Line around them, but cut around and follow the outer edge of the line. Trim close up to the Dresses, Coats, Suits, &c., leaving no white to be seen along the Outer Edge of the Garment. After the Doll and Dress is cut out place the Dress on the Doll, and turn the small tabs over on to the back of the Doll, and the tabs will hold the Dress, Hat, Coat, or any of the other articles on the Doll, as represented in the Illustration. If from long use, or any cause whatever, any of the tabs become worn or broken off, a small piece of thin card board can be pasted on in place of the worn one, and it will be as good as new.

DIRECTIONS TO AGENTS HOW TO SELL THESE DOLLS

And make a great many dollars with very little trouble. Take your Sample with you, and call at the residences in your own Town, or in any City or Village, in fact in any Store, Shop or Factory. Show them how many Dresses, Coats, Cloaks, Hats, &c., there are in the Wardrobe of these Three French Dolls. Ask every mother if she does not consider it her duty to her dear ones to order one or more Sets of these Dolls, for her Children to amuse themselves with during the long afternoons and evenings. Tell them how much enjoyment there is in this Beautiful little Novelty, and tell her that each child should have a Set, and convince them what a beautiful Present it is for a Boy or Girl. Ask them to allow you to put their name down for One, Two, Three or Four Sets, and that you will deliver them in a few days, and when you get 12 Names on your paper send us One Dollar, and we will send you 12 Sets, or you can keep on until you get 50 Sets ordered, and then send us $4.25 and we will send you 50 Sets, or you can wait until you get 100 orders, and send $6.00, and we will send you 100 Sets, for which you will get $15. But if you think you can sell them very fast we will tell you the best way to do, and the way most of our agents do, is to order 12 Sets for $1.00, or 25 Sets for $2.00, or 50 Sets for $4.25, or 100 Sets for $6.00, so as to sell and deliver and take your pay as you go. This saves going over the ground a second time. There are a great many persons that would rather buy than give their order. There are many people who will buy and pay for a thing when they see it (on the spur of the moment), rather than give their order. They have an idea that the Sample you show them is a little better, and they want the very one you show them. So you had better order a few immediately. But we only give this as advice. Of course you can do as you think best, either canvass by Sample, taking orders, and then order the Dolls and fill them, or order some of the Dolls and sell as you go. But whichever plan you work on it would be best to order a few of the Dolls to take along with you, for reasons given above. You can sell in your own town first, and then go to the next village or city, and keep on traveling and selling them every day until the whole country is supplied, and that will take so long that you will have steady employment for a year at least. Just try this, and see if you ever went at anything that you made money as fast. Begin at once, and work fast. Time is golden to you in this business, so push hard and fast. Work early and late. Call at every house in every town, and never appear in a hurry; talk with the people about the Dolls. Impress upon them that this is the Novelty of all Novelties to buy. Tell them it is intended for persons of every age, from 2 years up to 70 years, for it amuses every person that has examined it. Always keep right on, no matter what may happen, and be sure to keep your courage up even though you get a few rebuffs. After the first hour or two you will love to see them. You will get so engaged you will want to work late in the evening, for you will hear people remark, every step you take: "Oh, aint those Dolls elegant?—how much are they?—well, give me two Sets," and all such expressions of delight. Some will invite you to stay over night, and if you are travelling always accept, as it will save you paying out money. Experience is the best teacher, and in a short time you will know exactly how to talk and what to say to each person you approach. Persevere, for without that quality you can never accomplish much of anything. Always keep pleasant, and act with dignity. Never allow yourself to feel timid, but go right ahead as bold as a king. Pluck and perseverance will surely bring you success at this business. You never need be afraid to order these goods, for you are just as sure to sell them, if you follow the above advice, as that the sun rises and sets. We wish you every success, and hope your sales will run up to $20 a day. ☞ If you do not wish to sell these goods, kindly hand this to some worthy person out of employment, that needs a helping hand. The Dolls retail at Fifteen Cents a Set.

MONEY REFUNDED IF NOT SATISFACTORY.

No. 162. L. Ray's Directions to Agents; Henri, Louise, Marie. Anna Cappalonga collection.

Diane, the Bride is believed to have originated in Germany as *Her Imperial Highness, the Arch Duchess Dagmar Alexandria of Russia,* born December 28, 1868, the original doll 6⅛ inches tall. It is quite apparent that this was copied by McLoughlin Brothers as *Diane, the Bride,* perhaps under the assumption that this title would have added appeal in our country.

As pictured in Illustration No. 163, Diane is a four inch lithographed doll, the figure and costumes printed front and back, accessories front printing only, and are as they came with the doll some years ago. An uncut set might disclose additional ones, lost over the years.

Of the larger set, only the bridal gown is shown. This measures 6⅝ inches from the top of the headdress to the bottom of the veil, approximately the height of the missing bride who would be about one quarter inch taller than the German one. The bridal gowns of ivory satin and brocade, with the shimmering, diaphanous veils, are very lovely.

With Illustration No. 164 we picture an unlisted lithographed doll similar to others in this grouping. She is 4⅛ inches tall, printed double.

The same doll in 6¾ inch size, also lithographed but with front printing only, came with a penned notation, "The Bridesmaid for Dianne the Bride." Since no such listing is included with the bride in the catalogued group, we entertain serious doubt as to the accuracy of the title, and only mention on the chance that there may be corroborating evidence in the collection of some one of our readers. Again, the doll, so like the ones in the 247 group, may be the missing Virginie.

The late Mrs. H. B. Armstrong of Texas had in her collection the lithographed costume shown at upper right in our illustration No. 164 in an uncut portion of a sheet bearing a part of the W & S over a B trademark with "47" below, presumably the first two digits of the sheet number. This trademark definitely establishes the German origin of this doll, and that the company using the W & S over a B mark produced dolls in both the embossed and the lithographed media.

Subject doll's evening gown and the one with mask are in brilliant rose, the tiered skirt of the evening dress a soft contrasting pink. The jacket dress is an odd shade of green, almost olive, with brown fur trim. It would be helpful to have a definite designation for this particular doll.

Credit is given to Elizabeth Andrews Fisher, publisher, for release on the above material, similarly covered in a two-part article by this writer under the title "German vs. French Paper Dolls", in March and April, 1956, issues of THE TOY TRADER.

Once again, with *Pauline, Baby and Annette* (No. 165), a mere comma, in this instance placed where none should be, has caused confusion. Following the name "Pauline" in the 1894 catalog, it has led certain collectors to contend that the set should contain three dolls. However, it is noted that no comma

appears in the title on the envelope, and this, together with the fact that the several known sets consist of only two dolls, seems to verify that Baby Pauline and her nurse, Annette, comprise a complete set.

Like others of these so-called "French" paper dolls, this came out in the three media, a heavily embossed one presumed to be of German origin, (lower right in the illustration), and a large and a small set lithographed by McLoughlin Brothers of New York, these pictured at right and directly below the envelope reproduction. This 5⅛ by 7⅞ inch envelope is printed on a grayish stock, the border design in black and a medium blue; the entwined ribbon, and the semi-circle at lower right corner enclosing the name, "McLoughlin Bros.", are in dull gold, the title in black letters. Especially prized is the original pencilled price mark, 10, still legible in the upper right hand corner of the envelope.

Careful comparison of the three sets discloses minor differences in execution; in the embossed set pleasant "laugh" lines are faintly visible in the nurse's features, and her eyes appear to be closed as they gaze down upon the baby in her arms. The lithographed sets show no laugh lines, and the eyes are partly opened.

The embossed doll measures 6⅛ inches from top of her headdress to tip of her lower shoe, doll and costumes brilliantly colored. The dress of the baby held in the nurse's arms is a rose pink, her separate dress and the cloak a vivid blue. All parts have front and back views with the exception of the baby's extra cloak which has only the front design, since the baby is not a separate figure.

The larger lithographed doll, measuring 7 inches, is also printed both front and back, while the small 4⅛ inch one has front design only. The same color combination as used in the embossed set has been followed in these lithographed copies, though certain color shades in the latter are pale by comparison.

This particular text with accompanying illustration is included by courtesy of **HOBBIES** Magazine who published this author's article on the so-called French Paper Dolls of McLoughlin Brothers in their October, 1955 issue.

In Illustration No. 166 we have *Eugenia and Hortense. Eugenia,* 6¼ inches, shown in the lower row in the illustration, is represented as a German embossed set; the author's collection also includes a 4-3/16 inch lithographed one, presumably from a McLoughlin Bros.' six cent sheet.

The embossing of the German set is exceedingly fine, the raised ruffle, floral trim and other decorative touches seeming to stand apart from the costume foundations; backs are plain. As in all of these cut sets the accessories may or may not be correct. Two or more dolls were usually printed on the large German sheets from which the dolls were cut, and there is always the possibility that some small items were not assigned to the doll for which they were intended. Our illustration shows them as they came with this particular doll.

The apron pictured at extreme right seems somewhat inconsistent, but since it was included in both the embossed and the small lithographed sets, we have to conclude that it does belong. Ties of real string were added to the apron of the embossed set, perhaps by a child who had the pleasure of playing with this doll. If so, such activity must have been strictly supervised as the set is now in practically mint condition.

The two dressy costumes for Eugenia are in shades of pink and rose and are very elegant. The jacket and coat suits are in dark, somber tones.

Hortense, (in the upper row of the illustration), was acquired in all three forms, a 6⅛ inch heavily embossed doll, a 6¾ inch lithographed one, and a small 4⅛ inch figure, all three sets with plain backs.

McLoughlin Bros. have used the brighter colors in the Eugenia and Hortense sets, closely adhering to the beautifully colored costumes of the original embossed production.

While we have not personally seen an envelope for this set and cannot unqualifiedly state from personal checking that these dolls *are* Eugenia and Hortense, we have accepted identification as provided by an advanced collector whose authentication we do not question.

No. 163. Diane, the Bride, 4″. Author's collection.

No. 164. UNIDENTIFIED DOLL, 4⅛″. AUTHOR'S COLLECTION.

No. 165. PAULINE BABY AND ANNETTE. TOP DOLL 7″; LOWER 4⅛″ AND 6⅛″ RESPECTIVELY. AUTHOR'S COLLECTION.

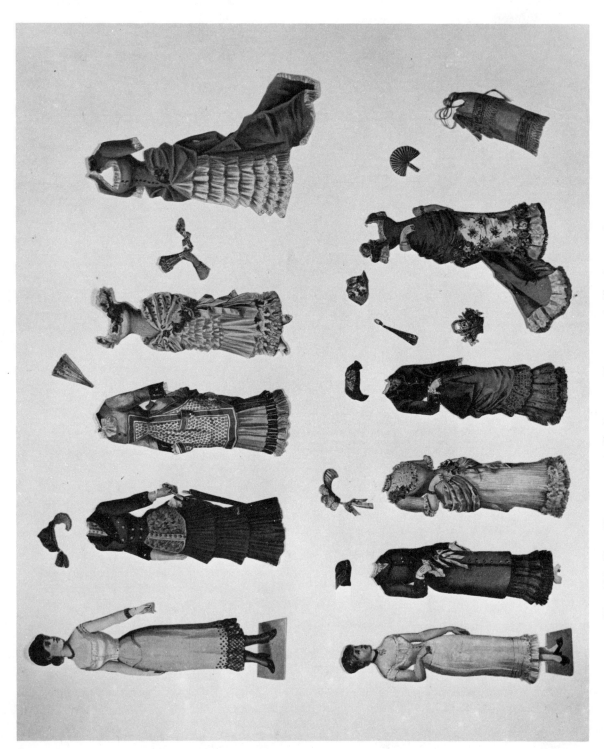

No. 166. Top, Hortense. 6⅛". Lower, Eugenia, 6¼". Author's collection.

Catalog item No. 248 cites "New Paper Dolls, Size 1", but fails to state the number of individual dolls included, nor does it give names by which they may be pinpointed.

The one specimen available which we firmly believe to be of this group is *Karl King* (No. 167). Measurements of both the doll, 6½ inches, (about seven with base), and the envelope, 6 - 3/16 by 11 - 3/16 inches, agree with the catalog sizes, and with the five costumes conforming to the catalog description (two hats are missing) seem to leave no question as to Karl King's rightful place in Group No. 248.

The envelope bears incription, "Copyrighted 1892 by McLoughlin Bros., Publisher, New York." This doll with his interesting wardrobe is lithographed in appropriate colors front and back, a helpful fashion guide for a boy doll of the Gay Nineties.

Item No. 249, "New Paper Dolls—Size 2", likewise fails to provide detailed information. However, we again present a doll having all the necessary characteristics to establish eligibility for inclusion. *Grace Green,* (No. 168), measuring 9⅝ inches with base, the 7¾ by 11¼ inch envelope, and the number of costumes, all conform to the catalog description, though three of the hats are missing. Notation on the envelope, "Figure cut out", emphasizes the publishers' description on this point. The same copyright information as appears on the envelope for Karl King is given on the envelope for subject doll, establishing publication date of 1892.

Doll and costumes are attractively lithographed front and back in color, and it is our considered opinion that Grace Green almost certainly was published as one of the No. 249 group of large paper dolls.

Fanny Field (No. 169), also is believed to fall into the No. 249 group. The envelope (not illustrated) is identical in all respects to that of Grace Green excepting only the doll name. Fanny is 9¼ inches, placing her in the correct size range for inclusion. Her wigs and the long hair provided with her hat match her own blond hair. Costumes, printed front and back, are beautifully colored. The soft tan dress in upper right of the photographic reproduction, with its deep rose color neck and sleeve ruffles, and the wide rose sash ending in the back with a large bow and streamer-type fringed ends, goes with the little pink bonnet at the immediate left, which originally had a white chin bow.

The cloak at lower left is a bright blue with white fur trim, while the one at lower right, showing both front and back, is in a lively shade of brown with dark fur trim.

These two sets, Nos. 168 and 169, represent choice paper dolls of the early 1890's.

Assuredly other dolls were published under these various classifications, and it is hoped a complete list by names may one day be forthcoming.

Four winsome little girl dolls named in alphabetical sequence, *Katie, Lizzie, Mamie,* and *Nellie,* were published by McLoughlin Bros., New York, circa 1899. These were printed on 12⅞ x 8½ inch sheets and sold for a penny. Each has a seasonable wardrobe comprising dainty summer dresses and a warm winter cloak with appropriate accessories.

These dolls are illustrated in Nos. 170 to and including 173 respectively. *Katie* is pictured in a cut set which may be incomplete, perhaps lacking some small garment or accessory. An uncut was not available for checking. The other three dolls are reproduced from original uncut sheets.

It will be noted that all but Mamie have free arms which can be drawn through slots spotted for the purpose in the dress sleeves and capes of the cloaks. Mamie's arms are fixed, and for that reason her costumes have printed arms and hands.

In addition to these arm slots, dresses are equipped with turnback shoulder tabs visible in the illustrations. Katie's cloak has an identified slot to be cut in the standing collar, while for Lizzie's and Mamie's cloaks, having attached hoods, separate back supports bearing printed instructions are supplied: "GUM on back of BROWN CLOAK at STARS", the stars being tiny matching identification marks for proper placing of the support on the back of the garment; the brown cloak is Mamie's, the instructions changed to read "Red Cloak" for Lizzie.

Only Mamie, clutching her favorite doll, has toys. She is the privileged owner of a skipping rope and a tricycle for summer outdoor activities.

Although as we have seen, McLoughlin Brothers produced paper dolls in alphabetical sequence beginning with the Alice to Dora series and the four subject dolls, there is no apparent connection between the two runs. If a complete alphabetical series was planned by the publishers, we are without a substantiating record.

Doll types were frequently changed, no doubt with a view to stimulating demand, and with the several penny productions available, no little girl need to have been without her paper dolls at the turn of the century.

No. 167. Karl King, 6½″.

NO. 168. GRACE GREEN, 9⅝″ INCLUDING BASE. COLLECTION LATE MRS. H. B. ARMSTRONG.

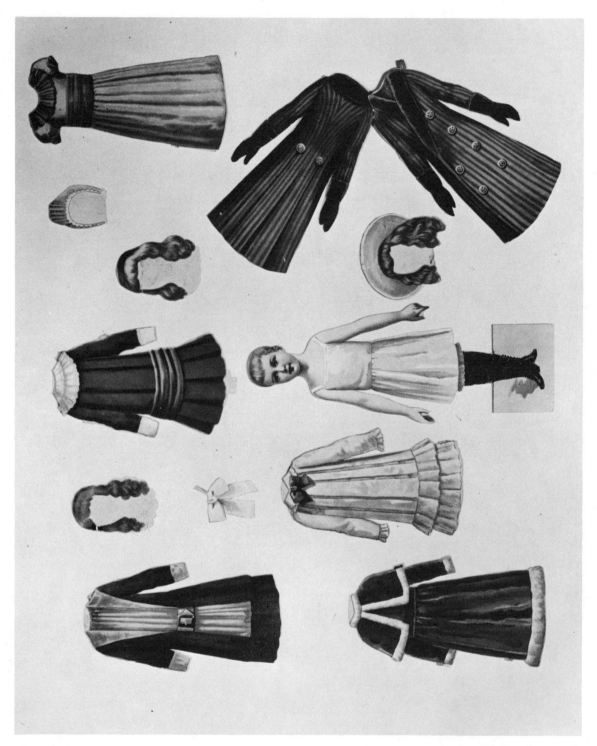

No. 169. FANNY FIELD, 9¼″. AUTHOR'S COLLECTION.

No. 170. KATIE, 6¼".

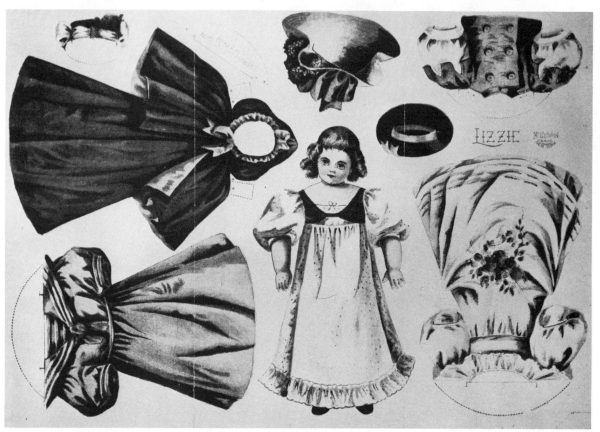

No. 171. LIZZIE, 5¾".

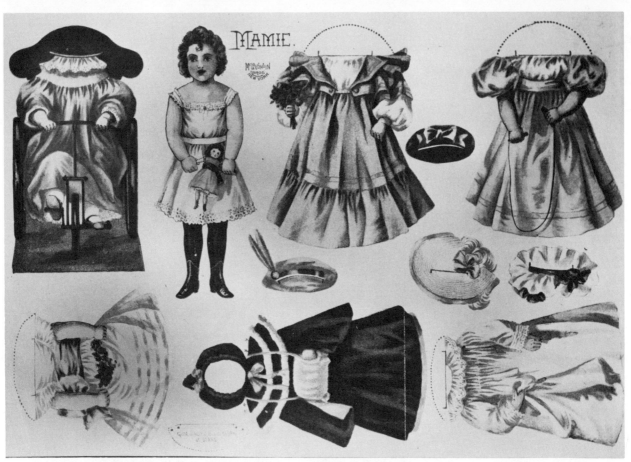

No. 172.   Mamie, 5⅛".

No. 173.   Nellie, 5⅞".

"OUR DOLLIES and how to dress them" was produced as a boxed set in 1905, copyrighted by Mc-Loughlin Bros., New York, an unique toy consisting of sectional parts to be assembled into complete dolls, all lithographed in color. The $9\frac{3}{8}$ by $12\frac{3}{8}$ inch box cover is reproduced in Illustration No. 174, an assembled doll 6 - 3/16 inches tall, together with various sectional parts in No. 175, while No. 176 shows remaining separate parts. As distributed, the legs and feet with a brief portion of petticoat in one piece, were printed on four lithographed bases, which in turn were tacked with nails barely a half-inch long to little wooden blocks fitted into a row of openings the exact size of the blocks in a built-up half-tray-like section of the box. These wooden blocks provided firm standing for the dolls.

There are four heads with neck-tabs, and twelve two-section dresses, slotted and tabbed for easy assembling. All parts are interchangeable. The four hats included indicate that seven have been lost. The paper backing of all pieces is especially interesting with its old-fashioned all-over design of the tiniest of brown flowers.

The pictured set has been removed from the box for purpose of mounting in a binder, and extra bases and one extra head from a different set were added, these said to be of a lighter stock than those which came in the boxed set, suggesting that the same figures may have been published in light weight die-cut sets, perhaps distributed in envelopes, or possibly in sheet form.

Circa 1911-1913 McLoughlin Bros., New York, issued an apparent series of paper dolls in numbered sheets, the first two digits of the several numbers being "01". There seems to have been no continuity of subjects, constituting a disorganized run.

Sheet No. 0101 is of a series titled "Dolls of all Nations", treated further on in this work.

Sheet No. 0102 portrays a bride of the period with her trousseau. Shown in Illustration No. 177, the sheet measures $10\frac{1}{2}$ inches square, the bride 7 inches, and all designs are lithographed in nice colors on a fair quality of light board or heavy paper. No selling price is known, but this certainly was an inexpensive toy. Bride dolls have special appeal for the young as well as for the older young-at-heart, and this dainty bride, with her charming trousseau, surely thrilled many a young girl of the early 1900's.

In Illustration No. 178 we have a similar sheet numbered 0106, the paper doll representing the ever-popular character of Grimms' fairy tale, Cinderella. The 6 - 3/16 inch paper doll itself is quite unlovely, reflecting her role of the weary, over-worked servant. Her wardrobe, however, covers the transition from this unhappy phase of her life to her triumphal rise to Princess, following the Prince's placing of the tiny slipper, "small and dainty and made entirely of gold", upon her slender foot. In play, her drab work dress and broom would be replaced first by two fashionable gowns, these in turn replaced by the

lovely Princess robe with crown, and many a Cinderella party must have been staged among little playmates some fifty-odd years ago.

Also in the early 1900's, McLoughlin Bros. frequently used the design of a paper doll wearing a white slip with ribbon trim, similar to certain ones attributed to Dennison Mfg. Co. While the latter known dolls were believed to have been assembled from imported parts, McLoughlin Bros. used the design in sheets of cutout dolls and in cutout books. Illustration No. 179 shows one of these sheets, the doll called "Celie", lithographed on a 10 - 7/16 inch square sheet, and which bears the inscription, "Copyrighted 1900 by McLoughlin Bros., 890 Broadway, New York". The doll, 8 - 9/16 inches tall, is printed as a complete figure, having no separate or movable parts, and in sheet form probably sold for a penny. Attention is called to the abacus in the hands of the upper costume, a counting system of sliding balls strung on wires said to have originated with the Chinese, but known in ancient times also to the Egyptians, Greeks and Romans. It is an unusual feature in connection with our paper dolls. And now there has been a revival of this ancient device in our present-day schools, chiefly employed in kindergarten classes.

Two other dolls wearing the ribbon-trimmed slips, named Edna and Ethel, were printed on sheets similar to that of Celie, bearing the same copyright inscription. These two were republished later under other names in a cutout book titled WIDE WORLD COSTUME DOLLS, duplicates of Edna and Ethel illustrated in Nos. 181 and 182 in our coverage of this book; all details coincide with the uncut sheets of the two dolls, with the exception of a different arrangement of the figures in the layout.

It will be recalled that reference was previously made to an uncut sheet numbered 0101 of a series called "Dolls of All Nations", published by Mc-Loughlin Brothers, 890 Broadway, New York. This particular sheet is also marked "Set—B", and a pencil date of 1911 apparently was added, perhaps a gift date.

Two other sheets in this series are marked No. 2 and No. 4, indicating a missing No. 3. Subject sheets are not illustrated in this work as "Dolls of All Nations", since they were republished in the cutout book, WIDE WORLD COSTUME DOLLS, wholly illustrated.

Sheet No. 0101, Set—B, is duplicated in Illustration No. 185; sheet No. 2 appears in No. 184, while Set No. 4 is like the doll in Illustration No. 180, which also provides the cover design for the cutout book.

Duplication of these dolls in different series is confusing, but perhaps can be explained by transfer of the company ownership to the new corporation owner. As aforementioned, a few of the original records of McLoughlin Brothers were taken to Springfield when the buyer took over, and they may have found it convenient to make a start by using existing designs. This is conjecture only.

WIDE WORLD COSTUME DOLLS

Cutout Book No. 538

McLoughlin Bros., Inc., Springfield, Massachusetts.

Publication date of this 10 x 13¼ inch book is established as 1920 or later by the Springfield source, cover design in Illus. No. 180. In this the 8¼ inch doll is named "White Cloud", costumes not labeled; however, the Indian one appears in the illustration directly below the title; the center one is Turkish, the lower, Japanese, all so designated on "Dolls of All Nations" sheet, Set—4.

On the inside pages of this book the dolls themselves are not named, but each costume is labeled with a name appropriate to the country represented; thus the doll changes her nationality with each change of dress. Since these labels may not be legible in the book reproductions, they are given below, the first listing the Americans:

Illus. No. 181, (doll like Edna): Next to doll—Dorothy
Top left—Helen
Lower right—Alice

Illus. No. 182, (doll like Ethel): Top right—Anna of Russia
Center—Jeannette of France
Lower right—Susan in Grandmother's Tennis Dress

Illus. No. 183, Top left—Johanna of Switzerland
Center—Mercedes from Madrid, Spain
Top right—Fifi from France

Illus. No. 184, Top left—Marie of Alsace-Lorraine
Top right—Claudette of Northern Canada
Lower—Frieda from Germany

Illus. No. 185, Top left—Jean of Scotland
Top right—Norah from Ireland
Lower—Mary from Wales

"White Cloud" (No. 180) was also produced as a nine inch doll on heavy paper, in quality coloring. A little larger than the same doll in the cutout book, she was presented to the writer with an interesting wardrobe fashioned of early tissue and the sheerest of flowered Japanese crepe-textured paper, creations of some little dressmaker in the early 1900's.

Another delightful production at the Springfield works, circa 1920, is their cutout book No. 544, and again we have dolls in ribbon-trimmed slips. This 9⅞ by 13 - 5/16 inch book, titled NURSERY

RHYME PARTY DOLLS IN COSTUME, designed by Queen Holden, must have given many a child hours of pleasure, recreating beloved characters of her nursery rhyme stories.

Illustration No. 186 shows the attractive cover design, executed in brilliant colors, while No. 187 gives the back cover consisting of two 10½ inch punch-out dolls, a blonde and a brunette. Sturdy bases are provided. Inside sheets of this beautiful book are pictured opened flat, each illustration showing two pages.

In No. 188 we have costumes for Little Polly Flinders; Marjory Daw; Queen of Hearts; and Red Riding Hood.

No. 189 includes costumes for the Queen Who Would a'Wooing Go; Snow White; Little Bo-Peep, and Mary, Mary.

No. 190 gives us costumes for Columbine; Little Girl, Little Girl; Gypsy Dancer, and Cinderella.

Certain, perhaps all, of these same dolls were produced in pre-cut form in fine high-gloss lithography with certain of the nursery rhyme costumes pictured in our illustrations. As are all paper dolls designed by Queen Holden, these are highly desirable adjuncts to our collections.

No. 174.   Box cover for "Our Dollies and how to dress them."   9⅜" by 12⅜".

No. 175.   Assembled doll and sectional parts for Our Dollies.

No. 176.   Remaining sectional parts for Our Dollies.

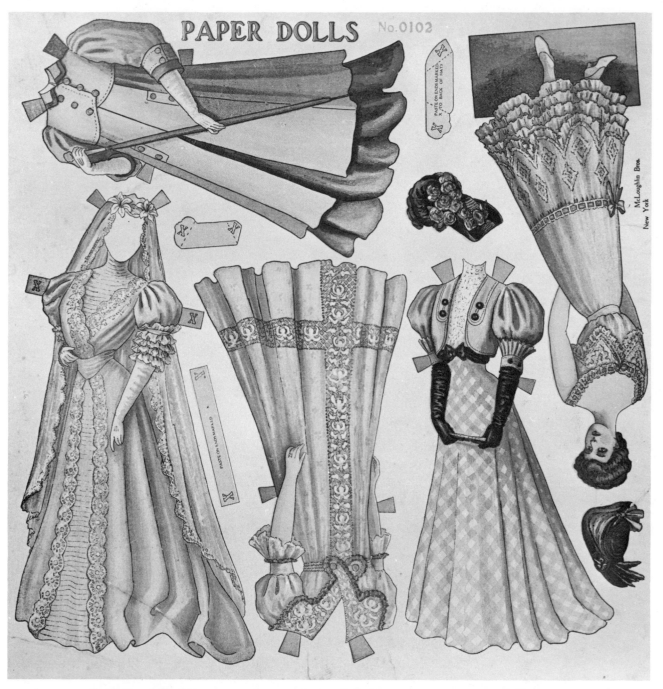

No. 177.   Bride No. 0102, uncut.   Circa 1911-1913 period.   Author's collection.

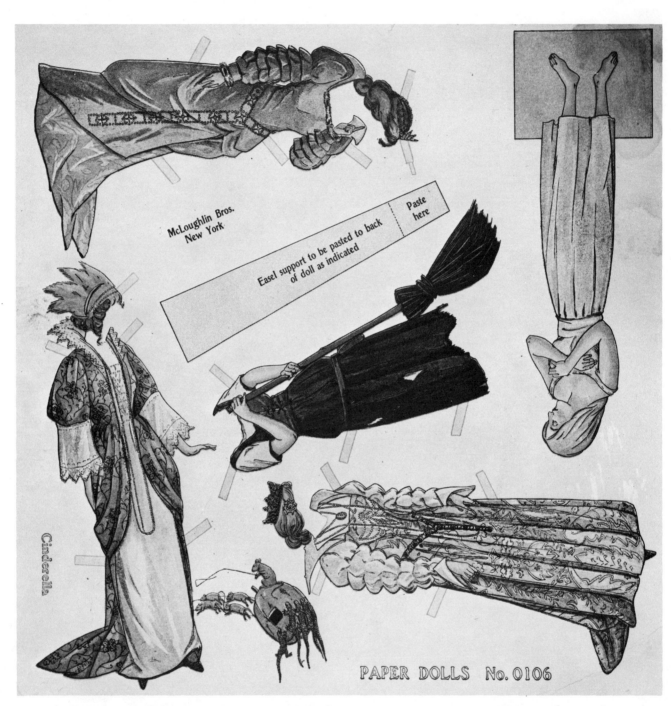

McLoughlin Bros.
New York

Easel support to be pasted to back
of doll as indicated

Paste
here

Cinderella

PAPER DOLLS No. 0106

No. 178. Cinderella, No. 0106, uncut.

Cut around the shoulder-tabs, leaving them
attached to the dress. Then fold them back.
Cut a slit in the hats along the forehead line,
for the head to go through.

Celie

COPYRIGHT 1900 BY
McLOUGHLIN BROS.
890 Broadway NEW YORK

No. 179. CELIE, 8-9/16″.

207

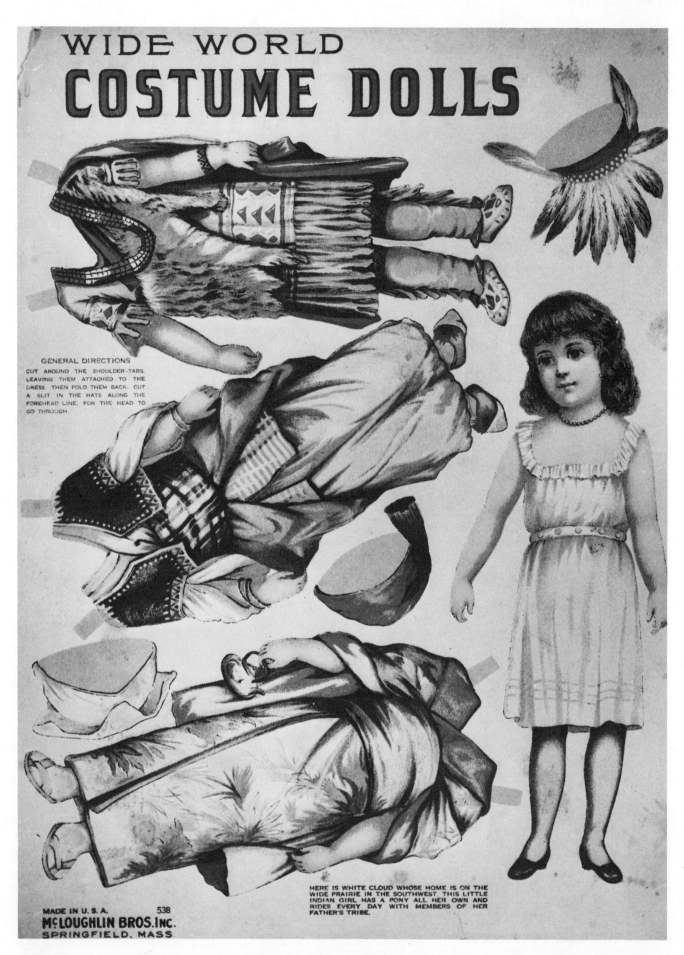

WIDE·WORLD
COSTUME DOLLS

GENERAL DIRECTIONS
CUT AROUND THE SHOULDER-TABS, LEAVING THEM ATTACHED TO THE DRESS. THEN FOLD THEM BACK. CUT A SLIT IN THE HATS ALONG THE FOREHEAD LINE, FOR THE HEAD TO GO THROUGH.

HERE IS WHITE CLOUD WHOSE HOME IS ON THE WIDE PRAIRIE IN THE SOUTHWEST. THIS LITTLE INDIAN GIRL HAS A PONY ALL HER OWN AND RIDES EVERY DAY WITH MEMBERS OF HER FATHER'S TRIBE.

MADE IN U.S.A.   538
McLOUGHLIN BROS. INC.
SPRINGFIELD, MASS

No. 180. COVER DESIGN FOR WIDE WORLD COSTUME DOLLS, WITH WHITE CLOUD. AUTHOR'S COLLECTION.

HELEN LIKES TO BLOW BUBBLES AND THEN WATCH THE SUN SHINE THROUGH THEM. BLOWING BUBBLES IS FUN. ISN'T IT?

THIS IS ALICE WITH HER PET BUNNY. HE LIKES TO BE CARRIED AROUND IN A BASKET FILLED WITH STRAW AND ALICE IS VERY CAREFUL NOT TO DROP HIM.

HERE IS DOROTHY, WHO LIVES IN THE COUNTRY. SHE HAS SO FAR TO GO TO SCHOOL. SHE HAS TO TAKE HER LUNCH WITH HER IN A BASKET.

No. 181.   Page from WIDE WORLD COSTUME DOLLS.

No. 182. Page from WIDE WORLD COSTUME DOLLS.

JOHANNA LIVES IN SWITZERLAND WHERE THE MOUNTAINS ARE SO HIGH THEY ARE COVERED WITH SNOW THE YEAR ROUND. THIS IS JOHANNA'S PARTY DRESS. DOESN'T SHE LOOK NICE?

THIS IS BRIGHT-EYED FIFI FROM FRANCE. FIFI IS VERY FASHIONABLE AND GAY AND SHE LIVES IN PARIS, ONE OF THE LOVELIEST CITIES IN THE WORLD.

HERE IS MERCEDES, THE LITTLE SENORITA FROM MADRID, SPAIN. LIKE HER FRENCH SISTER, SHE IS VERY GAY AND LOVES TO SING AND DANCE WHILE HER BROTHER PLAYS THE GUITAR

No. 183.   PAGE FROM WIDE WORLD COSTUME DOLLS.

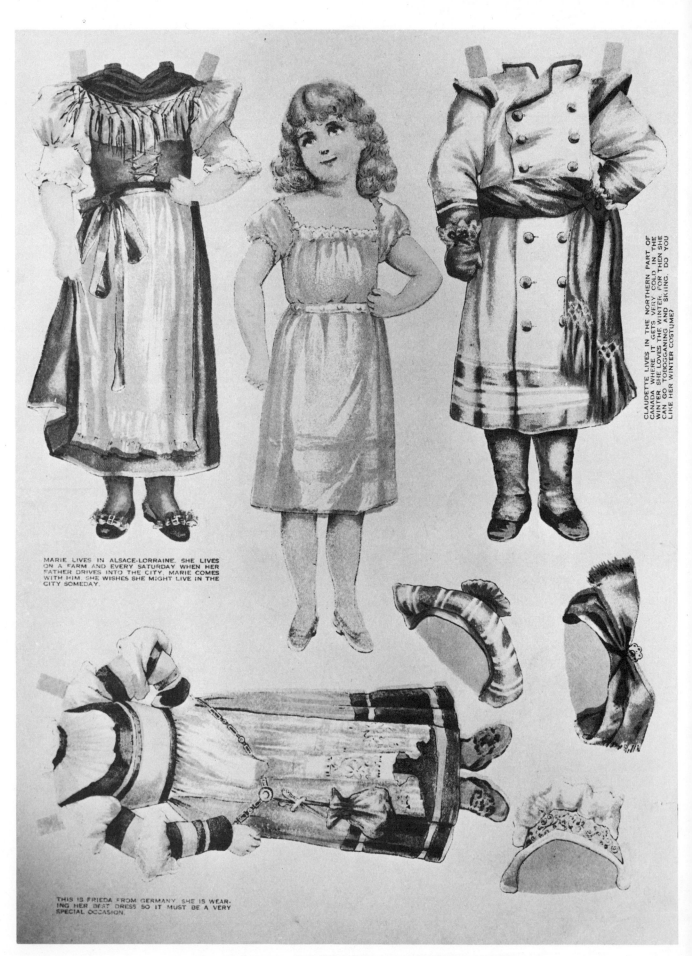

MARIE LIVES IN ALSACE-LORRAINE. SHE LIVES ON A FARM AND EVERY SATURDAY WHEN HER FATHER DRIVES INTO THE CITY, MARIE COMES WITH HIM. SHE WISHES SHE MIGHT LIVE IN THE CITY SOMEDAY.

CLAUDETTE LIVES IN THE NORTHERN PART OF CANADA WHERE IT GETS VERY COLD IN THE WINTER. SHE LOVES THE WINTER FOR THEN SHE CAN GO TOBOGGANING AND SKIING. DO YOU LIKE HER WINTER COSTUME?

THIS IS FRIEDA FROM GERMANY. SHE IS WEARING HER BEST DRESS SO IT MUST BE A VERY SPECIAL OCCASION.

No. 184. PAGE FROM WIDE WORLD COSTUME DOLLS.

YOU SHOULD SEE JEAN. THIS PRETTY SCOTCH LASSIE. DANCE THE HIGHLAND FLING. SHE IS VERY PROUD OF HER BIG BROTHER, WHO PLAYS THE BAGPIPES IN THE KILTIE BAND.

HERE IS NORAH FROM IRELAND, HOLDING FAST HER PET PIGGIE. NORAH LIVES IN A LITTLE WHITEWASHED COTTAGE WITH THATCHED ROOF AWAY OUT IN THE COUNTRY.

THIS IS MARY, FROM WALES WHICH, OF COURSE, YOU KNOW IS PART OF GREAT BRITAIN. MARY HAS JUST BEEN OUT IN HER GARDEN AND PICKED THESE LOVELY FLOWERS.

No. 185. PAGE FROM WIDE WORLD COSTUME DOLLS.

NURSERY RHYME
PARTY DOLLS
IN
COSTUME

QUEEN OF HEARTS

McLOUGHLIN BROS., INC.
SPRINGFIELD, MASS.

No. 186. COVER DESIGN FOR NURSERY RHYME PARTY DOLLS IN COSTUME. AUTHOR'S COLLECTION.

THIS BOOK CONTAINS FANCY DRESS PARTY COSTUMES OF SOME OF THE LEADING
CHARACTERS OF NURSERY RHYMES FROM THE MOTHER GOOSE STORIES. YOU WILL
FIND THEM QUITE ACCURATE IN DESCRIPTIVE DETAIL, AS BASED UPON THE ORIG-
INAL MOTHER GOOSE BOOKS.

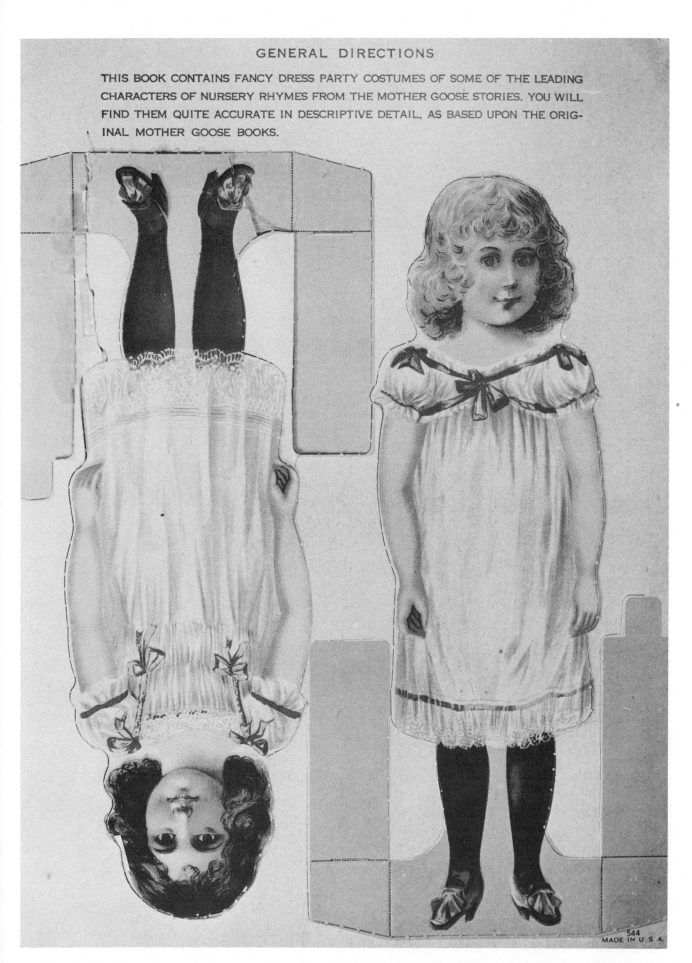

544
MADE IN U.S.A.

No. 187. BACK COVER WITH PUNCH-OUT DOLLS, NURSERY RHYME PARTY DOLLS IN COSTUME.

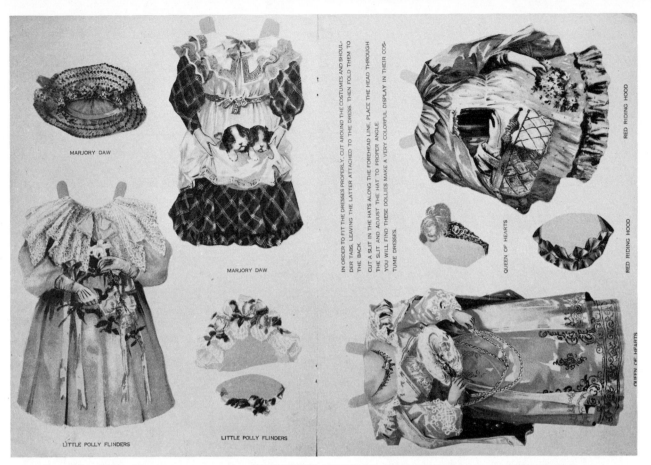

No. 188.   Double page from NURSERY RHYME PARTY DOLLS IN COSTUME.

No. 189.   Double page from NURSERY RHYME PARTY DOLLS IN COSTUME.

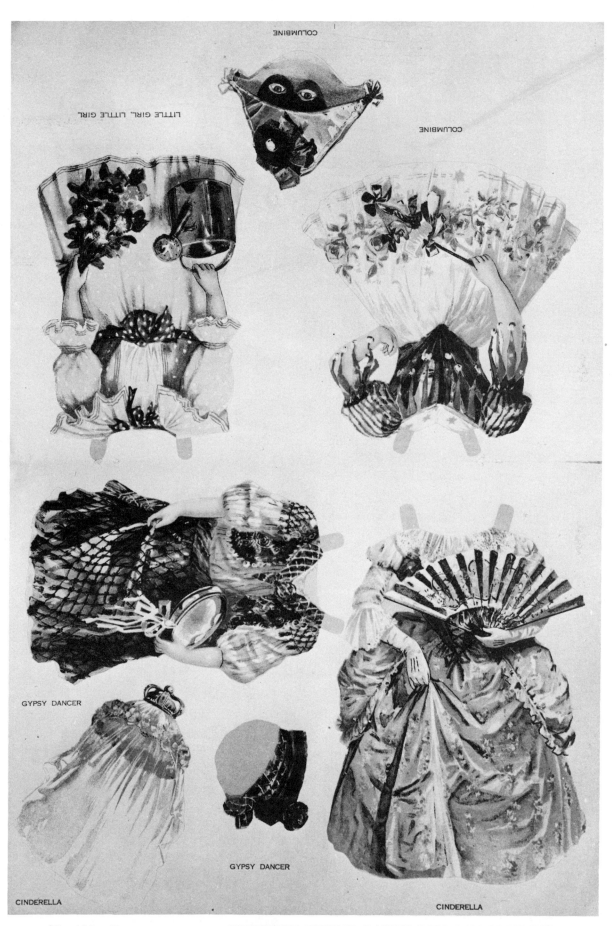

No. 190. DOUBLE PAGE FROM NURSERY RHYME PARTY DOLLS IN COSTUME.

McLoughlin Brothers' 4000 series, published at Springfield, Massachusetts, comprise dolls of poor quality, compared to the foregoing dolls. They are printed on sheets of pulp paper measuring approximately 10½ inches square, and because of this poor quality and resulting lack of value, collectorwise, we have included but two representative illustrations.

Each published set consists of four sheets, the numerical designation preceded by the letters A, B, C, and D.

Set A-4009 (Illus. No. 191) is the most interesting from point of subject, representing a tiny baby with wardrobe and nursery equipment. It has been reported that this same design was produced in a different printing, larger figures spread upon two sheets of a better grade of stock, a much more desirable one to cut out and play with. The pulp paper certainly would stand little fingering by small hands.

Set C-4011 (No. 192) consists of two unattractive dolls, a blonde and a brunette, and the placard in the hands of one costume commemorates, in a small way, the "Votes for Women" movement which reached a successful conclusion in the year 1920, approximately dating the dolls of these series.

Others in this 4000 series showed dolls in various poses, full front, profile and semi-profile. It is thought that any existing cut out dolls of any of the 4000 sets can be identified by the poorer quality pulp paper on which the unbeautiful dolls were printed. The letters "D.H." appearing in the lower left corner of the sheets presumably represent the designer.

In the 1930's McLoughlin Brothers, Inc., of Springfield, Massachusetts, published a series of three known portfolios under Patent No. 2028120, embracing "round about" dolls attractively designed by Betty Campbell, an accomplished portrait artist. All are cloth-bound, covers beautifully adapted from Miss Campbell's portrait paintings of living small girl models, as were all of her paper dolls.

The portfolios uniformly measure 10⅛ by 13⅝ inches, closed, and comprise extremely heavy board panels equipped with permanently fastened elastic bands to secure the removable contents.

These, as reported by Miss Campbell, immediately followed her first two published paper dolls, *Rosemary, the Round About Doll,* a beautiful set, copyrighted and published by her in 1932, a depression year, and *Jean and Joan and their friends,* also designed by Miss Campbell and published in 1934, "Patent Pending", by Milton Bradley Company of Springfield.

Incidentally, Miss Campbell's initial order from the Woolworth Company for 10,000 sets of *Rosemary* overwhelmed her, but with the cooperation of her lithographer, Einson-Freeman Co., Inc., L. I., N. Y., she was able to deliver.

The portfolio titled *The Fashion Book of the Round About Dolls,* dated 1936, consists of four panels, two of which contain a pair each of duplicate 10⅛ inch young girl dolls, the usual blonde and brunette, named *Diane* and *Daphne.*

A third panel carries six little girl dolls approximately six inches tall, while the fourth supplies two sets of eight round about costumes in color, labeled "For Diane and Daphne", with two sets of eight small costumes for the six inch dolls. This portfolio, housed in a sturdy slip-case, is a marvelous toy to delight the heart of any little girl.

In 1937 *The Sewing Book of the Round About Dolls* was published. Similar in format to the Fashion Book, the Sewing Book contains two pairs of differently designed 10¼ inch small girl paper dolls. One panel carries 32 patterns with detailed "Embroidery Lessons", the various stitches illustrated by enlarged drawings for the guidance of small dressmakers, patterns held in place by permanently affixed elastic bands. The fourth panel contains wool embroidery floss and crayons. Standards for the dolls, and blunt-nosed scissors, are included.

Not dated, but published under the same patent number, a three-panel portfolio of same general format appeared. Entitled *The Dress Parade of the Round Abouts,* it consists of one pair only of 10¼ inch dolls, duplicates of those in the Sewing Book. There are ten sheets of detailed patterns for round about costumes, adaptable to either cloth or paper dresses. One panel of this interesting portfolio contains cotton materials of the tiniest of designs, meticulously folded to disclose the various colors, carefully protected by cellophane wrapping. The cover design of a little girl embroidering a dress, her excited puppy trying to get into the act, is beautifully reproduced from Miss Campbell's appealing painting.

All dolls in this series of portfolios are of approximately ⅛ inch thick Tekwood, making them unusually sturdy for play, and whether or not other portfolios were published, the trio covered here represents an unusual and wonderfully interesting segment of McLoughlin Brothers' vast production of paper dolls.

Set-A —4009

PAPER DOLLS

McLOUGHLIN BRO'S, Inc.
Springfield · Massachusetts
Made in U. S. A.

No. 191. Set A-4009. Circa 1920.

219

No. 192. Set C-4011, "Votes for Women." Circa 1920.

PAPER FURNITURE

As with their earlier productions, McLoughlin Brothers included a limited amount of paper furniture with their later paper dolls.

In 1904 they published a cutout book under the title, A BOOK OF MODEL FURNITURE, containing furnishings for four rooms, parlor, dining-room, bed-room, and kitchen. (Hyphens are the publishers'.) While a complete book is unavailable, the writer has in her collection three sheets apparently either taken from this book or duplicated in loose-sheet form. Represented are the parlor, dining room and bedroom, (Illus. Nos. 193, 194 and 195), the kitchen unfortunately missing. A rich blue is the predominant color in the parlor pieces, red in the dining room, certain of the pieces carrying amusing mottoes. Note the "Music" book resting upon the blue fringed piano scarf, and, probably illegible in the illustration because of the fine print, the admonition on the alarm clock in the bedroom, "Improve each Hour". The top of the china closet carries the warning, "Haste Makes Waste", which might be interpreted, "Don't break the dishes". And of course there is a sampler counselling, "Live for Those who Love You".

Using a publication date of 1905, Katherine R. Hubbard vividly described a similar set in HOBBIES, August, 1943 issue, and, with their permission, partially quoted in THE TOY TRADER, June, 1965 issue. It is believed that the cut pieces she so interestingly covered were taken from a book, a duplicate of which is in Miss Louise Kaufman's collection. Ti-tled, THE DOLL HOUSE MODEL BOOK, published by McLoughlin Bros. in 1905, there exists a marked similarity to contents of the 1904 book, with some variations. Mrs. Hubbard describes the "five-piece 'parlor set' as red plush," coinciding with that in Miss Kaufman's 1905 book; the music book on the parlor piano becomes "Gem of Music", but she mentions the wall pocket labeled "Letters", (shown at left of the folding screen in upper right corner of No. 193). She tells of the marble-top dresser with its pitcher and basin; the commode with its "Good Morning" greeting, which does not appear on the 1904 washstand, nor do the tops appear to simulate marble. The 1905 alarm clock, however, carries the same "Improve each Hour" admonition, all of which seems to substantiate our assumption that the cut furnishings described in Mrs. Hubbard's article were taken from a DOLL HOUSE MODEL BOOK.

For the kitchen, Mrs. Hubbard tells of the spice box with its double row of tiny spice drawers, all labeled; the wooden ice chest with its appropriate motto, "No sauce like appetite"; a wooden water cooler mottoed, "Water is the best of all things"; stationary tubs proclaiming, "Water washes everything"; a dish closet topped by a sheet of speckled paper labeled "Fly Destroyer"; a coal range "Daisy", and other appurtenances of a 1905 "modern" kitchen. All of this arouses disappointment that this important room was not represented among the 1904 sheets illustrated.

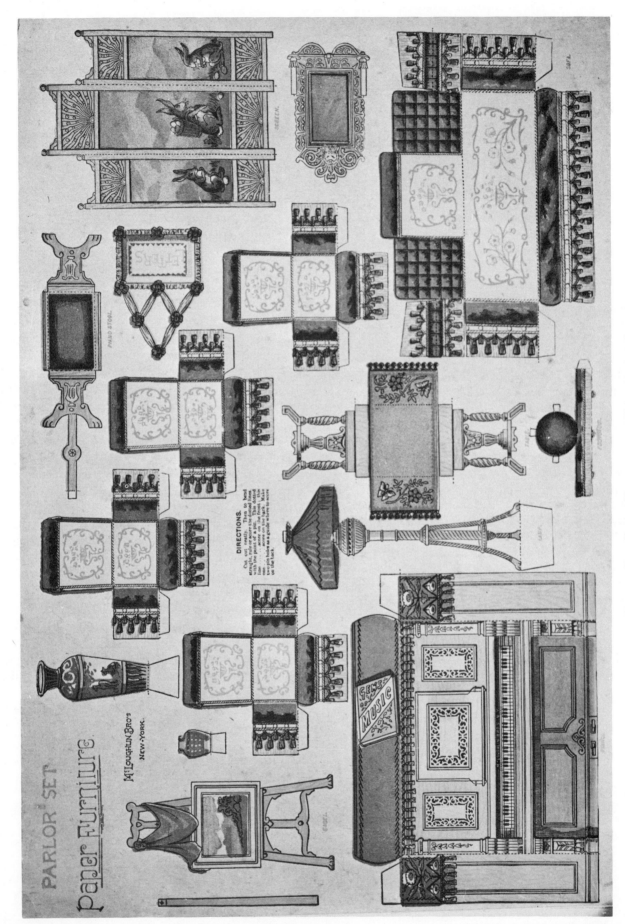

PARLOR SET

Paper Furniture

M'LOUGHLIN BRO'S
New York.

DIRECTIONS.

Cut out neatly. Then to bend straight rule or some dull edge lines with the point of a pin. The dotted line............ score on the front one...........run over the back. Make two pin holes as a guide where to score on the back.

No. 193. PARLOR SET, PAPER FURNITURE, 1904. AUTHOR'S COLLECTION.

222

DINING-ROOM SET.

Paper Furniture

McLoughlin Bros
New-York.

DIRECTIONS.

Cut out neatly. Then to bend straight, rule or write the dotted lines with the point of a pin. This dotted line.......... score on the face, this one.......... score on the back. Make ten pin holes as a guide where to score on the back.

LIVE FOR Those WHO LOVE YOU

HASTE MAKES WASTE

SIDEBOARD.

TABLE.

COUCH.

CHINA CABINET.

No. 194. DINING-ROOM SET, PAPER FURNITURE, 1904.

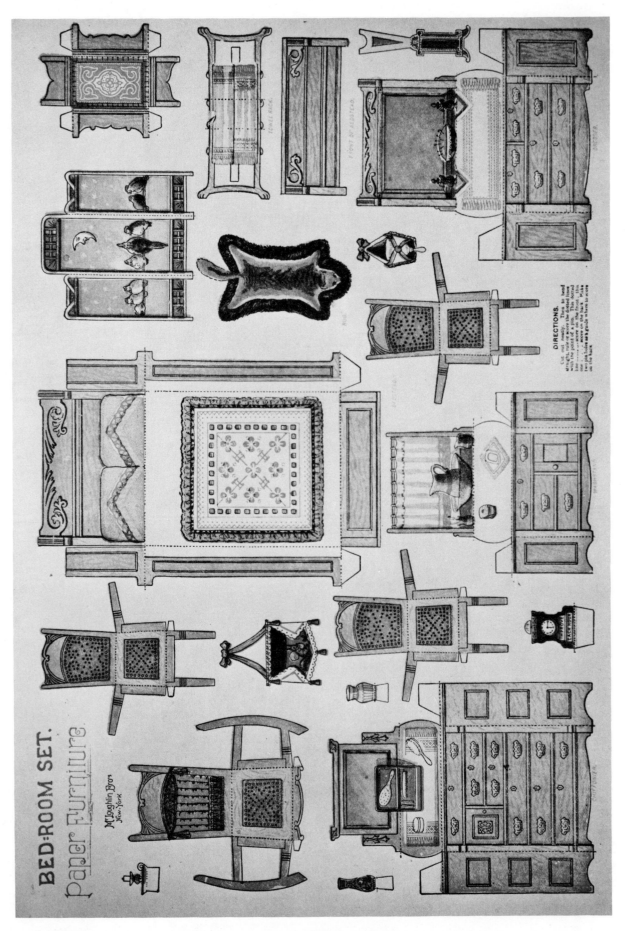

No. 195. Bed-Room Set, Paper Furniture, 1904.

In Sections A, B and C of this Chapter III, only the dolls listed in McLoughlin Brothers' early advertisements, and in their printed catalog for years 1875 and 1876 were covered, believed to incorporate the major portion of the firm's early production. It is a foregone conclusion that these listings do not include their entire output, as in the early days of any like organization there always are "trials and errors." A case in point is the Bride that obviously preceded the 1857 printing designated as Doll No. 1, yet the envelope bearing the inscription, "Improved Edition. New Dresses". Undoubtedly there were other similar instances among the early efforts of this company, a few specimens perhaps having enjoyed a limited circulation. Too, we have presented evidence that certain dolls were produced either for individual retail merchants, or that exclusive rights were purchased by them for the purpose of advertising their ladies'

wearing apparel. It is felt, however, that our coverage includes the McLoughlin dolls which proved to have sufficient merit, and to have enjoyed a degree of popularity, to warrant continued production and inclusion in a widely distributed wholesale catalog.

It is known that there also were many more late paper dolls published by McLoughlin Brothers than are covered in Section D of this third chapter. Indeed, we have a list of some 40 to 50 military sets alone, later printings included in museum and private collections. These include foreign units as well as United States Sailors, West Point Cadets, Rough Riders, Artillery, a Fife and Drum Corps, Boy Scouts, and others, too numerous to be included in this work. It would be impossible to cover in one book, the vast and scattered output of this prolific partnership, and this but emphasizes the need for further works on the fascinating hobby of paper dolls.

ARTISTIC PAPER DOLLS

Princes and Princesses Paper Dolls
Famous Queens and
Martha Washington Paper Dolls

Representing personages famous in history. With seven "Dolls" in a set, each with three costumes, making twenty-one "Dolls" in each set. The costumes and portraits are accurate, and these playthings become easy lessons in history, for home instruction or kindergartens.

A Year of Paper Dolls

With twelve designs of children, one for each month in the year.

Do not confound these with the cheap "Dolls" given away by advertisers.

Miss Tucker's water-color designs are exquisite, and have been perfectly reproduced. Each set in a beautiful box with colored covers. (The cut above roughly reproduces one of these.) **Price each set, 75 cents.** On receipt of the price these "Dolls" or any other of our publications will be sent to any address, postpaid.

Special attention is called to our **CALENDARS** the only important line designed and manufactured in America. Descriptive catalogue sent free.

FREDERICK A. STOKES CO.
27, 29 West Twenty=third Street, NEW YORK

No. 196. Advertising flyer of the Tucker Paper Dolls.

Chapter IV
Miscellaneous Paper Dolls

Among the loveliest of all paper dolls are the three sets designed and exquisitely executed in watercolor by Elizabeth S. Tucker, published by Frederick A. Stokes Co., New York, in the 1890's. Titles with brief details are given in our photographic illustration of an advertising flyer, No. 196.

Copyrighted in 1894, "A Year of Paper Dolls" consists of one seven inch doll and twelve separate costumes with front and back views, each appropriate in design to one month of the calendar year of 1895. A reproduction of the ten by eight inch box for this attractive set, together with the separate "leaf" of calendar cutouts, is given in Illustration No. 197. The fan for January had been cut from this sheet and is pasted in place.

For January the costume is a ball-gown with fan; February, postman's gray costume and a valentine; March, outdoor costume with kite; April, costume with umbrella; May, pale green costume with May basket; June, tennis outfit; July, red-white-and-blue dress with drum; August, seaside with net; September, school with slate; October, autumn with basket; November, cook's uniform with Thanksgiving menu; December, fur-trimmed outfit with a Christmas box.

Illustration No. 198 gives us the doll with costumes for January, February, March, and May, representative of the other eight not illustrated. Children's interest was stimulated by the intent of the calendar cutouts. On the first day of each month, the corresponding costume and the article from the

"leaf" pertinent to it were cut out, the calendar cutout pasted over the blank space provided on the costume, the doll then dressed for the entire month. This ritual was repeated on the first day of succeeding months throughout the year. Each month must have seemed to be a very long period of time to a child, eagerly awaiting the day when she could change the doll's dress, a delightful teaching method.

PRINCES AND PRINCESSES PAPER DOLLS

This beautiful set of seven paper dolls, copyrighted by Frederick A. Stokes Co. in 1895, was advertised, together with the other Tucker sets, in the December, 1895 issue of the LADIES' HOME JOURNAL. The dolls are not only historically interesting, but, supplied with three costumes each (front views only), they present past-century fashions for young royalty of various countries.

Pictured in the upper part of Illustration No. 199 is a paper doll representative of our own little girls of the Gay Nineties. Inscribed on the back, *An American Princess,* the 7 5/16 inch doll was included in the series as the American counterpart of small royal princesses, and she seems quite in character among them.

Infanta Marguerite of Spain appears in this same illustration, the other five in Nos. 200 through 204, identified by captions, the dates which are printed on the reverse of the dolls also given.

No. 197. Box cover design and calendar cutouts, A Year of Paper Dolls, 1894.

No. 198. Doll with January, February, March and May costumes, Year of Paper Dolls.

No. 199. Upper, An American Princess, 1895. Lower, Infanta Marguerite of Spain, 1422.

No. 200. Mary Queen of Scots, 1554. Three uncut title panels.

No. 201. Louis, Dauphin of France, 1739.

No. 202. Albert Edward, Prince of Wales, 1855.

No. 203. Crown Princess Wilhelmina of Holland, 1887. (Later, Queen Wilhelmina).

No. 204. Crown Prince Wilhelm Friedrich of Germany, 1890.

FAMOUS QUEENS AND MARTHA
WASHINGTON PAPER DOLLS

Copyrighted in 1895 by Frederick A. Stokes Co., this exquisite set of portrait paper dolls is vastly important, collectorwise. Portrait paper dolls always are eagerly sought and highly prized when acquired, and these of our own first "First Lady" and certain queens made famous in history carry special significance. Fashion-wise costume guides for each century from the fifteenth to the nineteenth with the one exception of the seventeenth, are provided.

The dolls and costumes were printed on sheets to be cut out, designations for the various occasions for which the dresses were designed printed on the backs, in each case including a court robe, a reception dress and a walking outfit. These are readily identifiable in the illustrations Nos. 205 through 209.

Of this series our own Martha Washington seems to have been published separately as a boxed set, later incorporated in the set, also boxed, titled as above.

While profiles of these royal personages have been omitted from our text in deference to reader interest, there are two perhaps less familiar incidents that we feel will be of interest.

Never a beauty, Queen Victoria nevertheless was attractive as a young woman, attested by a series of 31 photographic reproductions in the writer's possession, representing as many years in chronological or-

der, the first an 1838 likeness, the year following her succession to the throne of England. A close study of this series of likenesses reveals that the heavier features began to emerge in the year 1858, becoming more and more pronounced with the passing years, culminating in the extremely heavy features and the portly build so familiar to us today.

Not of the Elizabeth Tucker series, we are including a photographic reproduction of an engraving of Queen Victoria made especially for the LADIES' BOOK (Godey), March, 1838, (No. 210).* Note the raised waist line, apparently to offset in some measure the disproportionately short legs which, according to one contemporary writer, caused her practically to waddle when she walked. Not too intelligent, and imbued with a mean disposition, history records that her record reign of some 64 years still was marked by great achievements.

Tragic Queen Marie Antoinette of France went to the guillotine in October, 1793. At the time, Madam Tussau of the now famous wax works was in prison, and at the risk of the guillotine herself, was compelled to make a death mask of the severed head of Queen Marie, brought directly to her from the guillotine, a gruesome assignment indeed. This wax likeness, together with that of her husband, Louis XVI, who had been guillotined in January of the same year, are believed still to be displayed in the Tussau London Museum.

*Photograph by the late W. W. Howard.

233

No. 205. Martha Custis Washington, 1775.

234

No. 206. UPPER, QUEEN ISABELLA OF SPAIN, 1492. LOWER, QUEEN ELIZABETH OF ENGLAND, 1558.

No. 207. UPPER, QUEEN MARGHERITA OF ITALY, 1866. LOWER, QUEEN LOUISE OF PRUSSIA, 1797.

No. 208. Queen Marie Antoinette of France, 1789.

No. 209. QUEEN VICTORIA, 1837.

237

No. 210. Queen Victoria from engraving made for the LADIES' BOOK, 1838. Author's collection.

The name "Dennison" spelled magic for little girls who, sitting crosslegged on the floor, passed long happy hours, surrounded by a miscellany of pastel tissue and crepe papers, paper lace, gilt braids, with scissors and paste-pot at hand. Many and varied are the wardrobes, fashioned by childish fingers, finding their way into our collections; well-made or crude, all carry strong appeal, reflecting patient effort in the making.

A catalog, tentatively dated 1892, is shown in Illustration No. 211. This date derives from an announcement in a September, 1902 catalog, that the company imported crepe paper ten years earlier. The lone sample of pale yellow crepe paper included in subject catalog tends to date it as above. However, there is enclosed a price card of materials for making artificial flowers, also covered in the catalog, the card dated Sept. 1st, 1885. The quaint paper dolls illustrated surely are of this period. There also is a veritable rainbow of 126 swatches of different shades of tissue paper attached to the first page in vertical position, each shade overlapping the next by about an eighth of an inch, and numbered for convenience in ordering.

Under a sub-heading, *Doll Dresses in Tissue,* the Nursery Outfit was described as containing materials for making paper dolls and their wardrobes, the dolls available also separately. A doll eleven inches high, it is stated, has arms and legs cut in one with the body (their Illus. No. 9, our No. 212), stockings of black tissue, shoes of bronze paper with gilt dots to mark the flocking, gilt dots for the buttons. An easel rest was glued to the back of the body, the head an embossed picture. (Illus. Nos. 212 and 213).

In Illustration No. 214 we present a specimen of this construction, not authenticated as a Dennison product but with the characteristics to tentatively so designate it. The entire 10¾ body is die-cut from a lightweight, firm, linen-like board, the embossed head pasted to the background at the neck line, finished with a tissue neck-frill. The front of the nicely made and be-ruffled dress of light blue tissue paper is trimmed with small embossed rose buds, a belt of gold paper rosettes or stars, and gold paper braid. Only the shoulder of the dress and the bottom ruffles are carried to the back. The shoes are cut from black "leather" paper, pasted to the foundation on both the front and the back. An inscription handwritten in ink on the back of the body definitely dates her; "To Anna Belle Renfrew, brought by/Her Father from New Orleans' Exposition/1884".

An eight inch doll of exactly the same construction is given in Illustration No. 215, showing the one-piece die-cut body, and two of her five beautifully made front-and-back dresses. Shown with her is a smaller doll with printed bodice and black tissue stockings on a homemade body. The former doll appears to have been a commercially produced product, the latter homemade following the catalog instructions.

Quite the most elaborate of this general type of doll is the very grand lady with her colored maid (No. 216). The bodies are hand-cut from plain white cardboard in contrast to the previously described pre-cut linen-like foundations, but the costuming of each doll is perfect in all details.

The aristocratic lady is 11¼ inches tall, her body cut in one piece including the foundation of the long train; she has neither legs nor feet. The lithographed head in sepia is applied in the usual manner. Her gown is of pale tan tissue with embossed floral trim augmented by gilt paper rosettes and braid, and with full back treatment. A floral half-wreath dresses her hair.

The 11⅝ inch maid is of similar construction except she has feet and wears "patent leather" shoes. Her lithographed face is negroid in color, and her dark brown tissue dress with what originally were a white tissue apron and shirred tissue cap are appropriate to her station. Her dress also is carried to the back, the apron ties forming a bow with long, trailing ends. The heels of her shoes seem to indicate a date of 1890 or '91. While the bodies suggest homemade dolls, the perfection of the costuming appears to be commercial workmanship. If not Dennison dolls, surely they were Dennison inspired.

In a circa 1894 catalog in the collection of the late Mrs. H. B. Armstrong of Texas, addition of the swinging-limb dolls to the line of lithographed heads in five sizes, two of children, three of ballet dancers, was announced. These could be had with or without dresses. From this we deduce that the ballet dancers and certain little girl jointed dolls led the way to production of the large and varied assortment of this class of paper doll.

By 1905 the listing had grown to nine designs, including ballets in three sizes at 5, 8 and 10 cents each, and "Prima-Donnas, size 16¼ inches, three designs, 15c each".

Babies in two sizes, four designs, also were listed. These are extremely appealing. Acquired recently by

No. 211. Dennison Mfg. Co. catalog, circa 1892. Author's collection.

the manner of making these dolls and a few of the elaborate costumes.

A doll eleven inches high has the arms and legs cut in one with the body. (See illustration, Tissue Doll, No. 9.) The stockings are made of black tissue—No. 100—neatly gummed on the card-board. The shoes are of bronze paper, with gilt lines to mark the foxing

TISSUE PAPER DOLLS.

No. 7.   Size, 11 inches.
Price, 40 cents.

No. 8.   Size, 11 inches.
Price, 40 cents.

and gilt dots for the buttons.   An easel rest is gummed to the back of the body, near the shoulders.

The head is an embossed picture; but before it is attached to the body, a fine plaiting of white tissue is gummed to the under side

TISSUE PAPER DOLLS.

No. 9.   Size, 11 inches.   Price $1.25.
With two extra dresses and hat separate.

No. 212. Pages 24 and 25 of Dennison's 1892 catalog.

around the neck; the head is then attached in such a way that the top of the dress may be put under this plaiting; and each costume thus has the effect of a wide falling ruffle of white around the neck.

The dress forms for a doll of this size should be cut of stiff white paper, and be seven inches long, five inches wide at the bottom, and

TISSUE PAPER DOLLS.

No. 6   Size, 10 inches.   Price, 50 cents.

two and one-quarter inches at the waist-line, which is a little less than two inches from the top.   Do not forget to leave small tabs on each form, by which to hang the dress from the doll's shoulders. Each form should be covered with plain paper of the shade of which it is intended to make the dress.

TISSUE PAPER DOLLS.

No. 16.   Size, 6½ inches.
Price, 20 cents.

No. 17.   Size, 6½ inches.
Price, 20 cents.

No. 11.
Size, 4½ inches.
Price, 10 cents.

No. 14.   Size, 5 inches.
Price, 10 cents.

No. 12.   Size, 5 inches.
Price, 10 cents.

A dainty house-dress is of pale blue, in shade No. 36.   Cut a plain piece of tissue eight by seven and one-half inches, and fold and gum a narrow hem and three tiny tucks near one end.   Under the hem gum a fine plaiting which has been made of paper one inch wide. Shir this dress along the top, and also along a line two and one-half

No. 213. Pages 26 and 27 of Dennison's 1892 catalog.

No. 214. New Orleans 1884 Exposition Commemorative doll, 10¾ inches. Author's collection.

No. 215. Dolls with die-cut 8 inch body and a homemade body. Author's collection.

243

No. 216. Grand Dame, 11¾ inches; Maid, 11⅝ inches. Author's collection.

the writer, formerly familiar only with the type included in the later Dennison kits, 1905 babies in two designs came as a surprise, a smiling girl with a wispy curl and a sober boy. These have the same torso type bodies as the activated lady dolls, features those of real babies, heads, arms and legs flesh-tinted, attached to the bodies by eyelets, providing full freedom of movement. Possibilities for dressing these little tikes in long dresses of the period are titillating.

Taking into consideration this entire line of swinging-limb dolls, we are of the opinion that only the cardboard torsos and the metal fasteners were domestically produced, the dolls assembled and sold in New York City. Practically all of the beautifully executed heads and parts were produced by Littauer & Bauer, a Jewish firm in business in Germany from the late 1880's until into the 1930's when they were forced by Hitler to close. While no date appears on the imported parts, the torsos generally are stamped with the Dennison trademarks, some "Patented Aug. 24, 1880", others merely "Patented 1880", marks apparently carried on through from their earlier productions. It would appear therefore that the Dennison Company imported the parts, assembled dolls on their own torsos, marketing them under their own trademarks.

Illustration No. 217 includes a sheet of the Littauer & Bauer die-cut parts, the various members connected by small tabs to be broken for separating. Heads are embossed, limbs lithographed, the parts small to make six inch dolls; attention is directed to the dainty printed necklaces. The assembled doll pictured measures 5⅞ inches, and has Dennison's Aug. 24, 1880 patent mark on the back. The general construction of the doll, however, is unlike the more common type of activated dolls. Her white embossed panties are printed in one with the flesh colored torso which matches her limbs; legs are modestly encased in tights. The one-piece head and bodice is attached, together with the arms, to the torso by permanent ring type eyelets, allowing the arms and legs to swing while the head and shoulders remain rigid. These different features suggest the possibility that this particular ballet dancer may have been produced as a complete doll by Littauer & Bauer in Germany.

The same general type doll has appeared, also as a ballet dancer, measuring 9⅝ inches (No. 218). Her entire body is glossy pink, panties white and embossed; she does not wear tights, and the head and arms are attached separately to the body, the head-piece having one prong type fastener at the center shoulder line, allowing tilting as becomes a talented *ballerina*. This doll, dressed in unusual blue and

white paper lace, came as "The Flower Dancer", a title which may or may not be official. Note modeling of the hands to grasp the huge floral wreath.

Comparison of the heads shown in No. 217 with others to follow will disclose that identical ones were produced in the larger size, though without the necklaces.

In Illustration No. 219 we have two bloomer dolls wearing elaborately designed heavily embossed bodices and gloves, necessitating only a petticoat and a dress skirt to complete a costume. The dolls are approximately ten inches in height, the left one a blonde, the other a brunette. The embossed and lithographed parts are attached to the usual plain white cardboard torsos with prong type fasteners, and careful inspection will show remaining remnants of the small connecting tabs, establishing that the embossed and lithographed parts were distributed in sheets, or perhaps in connected pairs.

In more recent years these activated dolls, the same heads appearing both as slippered ladies and as ballet dancers, were sold by the late S. Burton, operating as *Burton's*, in New York City, and certain collectors have attributed to him the naming of certain ones for theatrical personages whom he considered they resembled, but actually the source of these designations is obscure. Names are penciled on the backs of the dolls in different hand-writing, and the one faint clue to the answer is the 1905 catalog listing by Dennison of "Ballet Dancers" and "Prima Donnas". How the dolls were distributed is not known, but if in some type of container, say an envelope, there is the possibility that the Dennison Company themselves assigned and printed on the container, names of various actresses. Confusion then arises when duplicate dolls appear with different name designations.

In Illustration No. 220 we have a 14⅛ inch blond doll assembled as a ballet dancer, slippers pink. Penciled on the back of her shoulders is the name, "Ada Rehan", stage-name for Ada Crehan, 1860,1916, an American actress who played juvenile parts, later starring in German and French society plays, and in Shakespearean comedies. Our source material makes no mention of ballet. An amusing incident is that in Dennison's 1905 catalog, "Ada Rehan" with ballet type arms raised in dancing position, appears as the central figure of a voluminous, fancy, circular crepe paper lamp-shade! A strange role for a "Prima Donna".

The separated parts shown in this same illustration No. 220 would make a ballet dancer of the same size, wearing black stockings and gloves. The hair is light brown, the L & B tab still attached at the shoulder. The name "Fanny Davenport" has been attributed to her, source unknown. A duplicate doll, assembled with parts wearing bloomers, slippers and gloves, is in the collection of Mrs. Charles Davis of Plant City, Florida, one of many such instances, emphasizing our assumption that these dolls were indiscriminately assembled at the Dennison plant.

Illustration No. 221 represents two fourteen inch so-called actress dolls, the blonde at the left having the name "Della Fox", an operatic actress of the 1890's, pencilled on the reverse.

The brunette doll at the right has the name "Maxine Eliot" written on the reverse, also in pencil. The same doll has appeared as "Rose Coughlin", and still another assembled with ballet parts. Confusion is rife.

In the case of Maxine Elliott (real name Gertrude Elliott), there may exist a slight clue. Born in 1871, Miss Elliott appeared in Shakespearean and other productions in the 1890's in New York and in London. In 1900 she married Sir Johnston Forbes-Robertson. A personal friend of King Edward VII, and extremely popular in England, she retired to that country shortly before the outbreak of World War I. Is there perhaps a possibility that, due to her residency and popularity in Europe, Littauer & Bauer themselves produced subject head as a portrait of the famous actress?

While these activated dolls do not enjoy the prestige of the now scarcer ones of the 1850's and 1860's, interest is increasing, and in time they too will fall into the category of the hard-to-finds. Beautifully executed, their activation imparts a certain life-like quality, and they lend themselves to glamorous costuming, both in crepe and tissue papers, and in satin and lace. Elaborately gowned and encased in a shadow-box, they can be spectacularly lovely.

Contained in our collection is a Dennison doll of a different type (No. 222). This eleven inch lithographed doll permanently wears a white slip trimmed with rose color ribbons, dark brown stockings and slippers. It will be noted that the slip is similar to that of McLoughlin Bros.' "Celie" (Pg. 207, Illus. No. 179), circa 1900. The body of the Dennison doll is in one piece of lightweight board, which includes the shoulder lines of the slip itself. The head, with a shortened shoulder piece, and the movable arms are attached by one eyelet at each shoulder, head placed on the back of the doll, arms at the front, the latter the only movable parts. Stamped on the back of the doll in blue ink is Dennison's trademark, "Patented Aug. 24, 1880", not necessarily dating the doll itself. Which one came first?

Whether or not the two-face baby heads (No. 223) were sold by Dennison Manufacturing Company is not known, but we include on the assumption that they may have been since the heads were produced in sheets bearing Littauer & Bauer mark. The separate heads, from the collection of Mrs. Robert Bowman, Ohio, measure 2-3/4 inches including the yokes, the made-up doll five inches, exclusive of the top ring added to accommodate a string hanger. It is odd that this particular doll was assembled with the crying baby holding the bottle while the laughing one lacks the staff of a baby's life. The bottle is solidly packed, probably with cotton batting, and tightly wound with tissue paper, now somewhat the worse for wear. The baby's right arm and hand are cut and brought forward to clutch the bottle. The body of this assembled doll certainly was commercially produced, seemingly pressed out of a cheap, fibre-like board. Plainly visible in the photograph and we hope in the illustration, is the board between the feet, scored, but which failed to loosen from the body when it was stamped out. The dress is a wrap-around of crepe paper. It is to be presumed that many of these L & B baby heads were mounted on homemade bodies.

At least one other pair of laughing-crying babies was produced by Littauer & Bauer. Beautifully embossed, the babies wear frilly bonnets, one with pink ribbons, one with blue. In contrast to the feet of the assembled doll shown in our illustration, this latter pair of heads are accompanied by little bare legs, feet dressed with booties and baby shoes.

The two charming young mothers pictured in Illustration No. 224, with their babies cozily tucked into carrying pillows, may or may not have been sold by the Dennison Company, but they were produced by Littauer & Bauer under their production number 30760, "Printed in Germany" appearing below the number. The figures are 5½ inches, with separate legs to enable assembling into complete dolls. These same figures came in the smaller size under No. 30762.

No photographic reproduction can do justice to the beauty of this pair. With the exception of the features, the stockings and the shoes, all parts, including even the wee hands of the babies, their bonnets and the pillows are beautifully embossed and brilliantly colored. One pillow has pink ribbons, the other blue, all flesh tones finely executed, the large, expressive eyes outstanding.

This German firm also produced other colorful, interesting cutouts, one outstanding one representing Hansel and Gretel, all extremely lovely examples of the workmanship of Littauer & Bauer, production ruthlessly terminated by order of Adolph Hitler.

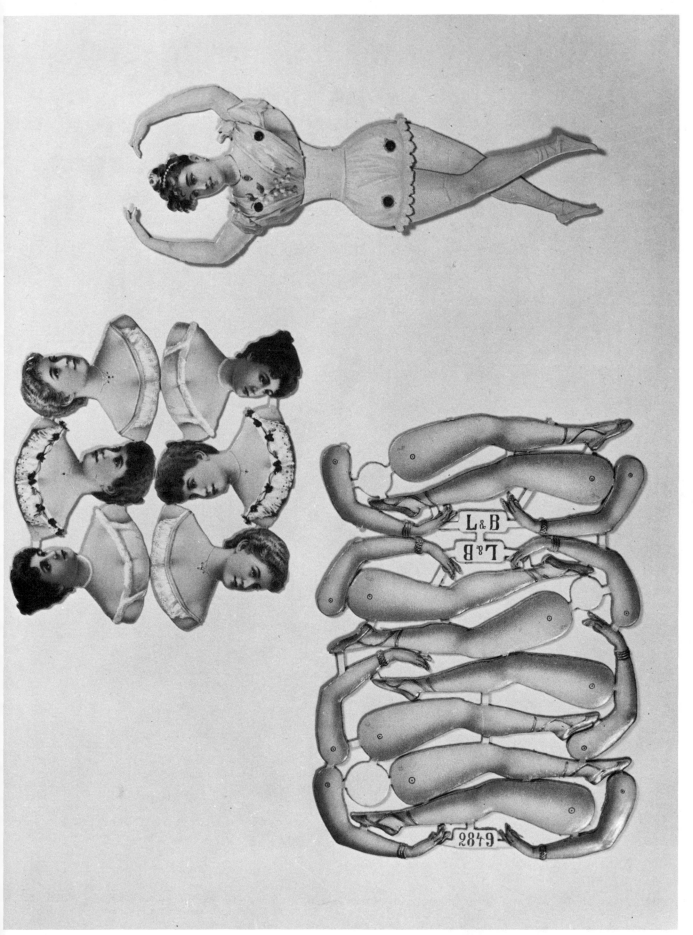

No. 217. Unbroken sheets of Littauer & Bauer heads and parts. Author's collection.

No. 218. "The Flower Dancer", 9⅝ inches. Author's collection.

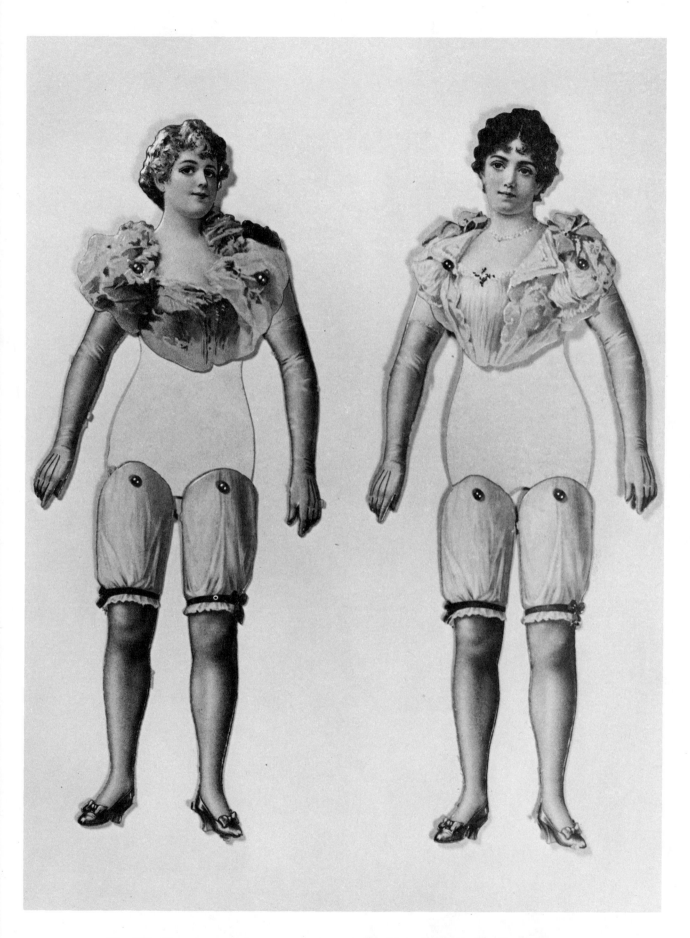

No. 219. Blond and brunette activated dolls, 10 inches. Author's collection.

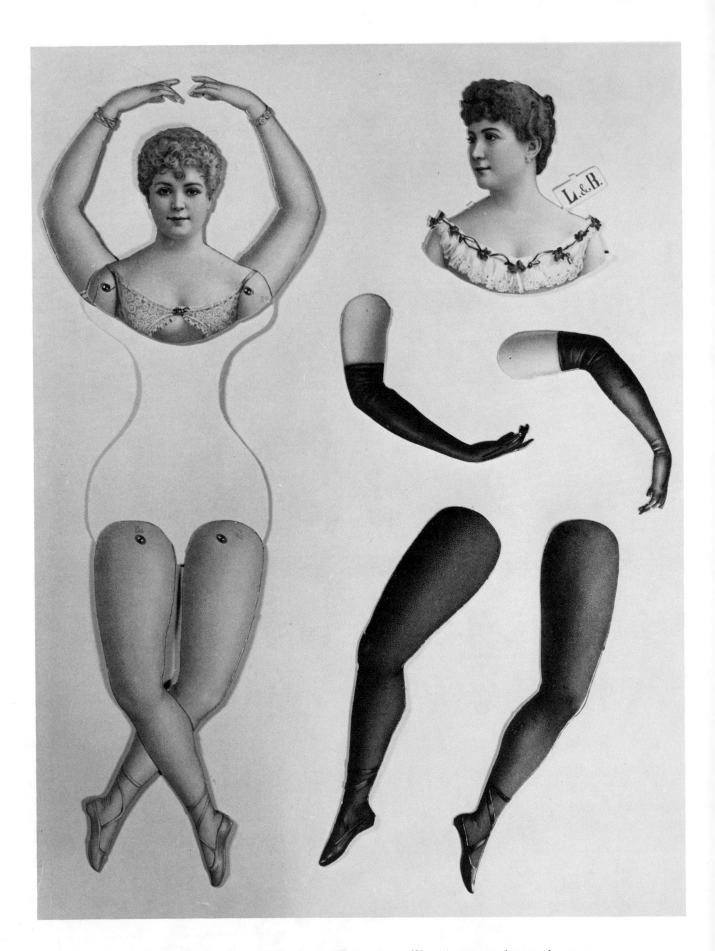

No. 220. L: Ada Rehan (?); R: Fanny Davenport (?). 14 inches. Author's collection.

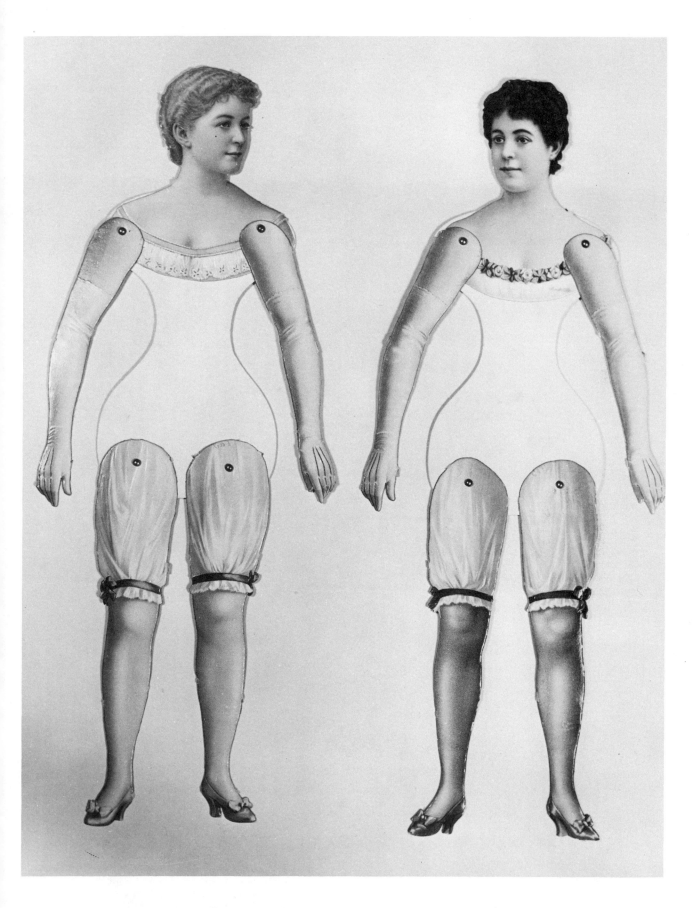

No. 221. L: Della Fox (?); R: Maxine Elliott (?). 14 inches. Author's collection.

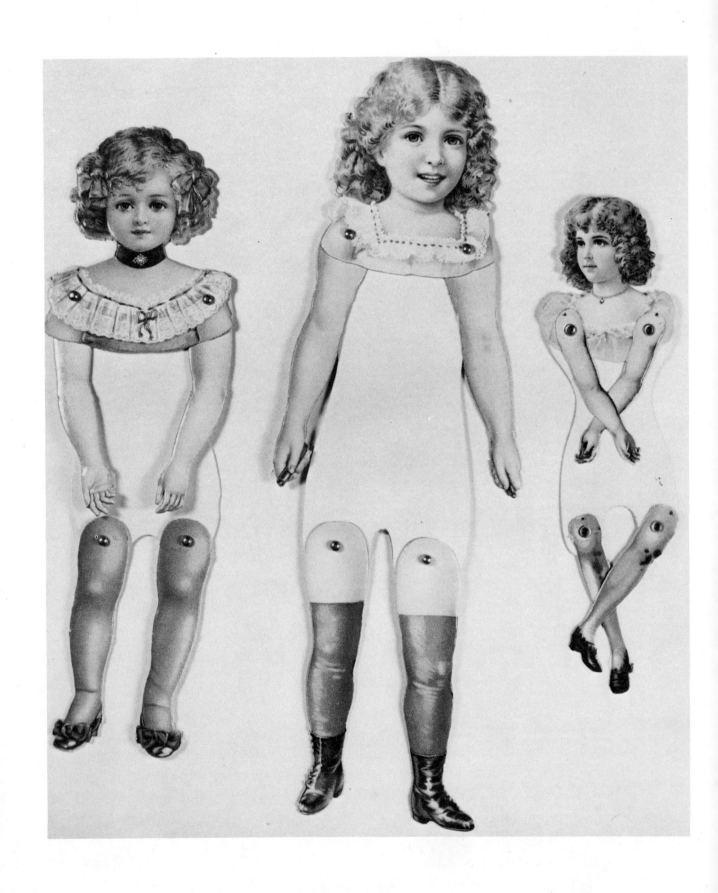

No. 221A. DENNISON ACTIVATED YOUNG GIRL DOLLS; L TO R: 8½″, 10½″, 6¾″.

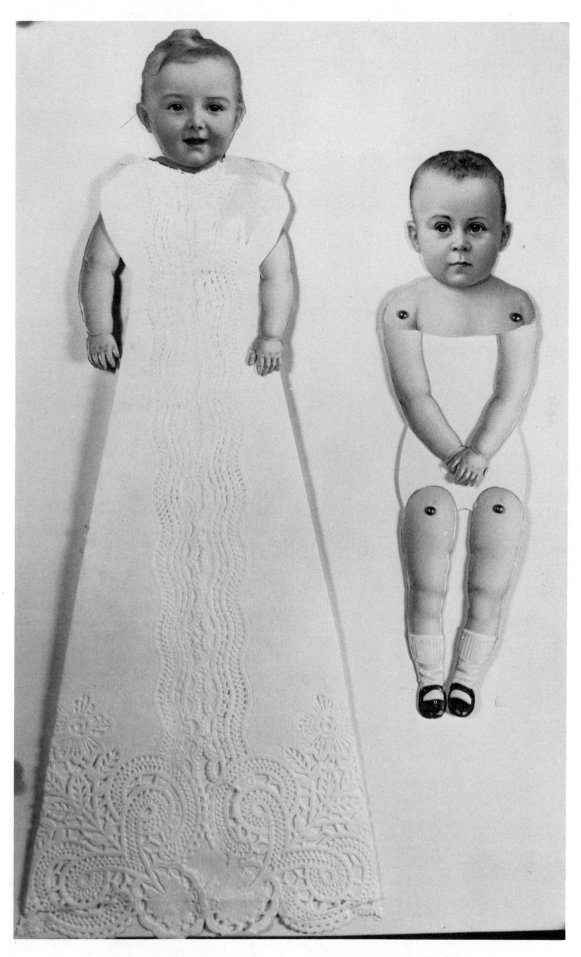

No. 221B. DENNISON ACTIVATED TWIN BABIES, APPROX. 9¼" INCHES.

No. 222. Eleven inch Dennison doll with activated arms. Author's collection.

No. 223. L & B TWO-FACED BABY. AUTHOR'S COLLECTION. SEPARATE HEADS MRS. ROBERT BOWMAN COLLECTION.

No. 224. L & B embossed cutout No. 30760. Author's collection.

The fully equipped dressmaking kits that so delighted children at the turn of the century are believed to have followed foregoing Dennison paper dolls. With patterns to assure perfect fit, it was possible to make dozens of garments and accessories from the generous supply of vari-colored papers and trimmings for the dolls accompanying each set.

The 8¼ by 14¼ inch box for Doll Outfit No. 31 bears neither date nor copyright inscription, but has characteristics to date it of the 1890's. The cover of this box is shown in Illustration No. 225, a representative assortment of the contents, including two paper dolls, in No. 226. The dolls as shown have been identified as assembled from L & B parts, but it is doubtful that they belong in this set. One at least is a replacement, since patterns and completed dresses are in two sizes, establishing that one of the dolls should be a larger one. Contents, however, appear to be original. There are 53 completed garments for practically all occasions, including two nightgowns. Some are well made, showing originality and care in the making and trimming; others are quite crude, suggesting efforts of a very young child. Other dresses and hats, cut out but not trimmed, along with many part-sheets of tissue and crepe papers in various lovely shades, still remain in the kit. There are also scraps of paper lace, simulated leather, bandings, a packet of parasol circles with wire for the "sticks", discs for making paper flowers for hat trimming, (one of these discs illustrated), together with ready-cut rufflings and bonnet strings. What more could a little girl ask?

Despite the close chronological order in the numbering, Dennison's Dolls and Dresses No. 34 is of a somewhat later date than Set No. 31, evidenced by the dolls themselves and the type and styling of the costumes. No. 34 is enclosed in an 8¼ by 11 inch decorated envelope. The sheet of "Patterns and Directions for Making Doll Costumes" lists contents as "1 (small) Doll No. 1; 1 (medium) Doll No. 2; 1 (large) Doll No. 3; 1 leaflet giving patterns of forms for dresses, coats and hats with instructions to follow; 8 pieces of white paper 6¼ x 10 from which to cut forms; 2 sheets of crepe paper printed with dresses, coats and hats".

The girl dolls pictured with the envelope in No. 227 wear pretty slips with panty lace and garter fasteners just showing, the baby a shirt and a diaper. He measures 6¼ inches, No. 2 doll 7⅝, while No. 3 is 8⅞ inches. All are nicely embossed, quality dolls, printed fronts only, as are the printed crepe paper garments needing only to be cut out and backed, no applied trimming required, an innovation.

Illustration No. 228 gives us the pattern sheet opened to disclose the directions, with patterns for Nos. 1 and 2 dolls, together with certain of the printed crepe paper costumes, cut out.

Dennison's Dolls and Dresses No. 37, not illustrated, consists of three named dolls, Eleanor 10 inches, Betty 8½, and a 7 inch boy named Bobbie. These are activated dolls printed front and back, wardrobes likewise printed double on crepe paper to be cut and backed; these fold at the shoulder line to slip over the dolls' heads. Sheets of plain crepe papers, backer papers, instruction sheet, and costume and hat patterns, plainly labeled by name for each doll, are included. As with the foregoing kits, No. 37 bears no date, but obviously followed No. 34.

These Dennison kits, complete and fascinating, provided hour upon hour of fun, and perhaps education in dressmaking, for probably thousands of little girls when they first appeared on store counters. Today they awaken nostalgic memories for many paper doll enthusiasts.

MILTON BRADLEY CO.

The above company of Springfield, Massachusetts, produced a splendid boxed dressmaking kit under the title, Bradley's Tru-Life Paper Dolls, intended to serve both as a toy and as an aid to teaching dress designing and making. The 14¾ by 11½ inch box (No. 229) originally bore the inscription, "Patent Pending", now all but defaced. The instruction pamphlet, however, bears copyright date of 1914 together with the inscription, "Trade Mark Registered", printed on the cover.

Contents of this set are amazing. There are twelve quality dolls equipped with easel standards, all in mint condition as if never played with by children, although a few crudely made tissue dresses are still in the box. An unusual feature is that the dolls in three sizes, 9½ inch, 7⅞ and two-inch toddlers, came in identical pairs, two blondes and two brunettes in each size. The girls' permanent slips have pink ribbons run through beading for the blondes, blue ribbon for the brunettes. Duplicate dolls suggest that the company thoughtfully planned the set, amply equipped to dress ten or twelve dolls, so two little girls could enjoy it together. Additional contents consist of two light-weight board sheets of background models to serve as patterns for dress foundations. As published there were eight sheets of brown paper patterns for each size doll, twenty-four in all, but in the writer's set, one pattern of each size has been cut out for actual use, these then enclosed in envelopes on the face of which are carefully pasted the costume designs and identifying pattern numbers. Four fashion plates in color plus many rolls of paper, glazed, "tweeds", flowered and striped, tissues, and others offer a challenge to little dress designers.

Illustration No. 230 shows the instruction pamphlet together with representative dolls, samples of two of the papers, a card of "buttons", background patterns, and one cutting pattern for a dress for the large dolls in No. 231.

A unique wardrobe in a slip case came as an accessory with the author's set. It consists of carefully designed pockets of paper with side and bottom folds to hold completed dresses, the several pockets assembled by prong type fasteners. The case is well filled with meticulously fashioned garments, assuredly the work of an adult. No mention was made of this case in Milton Bradley Co's. list of contents, and it is believed that it was added by the adult who obviously made the completed dresses. We reproduce it here, together with one of the colored fashion plates (No. 232), as a workable idea for similar storage of our own cherished dolls and dresses.

Under the same Tru-Life title, the Bradley Company. marketed a smaller, less pretentious boxed set containing fewer dolls and otherwise less elaborate to accommodate a more slender purse.

A still smaller set, simple and inexpensive, also found its way to store counters, a specimen now in the collection of Miss Leone Bemis of Oregon. Called *Cutie Dolls*, the 8½ by 4¾ inch box contains two 6½ inch girls wearing underwaist, petticoats and high-top shoes. There are four small rolls of paper, a fashion folder and two basic foundation patterns, a nice little kit for children denied the larger, more expensive sets.

Not forgetting boys, this versatile company published a boxed set of soldiers, date not established. Titled, *Bradley's Infantry*, the box bears the company's production number 4082, and measures 11 3/16 by 9 9/16 inches. The cover itself is a beautiful example of the printer's art, the three colorful figures printed on a gleaming gold background. The 25 figures include an officer 5⅞ inches tall, a 5 3/16 inch drummer, and 23 infantrymen each 5 11/16 inches. These figures are die-cut, beautifully lithographed, each tacked to a wooden standard which permits placing them in marching and other action formations. A small American flag came with the set, providing hours of playtime activity for boys.

In 1934, under production number 4396, Milton Bradley Co. published an attractive boxed set titled *Jean and Joan and their friends*, designed by Betty Campbell. Contents of the 16 by 12½ inch box include four lightweight board pre-cut dolls, front and back printing, two blondes alike, duplicate brunettes, arms free at the sides. Wrap-around dresses, made possible by the twelve "roundabout" patterns and attractive papers provided, completely encircle these double dolls. The box carries inscription, "Patent Pending, (c) 1934". This is a charming kit, reported to have been sold only in quality and resort shops, now out of production and on our "wanted" lists.

Another of Betty Campbell's designing, originally titled "Diane and Daphne", also came out in 1934 under a changed title, "*Peggy and Polly, Round About Paper Dolls*". The box measures approximate-ly 9½ by 13½ inches, the two appealing blond and brunette little girl dolls of Tekwood, strong and sturdy, supplied with wardrobes consisting of eight sheets of handsome roundabout costumes in color. While the dolls are plain on the reverse, the wrap-around feature of the costumes provides complete dresses. This is a delightful boxed set, the life-like child dolls reflecting Miss Campbell's portrait artistry, a complete set now in the collection of Mrs. Emma Terry of Louisiana.

The *Magic Mary* series is another of the Bradley paper dolls, published in 1950 under U. S. Pat. 2363914. Miss Campbell, who designed the originals, has offered the information that the first two of the four dolls in the series were posed by a now well known starlet, then a child of four or five years. Current sets under the Magic Mary titles, *Magic Mary, Magic Mary Ann, Magic Mary Jane,* and *Magic Mary Lou,* have been updated in styling, and while still interesting, do not have the appeal of the earlier portrait ones.

SAMUEL GABRIEL SONS & COMPANY

Among known paper dolls published by this company of New York is a series of child dolls printed in Germany and distributed by the Gabriel Company in the United States, probably in the first decade of the twentieth century. These uncut sheets carry the early Gabriel trademark, a "G" within a modified artist's palette. Four of an apparent set of six of these dolls are in the collection of Mrs. Allicia Fenton of St. Petersburg, Florida. Printed on lightweight board, each doll has three costumes with matching hats, and an easel for standing. The four dolls are named *Handsome Harold, Sweet Sallie, Pretty Pauline,* and *Jolly Jack*. We have no record of the names of the missing two.

A Gabriel doll independent of this series is *Susan,, a Rolling-Eye Doll,* 6 3/16 inches tall. A full length tab stapled at the neck line on the back of her slip can be swung back and forth, causing her eyes to move to the right and to the left, or they can be made to remain stationary. Each costume plate bears the early Gabriel trademark and the inscription, "Printed in Germany", the "something different" in paper dolls.

While it is likely that Samuel Gabriel Sons & Company issued other paper dolls in the interim, the next to come to our attention is *The Costume Party,* the first paper doll designed by Betty Campbell, an accomplished portrait artist, and a super-fine production it is in every respect. The interior of the attractive 16 by 10¼ inch box is divided into compartments to accommodate the various contents. Bearing neither date nor number, it was copyrighted by Sam'l Gabriel Sons & Company, New York, circa 1931. Included are two eight inch paper dolls, the usual blonde and brunette, posed as are all of Miss Campbell's dolls, by living models, and so beautifully reproduced by the Gabriel Company as to impart a delicate, lifelike glow to the features.

Accompanying the set is a booklet printed on pure white enamel paper, titled, *The Costume Party by Betty Campbell*. The story, however, was written by Susan S. Popper, describing the attic-treasure hunt embarked upon by two young girls who had been invited to a costume party. The twelve costumes, "discovered in dusty trunks", were reproduced by Miss Campbell's inimitable painting, with facial masks and headdresses applicable to the various garments. In addition to a gown "worn at one of Mrs. Lincoln's receptions", there are a Jenny Lind, one representing Gainsborough's "Blue Boy", another Sir Thomas Lawrence's "Pinkie", elaborate orientals and other foreigns, each on a separate sheet to be cut out. These are illustrated in the story booklet by figures wearing the costumes complete with masks. Bases allow the dolls to stand. The Gabriel Company magnificently reproduced Miss Campbell's superb paintings, resulting in one of the most exquisite sets of commercial paper dolls to come to our attention.

Outstanding among this company's productions is the later *Dolls with Williamsburg Dress*, (No. 233). Copyrighted in 1940, production No. D-139, this set represents a family of colonial days. The 16½ by 11⅜ inch box bears the above title with the added inscription, "Made under the Supervision of Williamsburg Restoration, Incorporated, Williamsburg, Virginia".

The family consists of Father, Mother, twelve-year-old Belinda, and ten-year-old Philip, together with two colored servants, Sukey the cook, and Moses the footman-butler. The dolls are cut from sturdy board, and range in size from approximately ten inches to 7 11/16 for Philip and 7⅝ inches for Belinda. Coloring is lovely, and the base of each doll is slit for inserting into a separate slotted standard, permitting the dolls to stand firmly.

Mother and Belinda each have four bouffant gowns, Father and Philip two suits each, while the servants have but one extra outfit each, a total of fourteen costumes in 1760 styling. Betty Campbell has generously supplied interesting details in connection with the designing of this handsome set of paper dolls.

As is generally known, Colonial Williamsburg was restored by Mr. John D. Rockefeller, Jr., and following an interview at the New York office of the Rockefeller Foundation, Miss Campbell went to Williamsburg to do the necessary research. While there she was domiciled in Raleigh Tavern, the official guest house of her host, The Restoration of Colonial Williamsburg.

At least two of the dolls fall into the portrait category. *Moses,* the paper doll footman-butler, is a likeness of Fleming, the butler at the Governor's Palace, (the Palace shown in the background of the box cover design), while the second cook at the Pal-

ace modeled for *Sukey.* Miss Campbell added that all costumes are authentic, passed on by a special Williamsburg Committee.

As part of the set there is a little booklet written by Mary Selby, titled *A Williamsburg Family, a Day in Williamsburg in the 18th Century.* The paper dolls seem to come to life in this little story, slanted to children, but of historical interest to adults.

Now operating as Gabriel Industries, Inc., trademark changed to a flying angel with trumpet enclosed, with the name "Gabriel", within a scalloped oval, the company has added materially to the volume of paper dolls and games which have long been a source of fun for children.

OLDE DEERFIELD DOLLS

In 1919 Mrs. Matilda Hyde of Deerfield, Massachusetts, now deceased, conceived the idea of commemorating, in paper dolls, the 1704 Indian massacre of the town of Deerfield. The resultant set, "Little Captives of 1704", now is a rarity.

On the last night of February, 1704, the horrifying Indian war-cry routed the inhabitants of Deerfield from sleep, and the raid which followed left the town in ruins, the populace either dead or captive. When the Indians departed, they cruelly carried away with them five terrified children, among them the son and daughter of Parson Williams, and tiny Abigail Nims, a mere toddler.

Paper dolls representing these pathetic little captives were lithographed in color by a six-stone process, each doll with costumes printed on a separate sheet; all have back views, the period costumes having one or more connecting points for folding front to back.

A sixth sheet represents Arosen the Mohawk, one of the Indian youths waiting when the raiding party returned with their captives. He was immediately attracted to the parson's daughter, Eunice Williams, and from the first showed her many special favors. As his story is told, he married Eunice when she reached the age of sixteen.

The handsome folder housing these six sheets of light-weight board measuring 22¾ by 10⅜ inches, too long and too narrow for photographing. Lithographed in soft tints, the front represents the Olde Deerfield Parsonage to be cut out and set up according to detailed printed marginal instructions. Dotted lines at each end indicate 3½ inch fold-back sections to give side views of the parsonage, and to permit it to stand.

The back cover is a gayly colored Indian wigwam with the same turn-back ends to provide side views, and with printed marginal instructions. For closing, a center flap on the back cover of the folder carries to the front to be slipped into a matching slot.

A prized accessory is a three by four inch double slip case containing six tiny booklets, covers in color, each titled with the name of the child whose history it contains, one being the story of Aroson the Mohawk. These interesting little stories were written by the late Mrs. Hyde, and, like the paper dolls, were copyrighted in 1919 by Olde Deerfield Doll House.

Fortunate indeed are possessors of this unusual and lovely historic paper doll set, now difficult to obtain.

COLONIAL WILLIAMSBURG PAPER DOLLS

Two delightful paper dolls were designed, copyrighted in 1939 and published by Williamburg Restoration, Incorporated. Distributed in envelopes, these represent a *Gentleman in 18th Century Dress as worn in Williamsburg in Colonial Days,* and a *Lady in 18th Century Dress,* each with separate period costumes, and a separate sheet containing *The Story of Eighteenth Century Costumes.* The Lady has seven bouffant gowns and a petticoat with hoops on which the torso is to be pasted to complete the doll. The Gentleman has six costumes of the knee-length pant and coat style, a dress wig, a tricorn hat, and riding boots. These dolls are most attractive, in nice coloring, inexpensive, and we are advised by the Williamsburg organization that they are continuously available on mail order from Craft House, Williamsburg, Virginia.

M. C. & K.

Identity of the company using the above initials has not been determined, the one known example of their paper doll output a "Set of 7 Dolls", published in 1895. The family members are Grandfather, 9⅜ inches; Grandmother 9¼; Father 9⅜; Mother 9 5/16; Brother 7⅛; Sister 6⅞, and Baby Sister 5¼ inches, (No. 234).

These head-and-shoulder dolls are lithographed in fine colorings appropriate to each member of the family on good quality light-weight board. Costumes are cut double to permit standing, backs plain, necks cut out for slipping over the dolls' heads; arms draw forward to overlap the garments. It would be helpful if this company could be identified, and to learn whether or not they published other paper dolls.

GODEY'S LADY'S BOOK

While we have shown that commercial paper dolls were published in our country as early as 1854, it was left to Mr. Louis Godey to pioneer the magazine doll. In the November, 1859 issue of GODEY'S LADY'S BOOK, four little girls and two boy paper dolls occupy one page, printed in black and white. A separate page provides a costume for each doll, these, like the famous Godey fashion prints, beautifully hand-tinted in attractive colors. The dolls measure from 3⅝ inches for the boy at the extreme left in No. 235, to 2⅝ for the toddler. Little gems of paper dolls that they are, they faithfully reflect fashions for children some 107 years ago.

FRANK LESLIE'S LADY'S MAGAZINE

The next magazine paper doll of which we have knowledge appeared in FRANK LESLIE'S LADY'S MAGAZINE in 1866. An inscription on an uncut sheet supplies the information, "Chromolithographed expressly for FRANK LESLIE'S LADY'S MAGAZINE, printed by The Major and Knapp Engraving, Manufacturing and Lithographing Company, 449 Broadway, New York, N. Y., 1866". This 4¼ inch little lady appears in Illustration No. 236, with an uncut sheet showing three of her six lovely dresses and several changes of hairdress, all in front and back printing, vivid coloring, a charming paper doll.

BOSTON SUNDAY HERALD

Supplemental to its Sunday issue of March 24, 1895, the BOSTON HERALD published a 10½ inch blond lady paper doll. Printed on a plate of medium weight white cardboard, she wears a corset and a four-ruffle petticoat. On June 16th of the same year a brunette doll of same pose and proportions was published. 38 known costume plates were distributed, one each Sunday, costumes interchangeable between the two dolls.

As a service to her subscribers, Elizabeth Andrews Fisher, publisher of THE TOY TRADER, reproduced the entire series, not in consecutive issues however; the first appeared in April, 1959, showing the blond doll with two costumes. In the accompanying article this writer specifically brought out that while all but one of the costumes had been authenticated by uncut plates, the one shown at right of the doll in the illustration was *presumed* but not definitely known to be the No. 1 costume plate issued on March 31, 1895. At the time this article was published, no uncut plate of the No. 1 outfit had come to light. It now is gratifying to be able to have reproduced in Illustration No. 237, an uncut plate of the No. 1 costume, dated, and labeled "Ladies Toilette". This verifies our former identification by process of elimination.

This series of fashion figures was printed by G. N. Buck & Co., N.Y., Lith. The late Mrs. Armstrong of Texas had in her possession a plate bearing only the lithographer's name, evidencing that blank plates were sold to various newspapers, each adding its own imprint. Newspapers other than the BOSTON SUNDAY HERALD known to have distributed these same dolls and costumes under their own assigned titles, as well as certain additional costume plates not appearing in the HERALD series, were the ST. LOUIS REPUBLIC, THE CHICAGO RECORD, THE WASHINGTON STAR, NEW YORK MERCURY, THE PHILADELPHIA PRESS, SAN FRANCISCO CHRONICLE, and there may have been others.

This series is attractive and helpful as a fashion guide of the Gay Nineties, costumes running the gamut from tea-gowns to sports wear, afternoon, reception, evening, luncheon gowns, riding habits, and others.

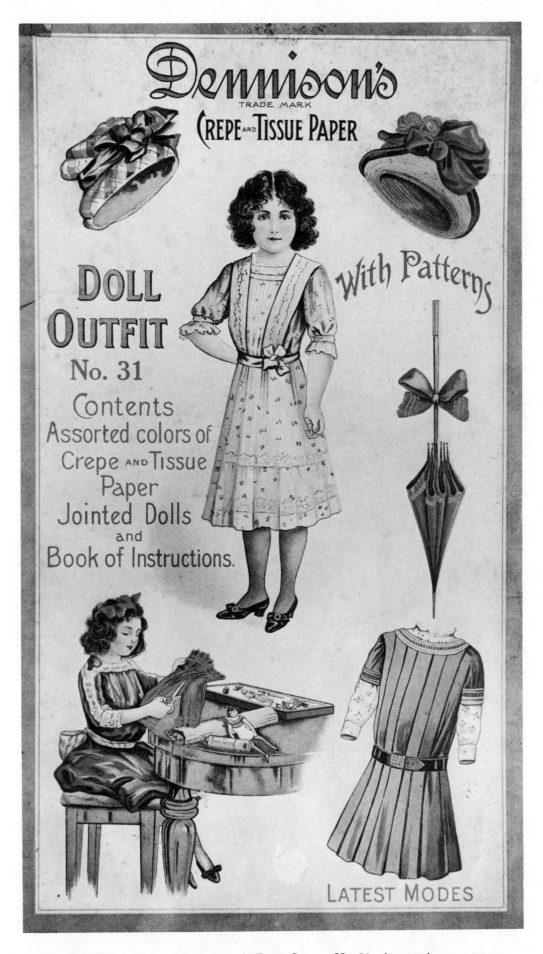

No. 225. Box cover for Dennison's Doll Outfit No. 31. Author's collection.

NO. 227. ENVELOPE AND PARTIAL CONTENTS, DENNISON'S DOLLS AND DRESSES NO. 34. AUTHOR'S COLLECTION.

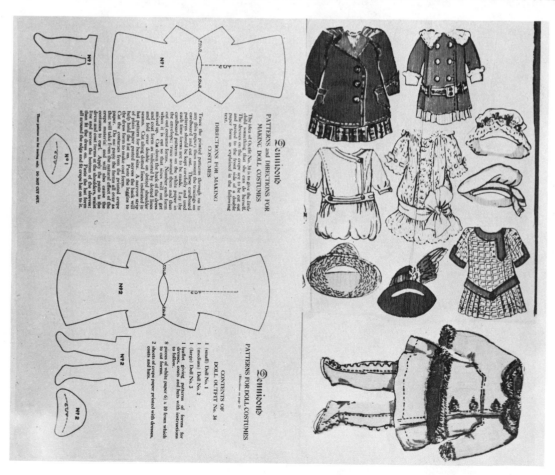

NO. 228. PARTIAL CONTENTS DENNISON'S DOLLS AND DRESSES NO. 34.

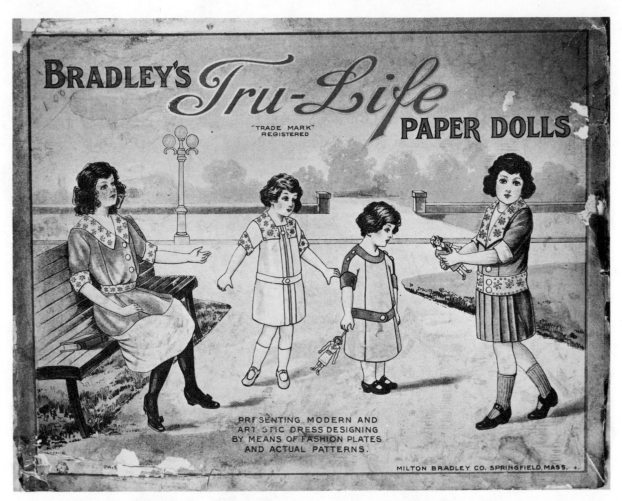

NO. 229. BRADLEY'S TRU-LIFE PAPER DOLL BOX. AUTHOR'S COLLECTION.

NO. 230. TRU-LIFE INSTRUCTION PAMPHLET AND SPECIMEN DOLLS.

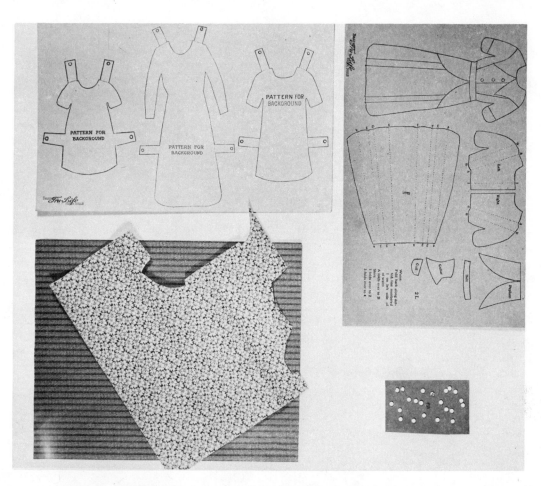

No. 231. PARTIAL CONTENTS, BRADLEY'S TRU-LIFE KIT.

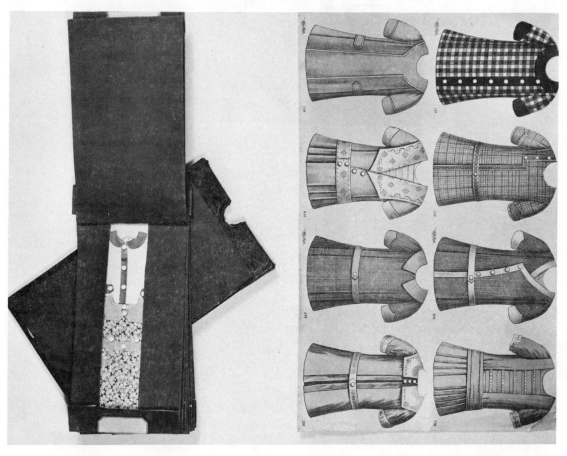

No. 232. COLORED FASHION PLATE AND WARDROBE CASE, BRADLEY'S TRU-LIFE KIT.

No. 233. Dolls with Williamsburg Dress, box and dolls. Author's collection.

No. 234. M. C. & K's. Family of 7 dolls. Author's collection.

No. 235. The Godey Children, November, 1859. Author's collection.

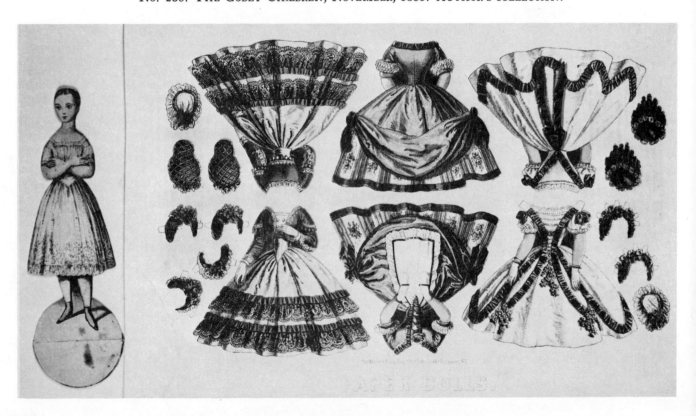

No. 236. 1866 doll from FRANK LESLIE'S LADY'S MAGAZINE. Author's collection.

THE SUNDAY HERALD.

MARCH.31.1895.   WEEKLY COLORED COSTUME PLATE,   NO. 1.

To fit Hat on Figure
cut on dotted Line.

Cut carefully around dress and tabs and secure to Fashion Figure
by folding the tabs behind back.

LADIES' TOILETTE.

A duplicate of the "Model Figure" will be mailed to subscribers of the Boston Sunday Herald
upon receipt of four cents (two 2 cent stamps) to cover postage and mailing expenses.

No. 237. SUPPLEMENT TO THE BOSTON SUNDAY HERALD, Costume Plate No. 1.

No. 238.   FEMALE PANTIN, CIRCA 18TH CENTURY.

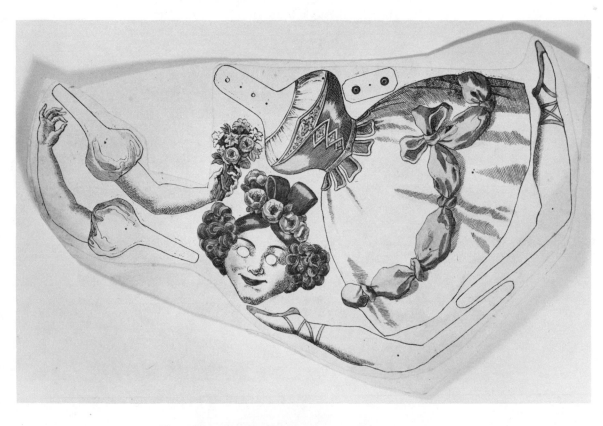

No. 239.   BALLET PANTIN, CIRCA 18TH CENTURY.

270

Chapter V
Foreign Paper Dolls

Pantins of the seventeenth and eighteenth centuries, playthings of adults including royalty, marked the beginning of paper doll production in Europe. Named for the area in which they originated, these activated figures, painted on thin paper by renowned artists in space-saving form, may have been the inspiration for our later "jointed" paper dolls. The sheets of pantins were pasted over cardboard for strength, cut out, and assembled at the joints by a series of threads; by manipulating a coordinating thread at the back, the figures could be made to dance and to assume all manner of grotesque positions.

Early specimens now are extremely scarce, and we are gratified to have the privilege of including photographic representations of three of these.

In Illustration No. 238 is shown a rare female specimen with elaborate costume. Printed in soft tones on a 12 by 14¾ inch sheet of very thin paper, it is said to have been executed as a companion to the Louis XV pantin illustrated on Pg. 42, DOLLS, by Esther Singleton, and in other books. Assembled, subject figure would be approximately twelve inches tall.

A second original specimen is the ballet dancer reproduced in Illustration No. 239. An unusual feature is that the separate eyes, shown just above the dress, can be made to move in addition to her activated dancing.

Still another splendid example of these meticulously designed and painted pantins is the violinist shown in No. 240. Said to date from the early nineteenth century, when cut out and properly assembled, he can be so manipulated as to draw the bow over the violin strings, nodding his head to the "music".

All of these assemble into very large figures, and fortunate indeed are the owners of these extremely rare, centuries-old activated paper dolls.

Popular also are the Imagerie D' Epinal sheets of paper dolls, and collectors who count one or more in their collections will be interested to learn of their origin.

Through United Press International we are able to include a history of the Pellerin family, together with photographic reproductions of the present M. Pellerin. In Illustration No. 241 he is shown operating the press first used in 1803, while in No. 242 he is pictured applying colors to a printed sheet through a stencil by use of a soft brush, the same basic technique as was employed by his forefathers. Separate stencils are cut to expose the different portions of the design, depending upon the number of colors necessary.

While comic strips did not originate at Epinal, a little French town in Western France at the foot of the Vosges Mountains, it was the home of the colored picture, and where stories in strip form with colored illustrations originated. It was there too that the first colored playing-cards were produced.

Picture-makers in the town, all belonging to the same family even to this day, began to ply their trade back in the seventeenth century, when they made religious pictures in quantity to illustrate prayer books and to decorate homes. The religious pictures appealed to the rural and working people, but after the French Revolution in 1792 the mood changed, and the Brothers Pellerin, who had by this time established a reputation in that line, started turning out illustrated stories—fairy tales, legends, fables, and stories of great battles, which appealed to grown-ups as well as children.

The first "Images D' Epinal" as they were known, and still are, were primitives. Only four colors were used, blue, brown, red, and yellow. Faces, legs and arms remained dead white until flesh pink was introduced about the middle of the eighteenth century.

Tools were equally primitive. Wooden blocks were engraved by hand, inked, covered with a sheet of paper, colors then applied as previously described...

The above information was released in May, 1951, photographs by Rene Henry.

Early Pellerin sheets are choice collector treasures today; two of a later printing, on heavier stock than the earlier ones, are illustrated in Nos. 243 and 244.

Poupees A Habiller/La Mode en France a toutes les epoques (No. 243) measures 11-11/16 by 15-7/8 inches. This includes a paper doll with seven costumes, six headdresses, all numbered for properly matching fronts to backs, as well as the correct hat or bonnet for each costume. Inset printing identifies the various costumes as—No. 1: X* siecle. No. 2: Renaissance. No. 3: Page Francois I.er. No. 4: Epoque de Louis XIV. No. 5: Republique. No. 6: 1830. No. 7: 1875. No hat or bonnet is included for dress No. 3, but do note the towering head-piece for No. 5.

Pellerin & Cie's sheet No. 117, (No. 244), is entitled "Grandes Constructions/Transformations/Faciles et Amusantes/*Mademoiselle Chouchou*/essays des Costumes pour le Carnival/Masques & Travestissements". The sheet is brilliantly colored, the costume emporium spread across the upper part, a display of carnival costumes and masques in the lower portion. The sheet measures 19-3/8 by 15-3/8 inches, and, with its unusual subject, is exceptionally inter-

271

esting. A sales woman is seen in consultation with a prospective customer, comfortably ensconced in an easy chair, while a fitter is engaged with a second customer whose features are blanked out for application of one of the masques. Were it not for the position of the feet, one would suppose this to be a rear view. Directions are printed in French, and should be decipherable for translation.

While none of these sheets is dated, inclusion of a dress and bonnet for 1875 in Illustration No. 243 evidences a printing of that year or later, but all of the designs are authentic styling for periods represented.

Over a span of more than two centuries, the versatile Pellerin family have produced picture-stories in a wide range of subjects. Known pantins include Columbine, Arlequin, Pierrette, and one combining Polichinelle with Arlequin. Also, Pierrot and Columbine appear on a single sheet, and there are many others. One elegantly designed and fabulously colored set consists of three sheets comprising a fascinating Salon. This is illustrated in HOMES FOR PAPER DOLLS AND KINDRED PAPER TOYS, Pgs. 32 and 33.

Two theatre sheets Nos. 1544 and 1545, in the author's collection, bear the title, *Nouveau Theatre Portatif A Rainures*. Perhaps Monaco? This collection includes many other Pellerin sheets, both the richly colored thin early specimens, and the reprints on heavier stock, and assuredly there are many additional designs extant. Contribution of the Pellerin family to our collections is indeed impressive.

Taglioni (No. 245) supposedly needs no introduction to paper doll collectors. The lovely set illustrated here is believed to be complete except for headdresses, of which there should be one for each costume. The dark "splotch" in the lower part of the illustration is the slotted wooden standard, allowing Taglioni to assume a realistic ballet pose. The exquisite box measures 4½ by 6-5/8 inches, the doll 5¼ inches. The six costumes, representing various roles in the dancer's career, are brilliantly colored, topped with a glistening egg-white coating.

Marie Taglioni, born in 1804, lived to be 80 years of age. Her father trained her for her career, and the training was strenuous and strict, however, justified by Taglioni's instant success in 1822 in a ballet which her father had composed especially for the occasion. Taglioni was not a beauty, but her great talent earned for her the title, "First Dancer of Paris". She married in 1832, retired in 1847. Following dissipation of the great fortune accumulated during her fabulous career, she supported herself in London as a teacher of dancing and deportment. In an article in the January 1952 issue of THE TOY TRADER, the late Darcy identified Taglioni as "Princess Victoria's" dancing teacher. By 1847, the year of Taglioni's retirement, "Princess" Victoria would have been queen for some ten years. It seems improbable that Taglioni would have interjected teaching into her dancing career, always unless perhaps it was deemed to be expedient to bow to the desires (or command ?) of royalty. Or perhaps *Queen* Victoria was the student.

In 1957 Herbert H. Hosmer of South Lancaster, Massachusetts, issued a reprint, ready for painting, of the larger set of Taglioni. This includes the six headdresses in addition to the costumes, together with a brochure on the life of Taglioni, and reproductions of four portrait prints of the famous *ballerina*. It is believed that these paper doll reprints are still available, a nice replica set for collectors not so fortunate as to possess an original.

The beautiful French paper toy titled *L'interieur de la poupee* (No. 246), first illustrated in May, 1957 issue of THE SPINNING WHEEL, is contained in a box measuring 13-7/8 by 12¼ inches, an inscription in the lower right hand corner reading, "Nouveau jeu d'occupation pour/les fillettes sages". The unidentified trademark is a monogram, either "J S" or "S J", encircled by two tiny rings topped by a crown, with "i.B." in extremely small letters below the double circle. This appears at center of the bottom of the box lid, "Depose" at extreme left.

With the exception of the arm chairs which are equipped with fold-back standards, the collapsible table with its two separate tops and the piano stool, all furnishings are printed on the brilliantly colored backdrop. Walls are papered in a grayish-green stripe pattern, the formal drapes and certain other parts highlighted by the egg-white treatment, imparting a gleaming sheen to the whole. Glimpsed between the drapes are a writing room and a dining room, the perspective adding a touch of realism.

With the table assembled, the separate cloth with its printed flatware laid, the tiny blue and white separate plates in place, a 26-1/8 by 11¾ inch dining room is provided. This then may be transformed into a beautifully appointed living room by substituting for the dinner cloth, the dark grained "wooden" table top shown propped against the box in No. 246. The sitting dolls are tabbed for occupancy of the slotted chairs and divan.

As originally distributed, the dolls and accessories, including the little blue plates, and foods to provide a dinner, were linked in one, or possibly two sheets by tabs to be broken apart for separation. These are visible in the separated set illustrated in No. 247.

With the exception of the studious girl, comfortably seated upon the divan, all dolls are in two positions, sitting and standing, outdoor costumes included for the latter. It is to be presumed that the one missing standing doll, and outdoor garments for the pianist (the standing figure at extreme left in the illustration), were originally included. The standing figures range in height from 3¼ inches for the little boy, 4-11/16 for the girls, to Father's and Mother's 6-1/8 inches, the train of Mother's dress excluded.

Inclusion in the box cover design of an assembled kitchen and a bedroom with this combination living-dining room, suggests probable distribution of a series of these fascinating toys, making possible the arranging of a splendid home for a fortunate paper doll family.

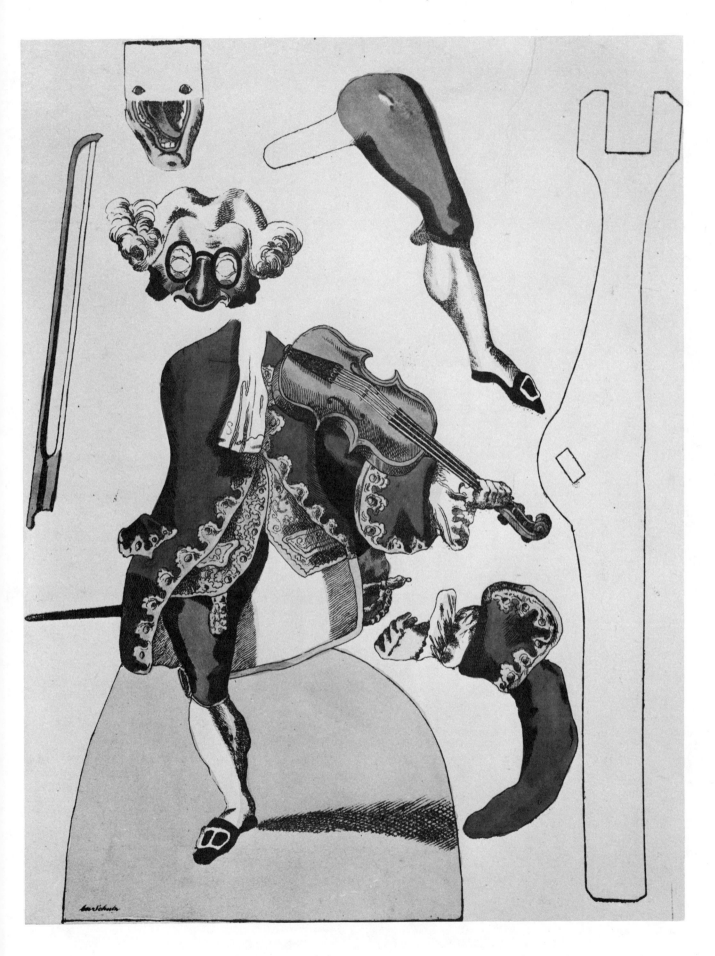

No. 240. VIOLINIST PANTIN, EARLY 19TH CENTURY.

273

No. 241.   M. Emile Pellerin operating 1803 press.

No. 242. M. EMILE PELLERIN APPLYING COLORS TO A PRINTED SHEET.

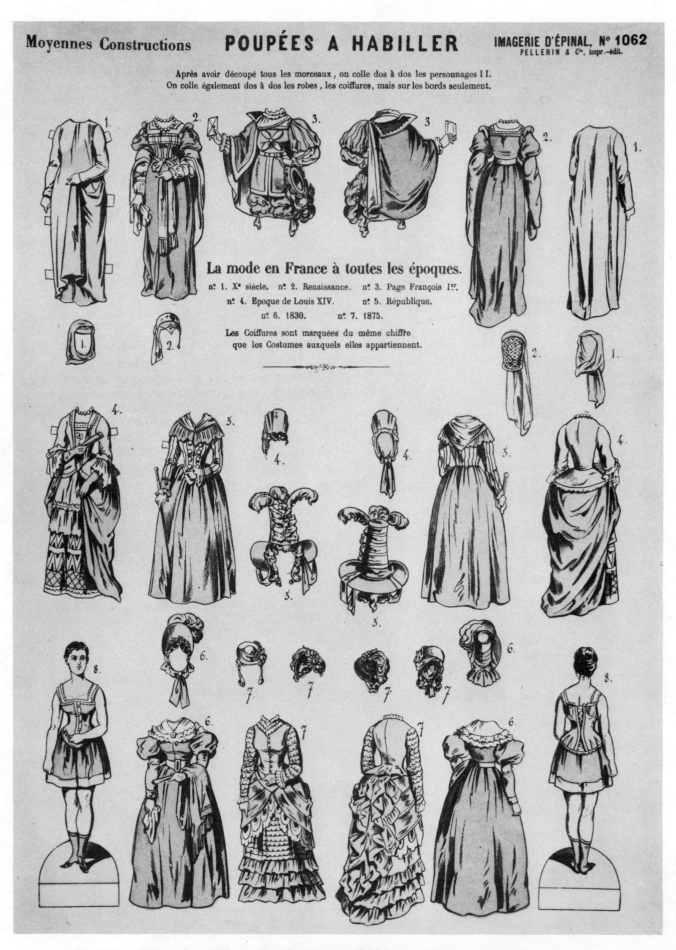

Après avoir découpé tous les morceaux, on colle dos à dos les personnages I I.
On colle également dos à dos les robes, les coiffures, mais sur les bords seulement.

La mode en France à toutes les époques.

n°. 1. X° siècle.   n°. 2. Renaissance.   n°. 3. Page François I°ʳ.

n°. 4. Epoque de Louis XIV.   n°. 5. République.

n°. 6. 1830.   n°. 7. 1875.

Les Coiffures sont marquées du même chiffre
que les Costumes auxquels elles appartiennent.

No. 243.   PELLERIN PAPER DOLL SHEET, POUPÉES A HABILLER. ALLICIA FENTON COLLECTION.

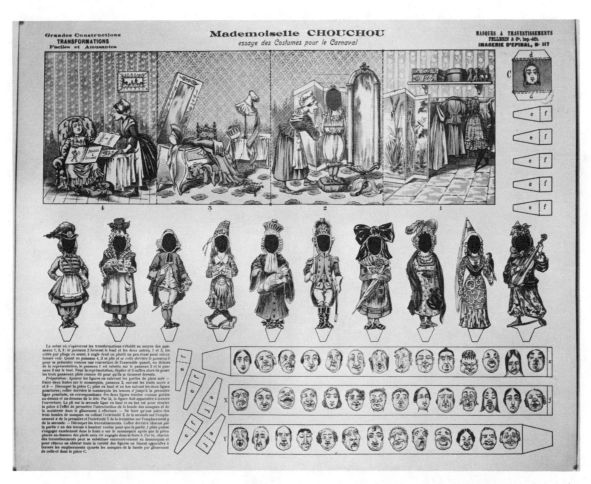

No. 244.   Pellerin Sheet No. 117, Mademoiselle Chouchou.   Author's collection.

No. 245.   Taglioni, First Dancer of Paris. 5½ inches. ca. 1830.

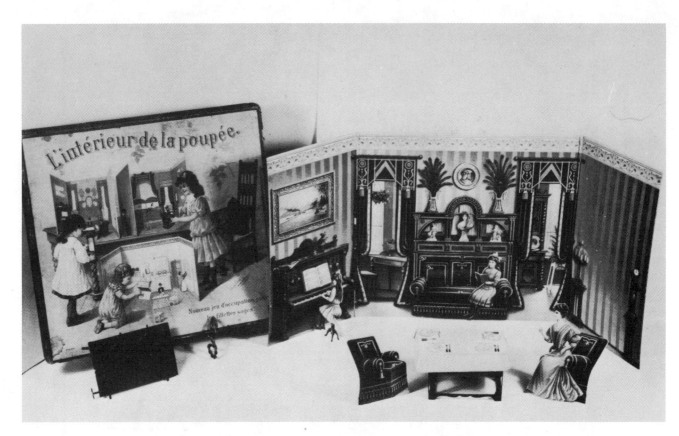

NO. 246. L'INTERIEUR DE LA POUPEE. AUTHOR'S COLLECTION.

NO. 247. DOLLS AND APPURTENANCES FOR L'INTERIEUR DE LA POUPEE.

GERMAN PRODUCTIONS

The circa 1830 doll pictured in Illustration No. 248 measures 9-3/4 inches "as is", her feet casualties of the passing years. Produced in Germany, the eight wondrous costumes show much fine detail in the designing, and are exquisitely tinted in subdued color tones. Four of these are reproduced with the doll, rear views of the costumes pictured directly below the corresponding fronts. The remaining four costumes, photographed in the same manner, are given in No. 249.

This doll was received with no identification, but when Miss Lillian Faffer visited several museums in Germany in 1960, she kindly carried with her, several photographs of the author's foreign dolls to attempt to establish origin and identification where lacking. In a museum in Munich she saw what she firmly believes to be a duplicate of this set, though comparison was somewhat difficult as it was displayed under glass. Titled *Die Aussteur der Puppe*, (The Trousseau for the Doll), there were the doll, the eight costumes, and the slip-case in which the set was distributed when published in Wien der Kunshandling der H. F. Muller am Kohlmarkt under number 1149. A very beautiful, rare paper doll.

Again substantiating the two-doll feature of many foreign produced boxed sets, a young mother in under-clothing is reproduced in No. 250, the three costumes and one doll establishing this as an incomplete set. This was identified by Miss Faffer at a museum in Nurnberg, Germany, as *The Virtuous Girl by eight representations to be changed*, duplicate dolls contained in the original box. The eight costumes were reported as printed front and back; presently known sets, including the one illustrated here, have only front printing with plain grayish green backing, a heavy neck reinforcement placed between the back of the doll and this green backing, features which will be noted in coverage of other dolls to follow. Dresses of the Virtuous Girl are lightly highlighted with the usual protective coating.

Cover of the museum box carries the title in five languages, costumes labeled respectively as, *Pretty; Diligence; Application; Patience; Clemency; Mansuetude; Candor;* and *Sincerity*. The three illustrated are *Patience* No. 4, (with the baby in an elaborately carved wooden cradle); *Clemency* No. 5, (with pot), and *Candor* No. 7, (with doves). The illustrated 6-7/16 inch doll with three costumes has "1" pencilled on the backs, evidencing the missing second doll.

The pictured set is as it came to this writer some years ago, and when a duplicate doll with three entirely different costumes came in, it went into the collection of the late Nellie MacLachlan. It was not until Miss Faffer returned from Germany that we learned this second doll and her three dresses would have brought the author's set to within two costumes of being complete.

Another feature in common with nearly all foreign paper dolls is the closely dressed hair, designed for applying various wigs and headdresses. None of these was received with subject doll, nor mentioned in connection with the Nurnburg set.

Of historical interest are portrait dolls representing the last Kaiser and Kaiserin of Germany, Nos. 251 and 252. No. 251 represents a cut set of William (Wilhelm) II, born January 27, 1859, the son of Friederick III and Victoria Adelaide Mary Louisa (Queen Victoria's daughter). William II succeeded his father upon his death in 1888 as Emperor of Germany and King of Prussia. He had married Augusta-Victoria of Schleswig Holstein in 1881.

Kaiser Wilhelm played an insignificant role in World War I, and when the great German drive of 1918 collapsed, and President Wilson stipulated that abdication of the Kaiser was a prerequisite of peace negotiations, the German people demanded such abdication. Not certain of support of his army, on November 10th, 1918, one day after the flight of the Crown Prince (Pg. 232, Illus. 204) to Holland, the Kaiser followed. Two weeks later he abdicated in his own name and that of his family.

The paper doll of this splendid embossed set stands 6-5/8 inches, and, with the seven resplendent uniforms, has been verified as correct by an uncut sheet bearing the German trademark "W & S" over a "B" contained within a palette, sheet numbered 858. The one discrepancy in the cut set is that it contains only three headdresses, while the uncut set shows seven, one for each uniform.

An uncut sheet representing the Kaiserin, the former Augusta-Victoria of Schleswig-Holstein, with two small princes is given in No. 252. Little Prinz Adalbert was born on July 14, 1884, Prinz August Wilhelm on January 29th, 1887. This rare sheet, titled *Augusta-Victoria, Deutsche Kaiserin und Konigin von Preussen*, bears a trademark of "J S" in what appears to be a tiny rolling pin, left half of the sheet numbered 71/1, the right portion 71/11. The publisher using this trademark has not been identified, but it has been suggested by an eminent researcher that he may have been Joseph Schreiber who has produced later printings of certain of these earlier productions.

As with all of these beautifully lithographed German sheets, the figures are richly colored, but without the coating of the earlier boxed sets. It will be noted that the Kaiserin and her wardrobe have front printing only, while the little Princes and their tiny garments are double throughout. The feminine styling of certain of the princes' costumes strikes an odd note today, but represents fashions for small royalty of the period. The sheet is undated, but the birth date of the sturdy little Prinz August Wilhelm, 1887, determines that the sheet would have been printed shortly prior to, or perhaps in early 1890.

These illustrations of the Kaiser and the Kaiserin, together with that of Crown Prince Wilhelm Friederick, (Pg. 232, Illus. 204), provide portrait paper dolls of five members of the family of the last Kaiser of Germany. Were there two other sons? Mrs. Jean Millen of California reports having read of five sons having been born of this union. This has not been verified by our source material.

No. 248. DIE AUSSTEUR DER PUPPE, CA. 1830. DOLL 9¾ INCHES.

No. 249. FOUR COSTUMES F. & B. FOR DIE AUSSTEUR DER PUPPE.

No. 250.   THE VIRTUOUS GIRL BY EIGHT REPRESENTATIONS TO BE CHANGED.   AUTHOR'S COLLECTION.

No. 251. Kaiser Wilhelm of Germany, 6-5/8 inches.

No. 252. Kaiserin Augusta Victoria, 6¼ inches, with Princes. Author's collection.

Two royal sisters appear in Illustrations Nos. 253 and 254, Countess Victoria of Burgundy, 6-1/8 inches, in No. 253, 5-7/8 inch Countess Wilhelmina of Burgundy in No. 254, measurements exclusive of bases. These were printed on one of the large German sheets, the trademark of W & S over B within a palette visible on the background of the costume at right of Countess Wilhelmina in No. 254. The cut edge of the sheet immediately below the base of Victoria, and the top cut line of the portion containing Wilhelmina, match perfectly, evidencing that Countess Victoria was printed on the upper portion of the sheet, Countess Wilhelmina on the lower part; dolls and costumes are heavily embossed, the dressy outfits brightly colored, outdoor garments in dark shades, brown for Victoria, blue for Wilhelmina. There should be more costumes for Victoria, and presumably additional accessories for both dolls. In common with others of these German sheets, accessories were scattered indiscriminately among the costumes, no guide given for assigning to a specific doll. Costume styling and the high-top button shoes, together with absence of the Printed in Germany inscription required by the United States after 1890, appear to date this production in the late 1880's. It is to be regretted that a complete sheet is unavailable to perhaps give us portraits of additional members of the House of Burgundy as well as missing costumes and accessories.

An uncut sheet bearing the "J S" mark and numbered 93 is shown in Illus. No. 255. Features of the dolls suggest that they too may be portraits, though not so identified. In any event, they constitute an interesting family group, the distinguished gentleman measuring 5-1/8 inches, his Frau 4-7/8. The two young women, 4-11/16 inches, appear to be twins, their separate garments designed alike, the two evening dresses in the same pale lavendar; evening jackets, however, while styled the same, are executed, one in white, the other pink. All four dolls and their wardrobes, including hats, are printed double.

The writer's collection includes several more of these beautiful large German sheets, and it is disappointing not to have space to illustrate them. Except for one sheet bearing the inscription, "Made in Germany" (illustrated in October, 1955 issue of HOBBIES), and with the further exception of the Kaiserin (No. 252), it is believed that most if not all were produced in Germany prior to 1890, certainly no later than the early 1890's.

The quaint boy and girl pair, produced as one figure, (No. 256), the boy 4-9/16 inches, the girl 4¼, have the grayish green backing already touched upon; however, this pair do not have the neck reinforcements. As the dual figure is slipped into any one of the seven delicately tinted costumes, the dolls automatically embark upon the activity represented by the particular garment. The flat soles of the shoes establish publication date as prior to 1860, and the action garments suggest the possibility that they may have been inspired by the illustrations of the toy books published in England by S. and J. Fuller early in the nineteenth century.

The illustrated dancing class (No. 257) is an unusually interesting group of lightly embossed paper dolls. A tiny circle enclosing a dot, printed on the bottom attaching-tab of the costume at upper left in the photographic reproduction, unmistakably identifies the group as having been cut from one of these German sheets. The dancing master, (French ?) with his violin, right forefinger emphasizing an instruction, measures 5-15/16 inches, the dancer in upper right 4-3/8, the others 4-5/8 inches, all bases excluded.

Attention is directed to the four costumes for the full-face student dancer, while one has three, one only two, showing this to be an incomplete set. The beautiful colorings of these German produced paper dolls prevail, shades varying in ivory and dainty pastels, a charming and treasured paper doll group.

No. 253. Countess Victoria of Burgundy, 6-1/8 inches. Author's collection.

No. 254. Countess Wilhelmina of Burgundy, 5-7/8 inches. Author's collection.

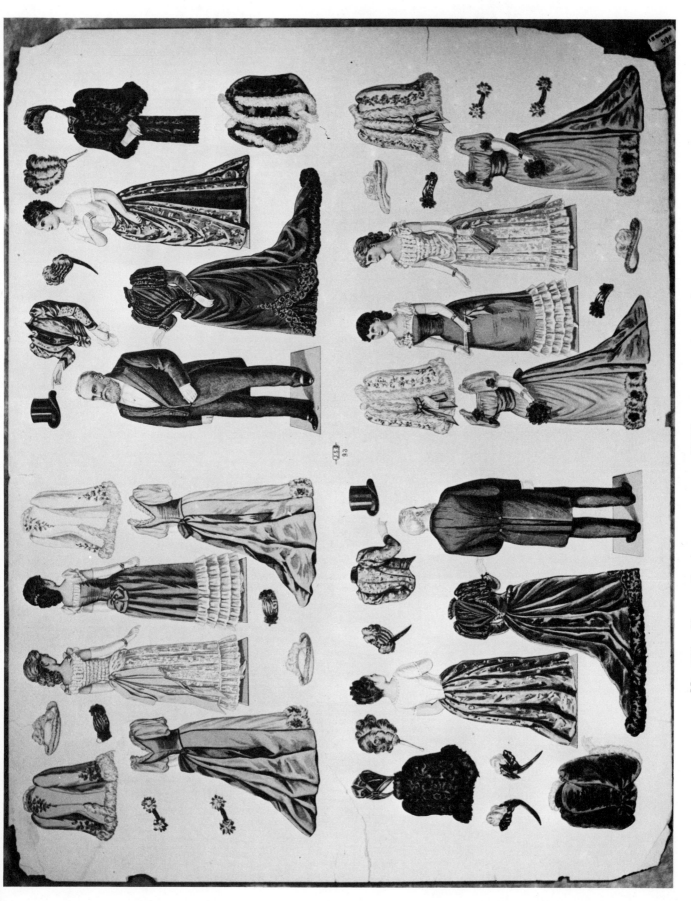

No. 256. Unidentified foreign paper dolls with action costumes. Probably German.

No. 257. A Dancing Class. Author's collection.

Paper dolls with removable costumes followed the French Pantin in rapid succession, the first known specimen published in England in 1790. The paper doll was eight inches tall with wardrobe to be cut out, on sale in English markets for three shillings. Advertised in *Journal des Luxus und der Moden* in France in 1791, the dolls were described as follows: "A new and very pretty invention is the so-called English doll which we have lately received from London. It is properly a toy for little girls, but is so pleasing and tasteful that mothers and grown women will likely also want to play with it, the more since good or bad taste in dress or coiffure can be observed, and, so to speak studied. The doll is a young female figure cut out of stout cardboard. It is about 8 inches high, has simply curled hair, and is dressed in under clothes and corset. With it go six complete sets of tastefully designed dresses and headdresses". An illustration in color of this doll, with three of her six costumes, may be seen opposite Pg. 150 in the English edition of Max Von Boehn's DOLLS AND PUPPETS. One fortunate collector has reported having an original set of the paper doll.

By the early 1800's paper dolls were being produced in various forms, one exquisite rare specimen, a wholly handmade, hand-painted soldier 5½ inches tall, under the title, *The Child of the Regiment* (No. 258). This was contained in a 4-5/8 by 7-3/16 inch wooden box with sliding cover, visible in the illustration, the date, 1810, marked on the bottom. Appearing just below the title at the top of the box cover, in script, is the declaration, "I will also be a french marshall", repeated, with the title, in German and French at the bottom of the box cover.

This young soldier is outfitted with seven uniforms, four shakos or busbys, (tall headdresses), and a drum, all beautifully painted front and back. The rear view of the uniform at lower left in the illustration is given to show the blanket or bed roll carried across the shoulders, together with the knapsack, attesting the meticulous attention of the artist to carrying from front to back all details of the uniforms. The ornate box suggests that this carefully made set may have been executed in perhaps a limited quantity as a commercial venture, as were the contemporary toy books with their hand-painted illustrations. This splendid little masterpiece, more than 150 years old and beautifully preserved, is a highlight in the collection of which it is a part.

Beginning about the year 1810 a series of toy books was published by S. and J. Fuller at the Temple of Fancy, Rathbone Place, London, "Where also are sold, Books of Instruction in every Branch of Drawing, Colours, and every requisite used in Drawing". Herbert H. Hosmer, Jr., lists the titles of several of these little books in his booklet, *A Brief History of Toy Books*. All of the Fuller books carried a moral theme, the hand-painted illustrations

tipped into the book, each one cut to form with a pocket on the back into which the pointed tab of the doll's head could be slipped; as the reader followed the story, the head was moved in sequence to the corresponding illustration, thus completing the paper doll figure. Books were enclosed in slip-cases, and so popular were they that at least one, *The History and Adventures of Little Henry,* had been published in seven editions by 1811.

A fabulous paper doll was published by S. and J. Fuller in 1811, one of the most sought after known paper dolls, *The Protean Figure or Metamorphic Costumes.* In a listing of "Juvenile Books, with figures that dress and undress", printed on the outside back cover of the 1814 booklet of Cinderella (immediately following), the Protean Figure is priced at 1£ 1s. In Illustration No. 259 this 8¼ inch figure is posed against the accompanying colorful landscape background, slotted for insertion of the heels of the paper doll. This splendid specimen of early English paper toys contains ninety different pieces, the twelve costumes with accessories enclosed each in its separate envelope type pocket, the thirteenth containing the scenic background. These pockets, opening flat for careful removal of the doll and costume parts, are tipped into a 9 by 4½ inch book, which in turn is enclosed in a slipcase. The title, *Metamorphic Costumes,* apparently stemmed from an accompanying figure representing *Proteus* rising from the sea, a prophetic old man of the sea in Greek mythology who tended Poseidon's seals on Pharos, an island off the shore of Egypt. If seized and held by an enemy, he would foretell the future, then to escape he would utilize his power to change himself into any shape he chose.

The twelve costumes are: A Walking Dress. Naval Uniform. Monk's Habit. Turkish Costume. Quaker's Habit. Mourning Suit. German Hussar. Full Dress in the year 1700*. Knight in Full Armour*. Officer's Dress (Land Forces). Gentleman's Evening Costume, and French Uniform (Imperial Guard). The two starred costumes are included in the photographic illustration.

It is quite evident that the stay-on tabs used on later paper dolls were unknown in 1811, since the ninety pieces comprising the wardrobe of the Protean Figure have no provision for attaching to the figure itself. Thus, with the scenic background laid flat on a table, the outfits are built up by laying the basic costume piece over the figure, adding other parts, each in its proper order, requiring care and utmost patience. This would provide a history of costume, but would preclude any usual playtime activity as was possible with the little toy books with their progressive illustrations, or with our later paper dolls. The Protean Figure now brings fabulous prices, an enviable treasure if and when one of the scarce specimens can be found.

Reverting to the regular toy books of S. and J. Fuller, we present the lovely one of *Cinderella*, 1814. The booklet containing the 79-verse story, 48 in "Part the First", 31 in "Part II", is titled, *Cinderella/or/The Little Glass Slipper/Beautifully versified and/Illustrated with Figures*. Illustration No. 260 shows the title page together with Cinderella's coach-and-four. A portion of Cinderella's ball dress is visible through the coach window, a pocket on the reverse into which Cinderella's head can be inserted; thus, in resplendent raiment, she is carried to the ball.

Illustration No. 261 gives us Cinderella's head with its pointed tab, and her six costumes running the gamut from pathetic drudgery to her beautiful wedding gown as she is triumphantly married to the Prince. This entire set is of the highest quality, all parts exquisitely tinted, a pocket on the back of each dress for insertion of the head-tab.

The story is recounted in the fanciful verse of the day. At the first ball given by the Prince, Cinderella is careful to leave before the stroke of twelve, but at the second dance, entranced by the Prince's love-making, she fails to heed time's passing, and as the clock strikes the midnight hour, she flies from the ball-room "as swiftly as the wind", losing a slipper in her flight. The work-a-day costume at lower left in the illustration depicts this flight, one foot minus its slipper, the pumpkin and scampering mice all that remain of the beautiful coach-and-four. The happy ending of the Cinderella story is familiar to all of us; in the 1814 version, in celebration of the royal wedding—"The cannon fired, the bells did ring,/Joy spread through all the nation;/And, lo! the palace one whole week,/Was one illumination".

The story of Cinderella has enthralled children since Jakob Ludwig Karl Grimm (1785-1863) included it in his collection of German folk tales, gathered and published in collaboration with his brother, Wilhelm Karl Grimm, under the title, GRIMM'S FAIRY TALES. The basic theme is the same in both of the above versions, but there is little similarity in the unfolding of the story. The little white bird of Grimm's tale becomes a fairy god-mother in the English version; Grimm's slippers are of pure gold, and there are other marked differences. However, the magical transformation of Cinderella from drudge to princess highlights both, brought to life in the lovely 1814 Cinderella paper doll in mint condition after a century and a half.

A splendid foreign paper doll, 7-13/16 inches tall, circa 1840, front and back printing, is reproduced in Illustration No. 262. The six costumes are beautifully colored and have the protective egg-white coating usual to foreign productions in the mid-1800's.

The source is unknown, and with no container, the doll cannot definitely be said to be a name doll; however, arrangement of the hair wound around exposed ears in the so-called "Queen Victoria" style, coupled with the fingers "loaded with rings" as the Queen's are said to have been, (three gold bands adorning the doll's right hand, four on the left, a bracelet on each arm), strongly suggests that the doll may have been produced to represent the young Queen shortly after her ascension to the throne of England in 1837. We do note absence of regal costumes, but since wardrobes of the majority of foreign paper dolls of the period consisted of eight garments, perhaps two royal robes were originally included. Whether representing royalty or otherwise, this is a fabulous paper doll, a gift to the writer from the estate of the late Margarett Dartt of California.

The American Lady and Her Children in a Variety of Beautiful Costumes (No. 263), was produced in two sizes, both boxed, country of origin undetermined. The title of the smaller set, illustrated, is printed on the 6½ by 8-7/8 inch box lid in five languages, French, English, German, Italian, and Dutch. The American Lady is 5-¾ inches tall, the children approximately 3-7/8, excluding bases. Dolls and costumes are printed front and back, costumes having the usual glistening coating.

The larger set of this interesting family (not illustrated) as described in a letter by the late Nellie MacLachlan in 1951, was distributed in a 9 by 12 inch box, title printed only in French, German and English. The dolls, measured to include bases, were reported as 9¾ inches for the Lady herself, her son 7¼ and the daughter 7 inches. Each was said to have four double costumes with the egg-white treatment; accessories included eleven hats, wigs and bonnets, with wooden bases in which to stand the dolls, all missing from the smaller set, but perhaps included when published.

The same children then were put out in boxed sets, *The Little Boy's Doll* and *The Little Girl's Doll*. The former is said to have been distributed in a 4¼ by 6-5/8 inch box, title in English, French, German, and Italian. The set consists of two boy dolls, the features varying slightly in expression from the boy in The American Lady set, and they have eight costumes as against four in the family group.

The box for *The Little Girl's Doll* is approximately the same as for the Little Boy's set, the design similar to that of the American Lady and Her Children, title in the same four languages, English at the extreme bottom of the lid. Lead title is in German. The doll measures 3-7/8 inches as in the family group, but with a second doll and eight costumes, emphasizing Miss Faffer's finding of two dolls in foreign produced boxed sets where only one character was featured. Four of these eight costumes are duplicates of the four in the American Lady set, all eight printed double, gorgeously colored, and coated. A small wooden standard also was included.

Our next presentation is *The Lady of London* set, comprising two dolls, similar but not identical as in certain other boxed sets. Doll No. 1 (Illus. No. 264) is 10-9/16 inches tall, No. 2 doll (No. 265) 10¾ inches. These dolls have the grayish green plain backs previously defined, with the same sturdy neck reinforcements. The elaborately designed and handsomely colored costumes, with the exception of the bridal gowns, are highlighted by the usual protective coating rather than solidly coated as in, say, The American Lady and Her Children set. Neither of the Lady of London bridal dresses is coated. The general characteristics of the box in which these lovely dolls were distributed are similar to those of other foreign sets, certain ones represented in this work. In the central cover design picturing the two ladies, the little boy and girl who comprise a part of two of the costumes for Doll No. 1 are shown. The title is printed in a curved line, in English at the top of the cover, below which, also in English is printed, "Newest English Doll of Fashion", all repeated in three foreign languages below the center design.

It has been generally supposed that the foreign dolls of this quality and with the strange shade of green backing, were produced in Germany, but in this instance, the lead title, printed in English, and the "Newest English Doll . . .", may raise a question of origin. However, since some are known to have been produced in Germany, it is quite possible that all originated there, featuring dolls of other countries, the dolls believed to have been printed in sheets, cut, backed, the numbers 1 and 2 as designated on the uncut sheets pasted on the backs of respective dolls, then distributed among represented countries. In cases of split sets, like The Virtuous Girl (No. 250), the original set printed double, it is possible some enterprising merchant may have divided sets, backed the figures with the green backing, and sold as two separate dolls at additional profit. All conjecture only.

Miss Faffer reported having seen a "Lady of London" puzzle in the museum at Nurnburg, but this still does not definitely establish country of origin.

The Lady of New York (not illustrated) has been defined as contained in a 5¾ by 7¾ inch box, the lead title in English, repeated in three foreign languages. The box cover design depicts three ladies with a boy and a girl. The set consists of the usual two dolls, slightly different, printed front and back; features and the under-clothing are the same, the feet placed in the same position, hands varying; dressing of the back hair differs, one with side curls falling to the shoulders, the other resembling a French twist. The dolls are small, 4-3/8 inches excluding bases. The eight dresses are printed front and back, heavily glazed. Miss Faffer had reported seeing this set in the Nurnburg Museum, this detailed description supplied by one of our own paper doll collectors who only recently acquired it, unfortunately too late for photographing.

Recently mentioned is *The Lady of Boston,* for which we have no details. It is apparent that a series of these foreign-produced "Lady" fashion paper dolls was distributed, designed with the United States market in mind.

An interesting cardboard theatre with paper doll characters is reported by Mrs. Donald M. (Sallie Lindsley) Black, who kindly traced the 14 by 10 inch box cover in color for inclusion here. The box cover design shows Little Red Riding Hood, napkin-covered basket at her feet, having her red cape tied under her up-tilted chin by her mother in preparation for her trip to Grandmother's. The box bears title, "The Story of Little Red Riding Hood with movable lifelike figures and scenery". Below this, "Spears Series" in an elongated scroll frame, and at the bottom, "Complete with book of Words/Manufactured at the Spear Works, Bavaria. Copyright in the United Kingdom, etc."

As is usual with these early cardboard theaters, the floor is wooden, grooved for movement of the characters by means of thread or string across the stage. A three-fold backdrop, the center section same size as the box, is reversible for setting up both exterior and interior scenes. The former provides the woods on the two side panels, a center path leading to a cottage at the rear. The interior has a door, a window, grandfather's clock, a warming pan, and two pictures. A two-section tray contains the paper doll characters and appurtenances for staging this beloved story as a play. All doll characters are fully jointed, and many an hour's enthralling entertainment must have been provided by this lovely theater. Undated, Mrs. Black tentatively dates it as circa 1900.

Also published by J. W. Spear & Sons is a marvelous 10 inch paper doll (No. 266). The name "Dorothy" appears in large script on the back, followed by "J. W. Spear & Sons, Manufacturers of the famous 'Spear' Series of Games, London. Designed in England, Copyright in the United Kingdom, etc." The box measures 12 x 6¼ inches, 2-5/8 inches deep, with a horizontal-opening lid, the title in gold in vertical position, "Dolly's Wardrobe", below which the same scroll type frame as on the above covered theatre box contains the inscription, "J.W.S.&S., Bavaria". The doll and the many accessories are perhaps the most colorful of paper dolls covered in this work; they are very heavily embossed on sturdy board, colors exceptionally brilliant. This is a work of art, circa 1900's.

A second paper doll set titled "Dolly's Wardrobe" was produced by Dean & Son, Limited, 160A Fleet Street, E.C., London/Printed in Germany". An inscription at the bottom of the wardrobe type folder reads "Wolfe & Co., Philadelphia, New York and Chicago", denoting this company as United States distributors.

From the collection of Helen Jane Biggart, Bloomfield, New Jersey, the container represents a wardrobe 8¾ by 17-3/8 inches, with vertical openings to simulate doors. Due to the tremendous size of the various parts, a dressed doll measuring 15½ inches, only a representative portion of the set is shown in Illustrations Nos. 267 and 268. The dual heads shown in Illus. No. 268 are nine inches over all, printed on both sides to provide four faces. Eight costumes are provided by double printing of the four skirts; Blouses are printed on one side only, equipped with loops on the backs to permit inserting the heads, the flange on the double heads acting as a stopper when a given head is in place in any one of the blouses, of which there is one for each complete costume. No date is given, but a like set in the collection of Mrs. Stephen J. Lindsley of Glen Ridge, New Jersey, was purchased for her in 1893, when she was a child. This approximately dates Dolly's Wardrobe of Dean & Son. Mrs. Lindsley calls attention that the two hats shown at upper left in Illustration No. 268 are erroneously included, actually belonging to another large, domestically produced set, "Our Favorite Dolls".

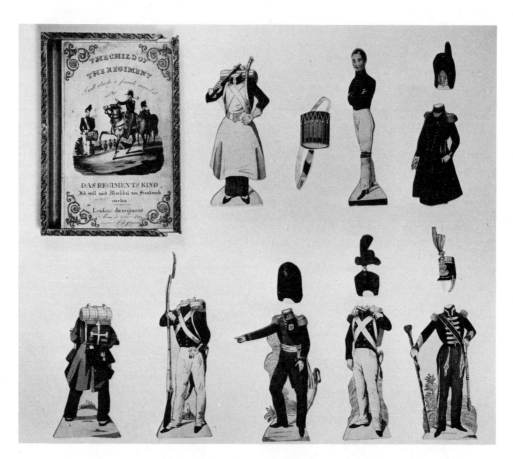

No. 258. THE CHILD OF THE REGIMENT, HANDMADE, 1810.

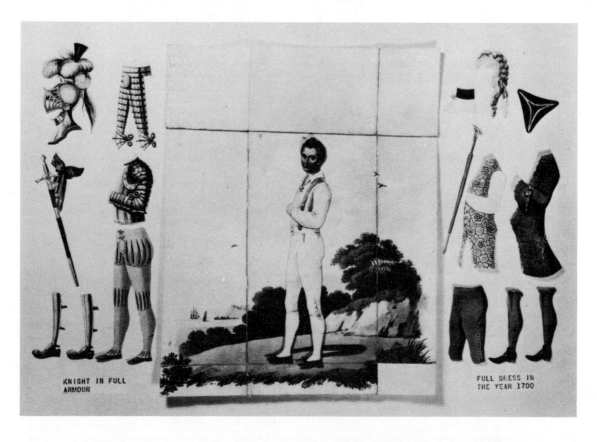

KNIGHT IN FULL
ARMOUR

FULL DRESS IN
THE YEAR 1700

No. 259. THE PROTEAN FIGURE OR METAMORPHIC COSTUMES, 8¼ INCHES.

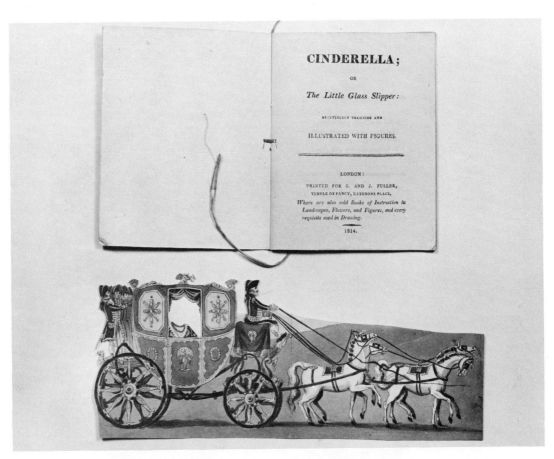

No. 260.   Cinderella Booklet and Coach-and-Four.

No. 261.   Cinderella and her Wardrobe.

No. 262. Ca. 1840 paper doll, perhaps representing Queen Victoria.

No. 263. The American Lady and Her Children in a variety of beautiful costumes. Author's collection.

No. 264. THE LADY OF LONDON, DOLL No. 1. AUTHOR'S COLLECTION.

No. 265. THE LADY OF LONDON, DOLL No. 2, AUTHOR'S COLLECTION.

No. 266.   Dolly's Wardrobe, by J. F. Spear, London. Author's collection.

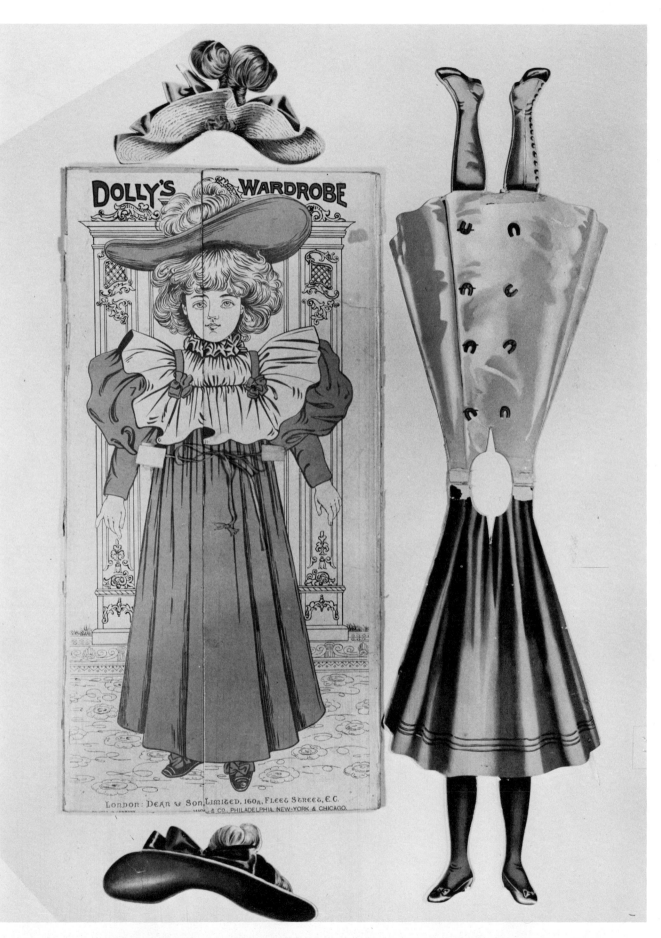

No. 267.   Dolly's Wardrobe, by Dean & Son, Limited, London.   Collection Helen Jane Biggart.

No. 268.   DOUBLE HEADS AND PORTION OF DOLLY'S WARDROBE, BY DEAN & SON.

Attempting to compile a comprehensive history of paper dolls of Raphael Tuck & Sons Company, Ltd., poses baffling problems. Duplication of certain dolls in different series, lack of identification on both dolls and containers in many instances, and other lapses, cause much confusion. It would require a sizeable volume to include even the information we have been able to gather from various sources; therefore, to keep within space limitation we are covering what we consider to be the most informative and helpful.

An unusual Tuck doll, apparently published prior to patented series, is an approximately 12¼ inch school girl, her doll clutched in her two hands (No. 269). Her five costumes range in succession from school days to maturity, including a beautiful bridal dress with a separate full-length veil having the traditional orange blossom wreath. A controversial dress is the dark, practically black one, the last of the serial garments. Some collectors have felt that this represented a mourning dress, identifying the costume series as one from school days to widowhood. Others feel that because the dress is not dead black, and carrying a handkerchief and a Bible (?) in hand, it was designed as a Sunday go-to-meeting dress.

The publishers' inscription on the reverse reads simply, "Art Publishers by Royal Warrant", no mention ". . . by appointment to their Majesties . . ." as in other and presumably later series of paper dolls. The easel trademark in less ornate form than the later one appears, which, coupled with the above omissions and with no patent information, seems to bear out our calculated opinion that this doll preceded the various series carrying such identifying data. This exceptional paper doll has been presented to the Chester County Historical Society in memory of Mrs. H. B. (Willie) Armstrong who had expressed special appreciation of its beauty.

Also believed to have preceded the Tuck patents are dainty little girls approximately seven and eight inches in height with background fences that tilt to form standards. The first one acquired by the writer some few years ago, her pink and white dress of Kate Greenaway styling, the latticed fence overgrown with wild roses, semed to be more of a decorative figure than a paper doll. She has no separate costume, and there are no publishers' identifying marks, the one printed label giving the doll's name, *Miss Wild Rose,* on the base of the fence.

When a second similar doll came with a separate blue dress, her white lace-trimmed apron caught up to form a pocket for three beautiful white doves, a fourth with spread wings resting upon her arm, it was possible to class these figures as paper dolls. This second one, with Tuck's easel trademark, is inscribed "Art Publishers by Royal Warrant/Raphael Tuck & Sons Ltd.,/London/Designed at the Studios in England and printed at the Fine Art Works in Saxony".

A third doll of this same type was recently reported, representing a little farm girl, her hair in a pigtail over her shoulders, rabbits, chickens and lambs forming part of the designs of her three costumes. This doll bears the same mark and inscription as the foregoing one. No patent date or "Patent Pending" appears on either. This omission, and the inscription "Art Publishers by Royal Warrant", (as on the school days to maturity doll), seem to place these fence-supported dolls as among the first of Tuck's paper doll productions. Perhaps a more extensive series of these dainty dolls was published.

We are indebted to Luella Hart for supplying details of the first patent taken out by the Tucks. On page 19, DIRECTORY OF BRITISH DOLLS, she shows a baby paper doll with a nursing bottle having a long drinking tube rather than the close fitting nipple familiar to us. This was covered by Patent No. 11367, issued to A. Tuck & F. P. Scott on June 9, 1893, A. Tuck believed to be the forerunner of the Tuck Company.

On November 30, 1893, Patent No. 23003, the second Tuck patent for paper dolls, was issued to A. Tuck for "Dolls printed in colours upon cardboard with a number of changeable dresses, hats, etc." The doll is illustrated, dressed and undressed, on Page 20 of the British Directory. This doll later became *Lady Edith,* published by Raphael Tuck & Sons Ltd. in three sizes, the two larger under different numbers, one No. 4 (Arabic), the other Roman Numeral No. I of the Artistic Series. The third small doll was issued as No. 101.

Lady Edith No. 4 of "Our Pets Series of Dressing Dolls" is so identified on the reverse of the doll's head. She measures 9¼ inches, has four known dresses and hats numbered 4a through 4d. Costumes are equipped with shoulder tabs to slip through slits in the doll's long hair, doll and costumes inscribed on the backs, "Publishers to their Majesties the King and Queen Alexandra" in addition to the company's name, and, "London, Paris, New York, designed at the Studios in London and printed at the Fine Art Works in Bavaria". No mention is made of a patent having been applied for, which seems to bear out our belief that this particular printing preceded the *Lady Edith* of the Artistic Series. Indications also are that a second printing of the No. 4 doll was issued between the above two printings. The late Mrs. Hackett of Austin, Texas, had reported her No. 4 Lady Edith as of the same series as the foregoing No. 4, but inscribed "Publishers to Her Majesty the Queen".

The Roman Numeral Artistic Series is divided ínto four sub-series, dolls and costumes numbered in Roman Numeral characters on the reverse, but not identified by the doll's names, these appearing only on the cardboard folders which also bear a likeness of each respective doll, providing authentication. For benefit of those collectors who may have dolls without containers, a listing follows:

I. Lady Edith

II. Doll familiar but name unavailable

III. Doll familiar but name unavailable

PRINCE AND PRINCESS SERIES

IV. Royal Reggie

V. Lordly Lionel

VI. Sweet Abigail

VII. Courtly Beatrice. (One doll marked A.S. VII has been reported as labeled "Princess May Blossom").

FAIRY TALE SERIES

VIII. Mother Goose Characters. (Costumes for Mother Goose, Little Miss Muffet, Bo-Peep, Little Red Riding Hood).

IX. Cinderella at Home. (Costumes for Cinderella, Fairy Godmother, Cinderella's Ball Dress, Goody Two Shoes).

X. Prince Charming. (Costumes for Prince Charming, Little Boy Blue, Dick Whittington, Little Jack Horner).

XI. Neither doll nor container for XI is known to us.

BLONDE AND BRUNETTE SERIES OF DRESSING DOLLS

XII. Belle of the South   XIV. Belle of Newport

XIII. Belle of the West   XV. Belle of Saratoga.

All dolls in this series measure nine to ten inches tall, distributed in folders.

Unlike costumes for Lady Edith No. 4, the six in the writer's set of Artistic Series I *Lady Edith* (complete except folder lacking) have extended neck tabs to slip under the chin of the doll's tipped on head, also equipped with shoulder fold-back tabs for added security. Three of the costumes are marked "Copyright. Patent applied for". The doll itself and one costume have an added rubber-stamped inscription, "Copyright, 1894, by Raphael Tuck & Sons Co., L't'd". Costume No. IB is marked "U. S. Patent February 20th, 1894/Copyright 1894 by Raphael Tuck & Sons Co., Ltd." These varied inscriptions indicate a mixed set, but all bear Artistic Series I, perhaps dating inception of the series as February 20th, 1894, the patent having been issued while the Roman Numeral No. I doll was in process of manufacture. This is conjecture only.

Artistic II doll has not been definitely named in any of the many collections reported to us, but a tentative designation was suggested by Alberta Anderson of Bothell, Washington in 1954. She reported having a doll with the envelope titled "Lady Betty, with Dresses and Hats. No. 2 of our Pets Series of Dressing Dolls". The company's name with that of the artist followed, "Printed in Germany" appearing in the lower right hand corner. This doll is a duplicate of Artistic Series II except is slightly smaller. (Lady Edith No. 4 is slightly smaller than Artistic Series I Lady Edith). Costumes of the Roman Numeral No. II and the No. 2 are identical, and it may follow that Artistic Series II may also have been titled *Lady Betty,* but only a folder would verify this point.

An interesting situation exists in connection with the Artistic Series dolls. *Lady Clare* is the English edition of the paper dolls comprising the Blonde and Brunette Series of Belles. *Lady Clare,* at one time in the writer's collection, has six costumes Nos. XIIIa through f, the doll becoming *Belle of the West,* in the Belle series. Lady Clare's costumes were assigned to the latter as follows:

XIII-A, Country Walking Costume	to	XV-D, Belle of Saratoga
XIII-B, Garden Party Costume	to	XII-C, Belle of the South
XIII-C, At the Opera	to	XIII-C, Belle of the West
XIII-D, Afternoon Costume	to	XII-B, Belle of the South
XIII-E, Brighton Costume	to	XIII-A, Belle of the West
XIII-F, The at Home Dress	to	XII-D, Belle of the South

Additional costumes then were supplied to provide each Belle with her quota of four, with hats.

Confusion is utter when we come to the six inch Artistic Series dolls. No. 101 is a duplicate of A. T. No. I except for size, but others of the small dolls do not conform to the Series I dolls as to numbers. Those reported, some checked from writer's collection, follow: No. 102, My Lady Betty. No. 103, Winsome Winnie. No. 104, Winsome Winnie, doll similar but slightly different than No. 103, dresses unlike those of No. 103. No. 105, reported to be like Dolly Delight #3 of "Our Pets Series of Dressing Dolls". No. 106 received in an envelope marked "Dolly Delight and Her Dresses, Our Pets Dressing Series No. 106". No. 107 like Royal Reggie, A. T. Series IV. No. 108 like Lordly Lionel, A. T. V. No.

109, like Sweet Abigail A. T. VI. No. 110 like Courtly Beatrice A. T. VII.

Inconsistencies exist also in other series. One, The Bridal Series of Dressing Dolls, boxed, Pat. Feb. 20th, 1894. Under above heading, No. 600 is The Bride and Her Trousseau; No. 601 the Bridegroom; 602 and 603 Bridesmaids. In the writer's collection is a bridesmaid marked "Artistic Series 602". One sales list indicated dolls of two separate series, but this is uncertain at this time. Apparently if there were two series, both bore the same numbers.

With the 20's, we again have confusion, rather, room for uncertainty. These are nine inch dolls, marked Artistic Series No. 20 and so on, Pat. Feb. 20th, 1894. Our available information follows:

No. 20: Said to be a blonde, name not definitely known, but may be "Darling Hulda", but which of the two types?

No. 21: When printed in one piece with shoulder slits to accommodate dress tabs, is said to be named "Darling Maud".

With tipped on head?

No. 22: With tipped on head, said to be "Darling Edith with her Wardrobe".

Printed in one piece with shoulder slits, "Darling Marjorie".

No. 23: With tipped on head, "Darling Gladys".

In one piece with shoulder slits, name?

One source reports that these dolls were issued under the heading, "Little Darling Series of Dressing Dolls", but whether this applies to both types, those with tipped on heads and those with the shoulder slits, we do not know, nor have we verified the above information. Those in the writer's collection have tipped on heads, but there are no containers.

Dolls "in one piece with shoulder slits" can be defined as having slits at the shoulder line cut through the long hair for costume tabs, whereas extended necks slip under the chin of the tipped on head. All of these Tuck dolls were of course designed with children in mind, and apparent discrepancies seemed unimportant, but to collectors they are disconcerting.

One splendid set of portrait dolls is known. Issued under the heading, "Favorite Faces, Novel Series of Dressing Dolls", Pat. Feb. 20th, 1894, Box No. 1 contains Miss Ada Rehan. Box No. 2, Miss Maude Adams. Box No. 3, Miss Julia Marlowe. Box. No. 4, Mrs. Leslie Carter. This set would add prestige to any collection, specialized or general.

A further beautiful set difficult to accurately identify is the 500 series, dolls approximately 13 inches tall. The four dolls known to comprise the series are numbered on the backs with no names given, while the boxes bear the title, "Dolls of all Seasons" with the dolls' names, but with no matching number. Therefore there may be room for question in the following listing, though compiled in collaboration with several advanced collectors, and felt to be correct: No. 500, *Dear Dorothy*. 501, *Rosy Ruth*. 502, *Merry Marion,* the one doll reported in an important collection as having both the name and the number printed on the reverse, unquestionable authentication. No. 503 is believed to be *Sweet Alice*. Dolls have wardrobes of four costumes with matching hats, are beautifully executed.

There were other series of these large dolls produced, but the number is not known. One, "Little Maids New Series of Dressing Dolls" is also distributed in boxes, 9 by 12 inches. No. 41, *Sunny Susan* is 12 inches, wearing a medium blue petticoat with bottom plaiting, a white underwaist with blue ribbons run through beading as trim. Her stockings are brown, low-cut shoes extending over the instep with four buttons. Arms are bent at the elbows, drawn across her body, a long-stemmed flower in her right hand, supported by her left at chest level. Her wardrobe consists of four charming costumes with four hats.

No. 43 of this series is titled *Playful Polly,* contained in Miss Louise Kaufman's extensive collection, an interesting feature the original price mark, .35¢ still legible on the box.

Miss Kaufman also has an unidentified 13½ inch young girl paper doll. She wears petticoat and underwaist, low slippers with buckles. Her hair is dressed high in front, a yellow flower at the left, two curls extending vertically across her forehead. She has three dresses, one a school dress, a typical feature of these large, young girl dolls.

A fourth large doll, perhaps of the same series as above doll or dolls, measures 13 inches, illustrated in No. 270. We have no identification for this winsome little girl, in the writer's collection. She holds a comb in her right hand, and her wardrobe con-

sists of three dresses, an ermine-trimmed coat, and two hats, other hats missing. The photographic reproduction shows details of this lovely set, and it is hoped identification may be forthcoming.

A fifth 12½ inch doll in our collection is of a different type, a young lady doll with tipped on head, luxuriant dark hair, wearing a pink petticoat, pink ribbons run through beading trimming her white corset cover. Slim of body, her name, *"Marion Manners,* Maidens Fair Series of Dressing Dolls" is printed on the reverse. The easel trademark is given, below which is the inscription, "Art Publishers to their Majesties the King and Queen/Pat'd. Feb. 20th, 1894". Printed at the bottom of the skirt is the company's identification, "Raphael Tuck & Sons Co., Ltd. New York, London, Paris, Berlin, Montreal/Designed at the Studios in New York and Printed in Germany". Only the top of an easel standard remains, adhering to the body. The four elegant costumes, richly colored, reflect New York designing of a wardrobe for a young lady of social distinction. (No. 271).

A set of four small dolls (not illustrated) designed unlike any other Tuck production we have seen is a cardboard folder titled, "Dollies on their Travels". Closed, the folder measures 9-5/8 by approximately 5¾ inches, 21 inches long when side panels are swung open. Description of the set is printed on the reverse side of the folder: "Contents Four Dollies, One Trunk, One Suit Case, One Bag, Eight Dresses, Four Hats". The luggage is attached to the three panels of the folder by expanding hinges for storage and removal of the hat and extra costume provided for each doll, they themselves consisting of three little girls and one little boy, perhaps four or five years old, each wearing a removable costume. The dolls are pasted by their feet only to the backdrop, the little boy supplied with a traveling bag, the center trunk flanked by two of the little girls, the suit case assigned to the third. An ocean scene decorates the backdrop, suggesting a contemplated sea voyage. The usual easel trademark is given with the inscription, "Art Publishers to their Majesties the King and Queen/Raphael Tuck & Sons Co., Ltd., New York, London, Paris, Berlin, Toronto". This is a delightful and quite different paper doll set.

An especially interesting paper doll was recently acquired by the writer, published at Tuck's Paris establishment. Titled *Enfante de Tous Les Pays. Nouvella Poupees habiller No. 3".* This bears inscription at the bottom of the sheet on which it was printed, "Edition de la Librairie Artistique de La Jeunesse". Surprisingly, this was found to be a duplicate of McLoughlin Bros.' Wide World Costume Doll shown on page 212, with one added costume labeled "Holland-aise", to make a total of four costumes and hats. While we learned that McLoughlin Bros.' cutout book was published circa 1920, we also determined that the book was a reprint of "Dolls of the Nations" printed on sheets by McLoughlin Bros. in 1900. Thus, the Paris edition could have been marketed shortly after the turn of the century, or even earlier if the design originated in Paris. There is no way of establishing which set preceded the other. The French doll measures 8¾ inches, printed on heavy cardboard. The figures have been cut apart but not to form, the cut edges fitting perfectly to form a sheet 18 inches long by 9-7/8 high. The surface is dull rather than glossy, but colorings are very good, the doll in particular executed in delicate, lifelike tints. Labeling of the various costumes for the country which they represent is of course in French. This surprise paper doll is a most pleasing acquisition.

The few instances of duplication and other confusing features of Tuck's paper dolls, cited here, emphasize the difficulty of attempting an over-all coverage of their paper doll production. Such a work not only would fill a volume in itself, but it is extremely doubtful if any writer, or even a collaborating group could compile a really comprehensive, all-inclusive record of the enormous output of this company. However, such a compilation, if one could be achieved, would prove of inestimable value as reference material.

It might be well to add that no assistance could be expected from the Tuck company. In a letter addressed to Mrs. Armstrong under date of 26th March, 1945, they advised that they could offer no information on dolls published prior to 1900, as their records were destroyed by enemy action. Thus the early dolls in today's collections are the sole remaining record of the initial production of Raphael Tuck & Sons Co. Ltd., treasures to be preserved.

Our final presentation is a paper version in miniature of Japan's, The Festival of the Dolls, or, as often referred to, The Peach Blossom Festival, held annually on March 3rd, Illustration No. 272. This little gem was printed in Japan as noted in English on the back of the container. The printing in Japanese on the front is assumed to be the title.

The Festival setting is encased in a satchel type folder with a closing flap and a double carrying handle. When the case is opened, the series of red steps, each with its setting of traditional festival dolls and appurtenances, pops into a 3-D display as shown in the lower portion of the illustration. The folder design is brightly colored against a vivid red background, the case measuring 10¼ by 5-7/8 inches exclusive of the handles; the tiny paper figures, all in color, average an inch in height.

Though a modern creation, this lovely miniature paper specimen of the ancient *Hina-Matsuri* (Doll Festival), of interest to doll collectors and paper doll enthusiasts alike, is felt to be a fitting finale to this work.

No. 269. Tuck's "School Days to Maturity" doll, 12-3/4 inches. Courtesy Chester County Historical Society.

No. 270.   UNIDENTIFIED 13 INCH PAPER DOLL BY TUCK. AUTHOR'S COLLECTION.

No. 271.   MARION MANNERS, 12½ INCHES, BY TUCK. AUTHOR'S COLLECTION.

No. 272. THE FESTIVAL OF THE DOLLS, JAPANESE POP-UP. AUTHOR'S COLLECTION.

Index of Names of Dolls and Manufacturers

Note: Dolls with both given and surnames are indexed under given name only, i.e., Bertie Bright, not Bright, Bertie. References to illustrations are printed in italic numbers.